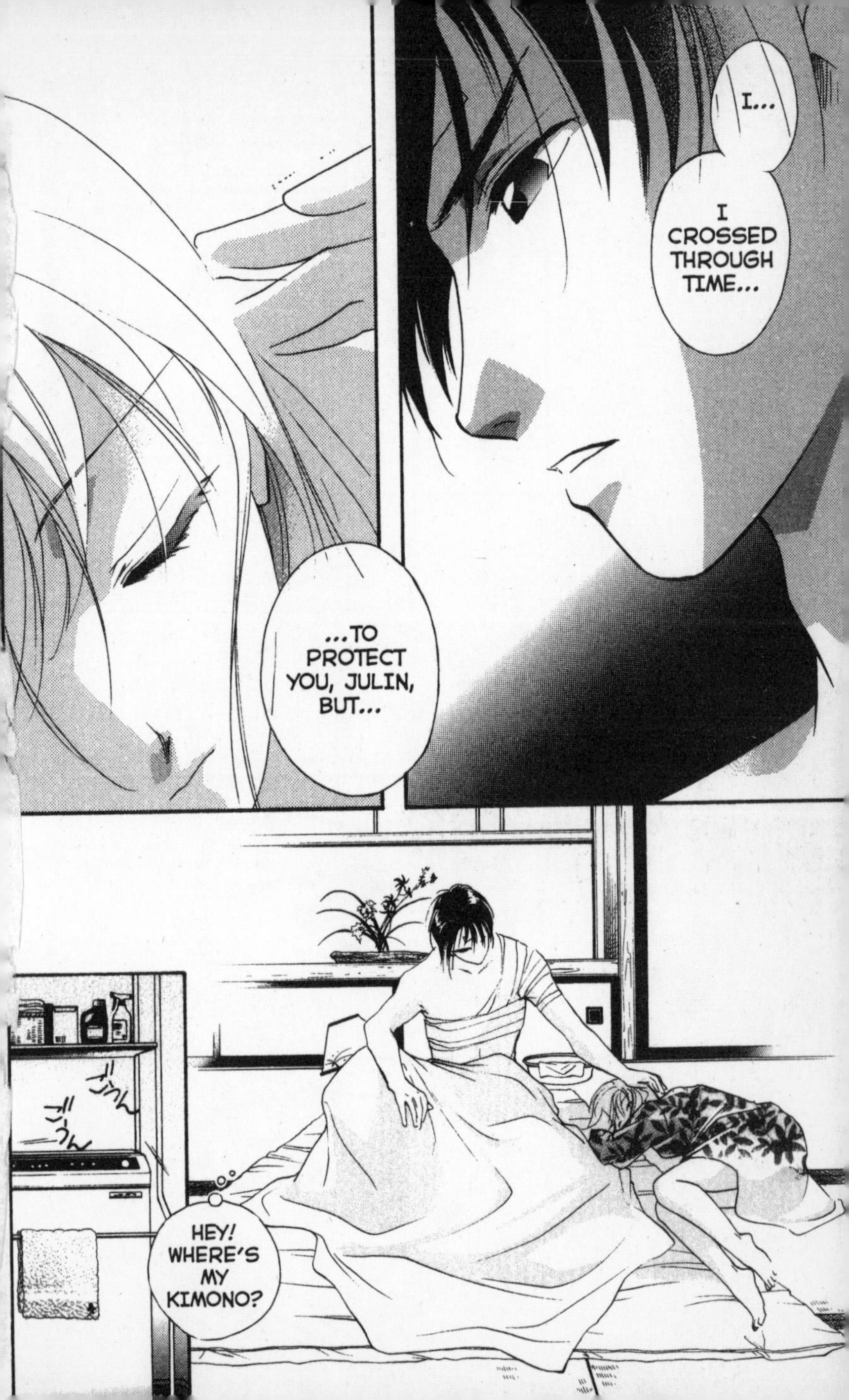
I...
I CROSSED THROUGH TIME...
...TO PROTECT YOU, JULIN, BUT...
HEY! WHERE'S MY KIMONO?

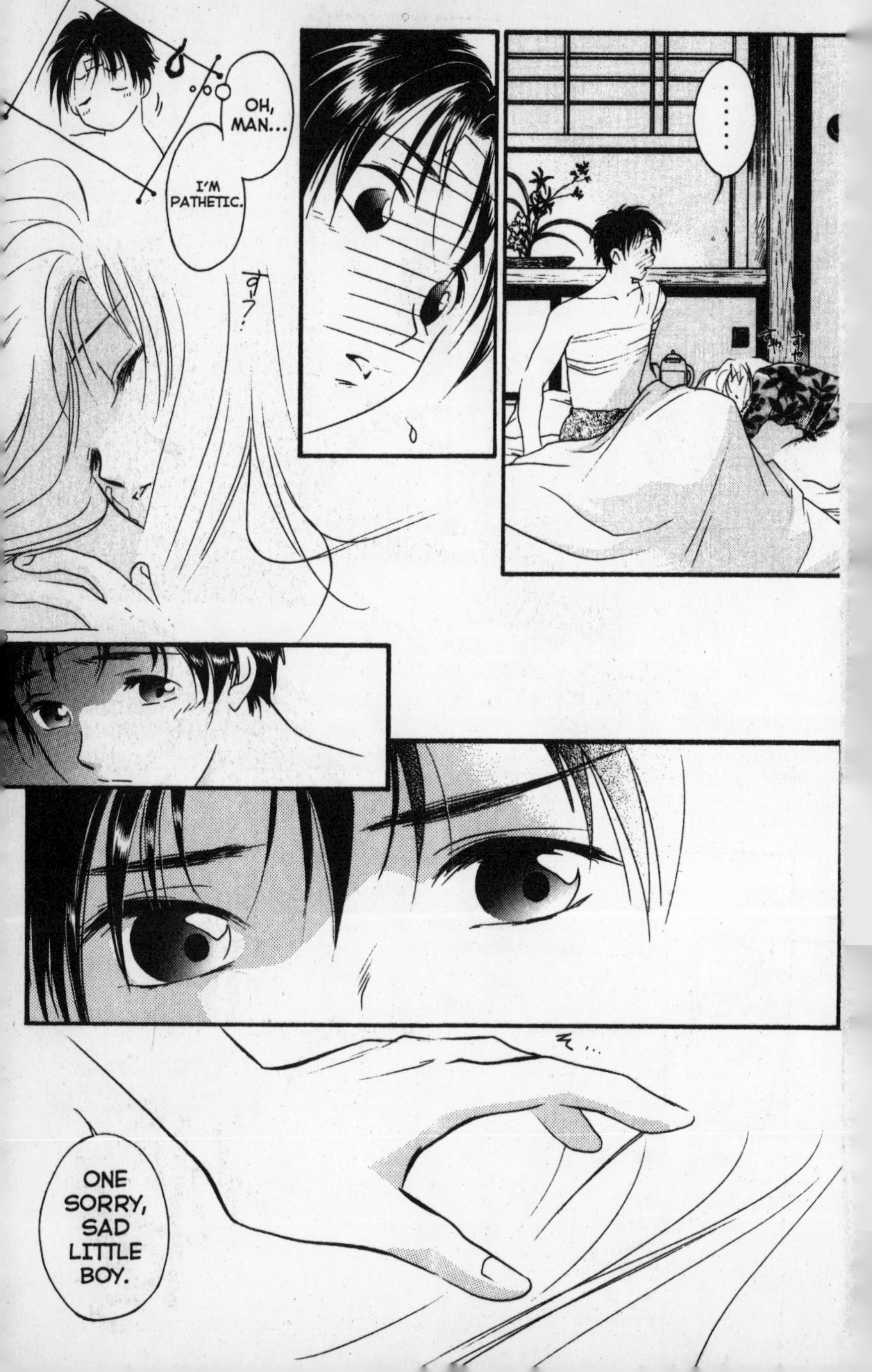
......
OH, MAN...
I'M PATHETIC.
ONE SORRY, SAD LITTLE BOY.

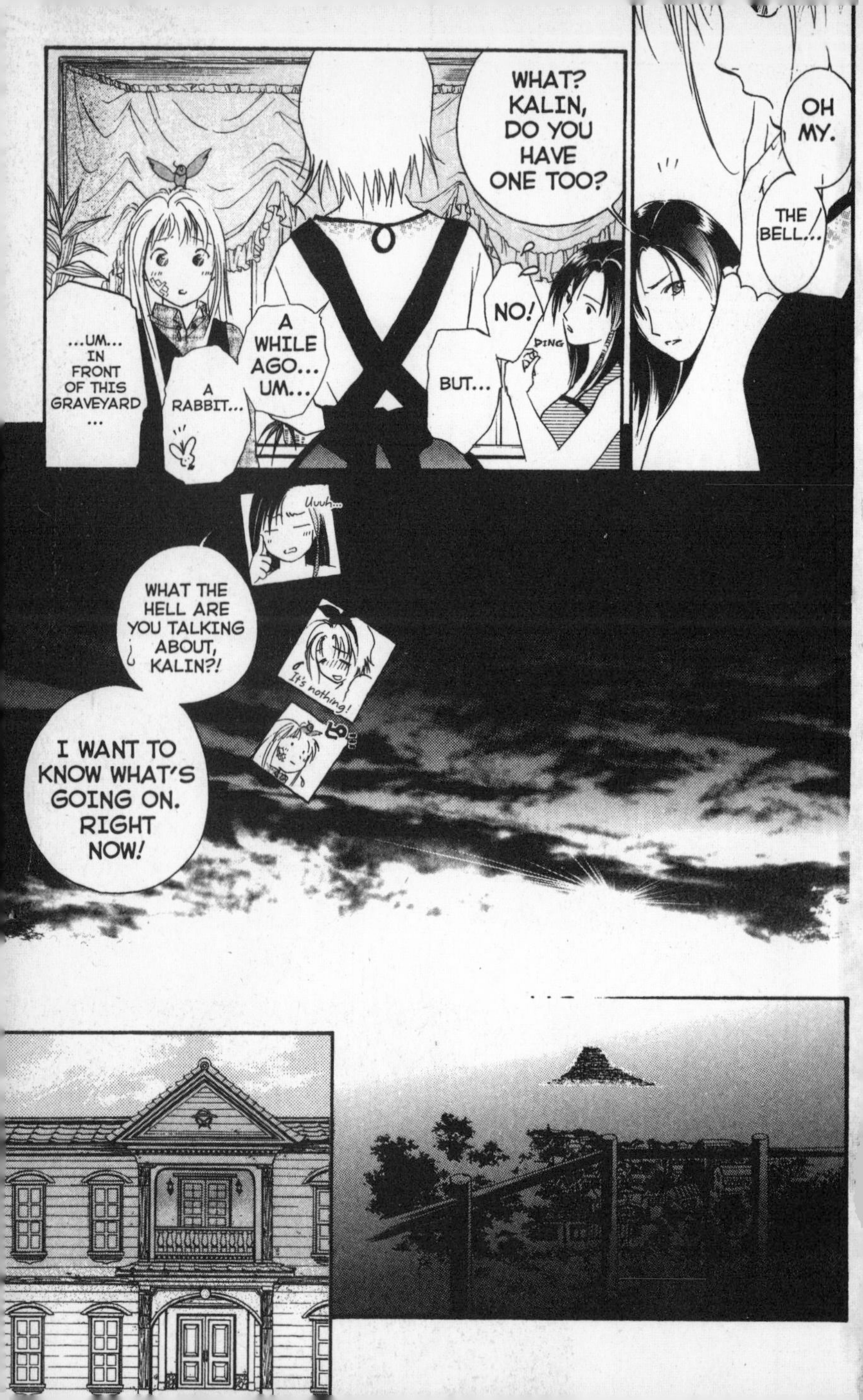
OH MY.
THE BELL...
WHAT? KALIN, DO YOU HAVE ONE TOO?
NO!
DING
BUT...
A WHILE AGO... UM...
A RABBIT...
...UM... IN FRONT OF THIS GRAVEYARD ...
Uuuh...
WHAT THE HELL ARE YOU TALKING ABOUT, KALIN?!
It's nothing!
I WANT TO KNOW WHAT'S GOING ON. RIGHT NOW!

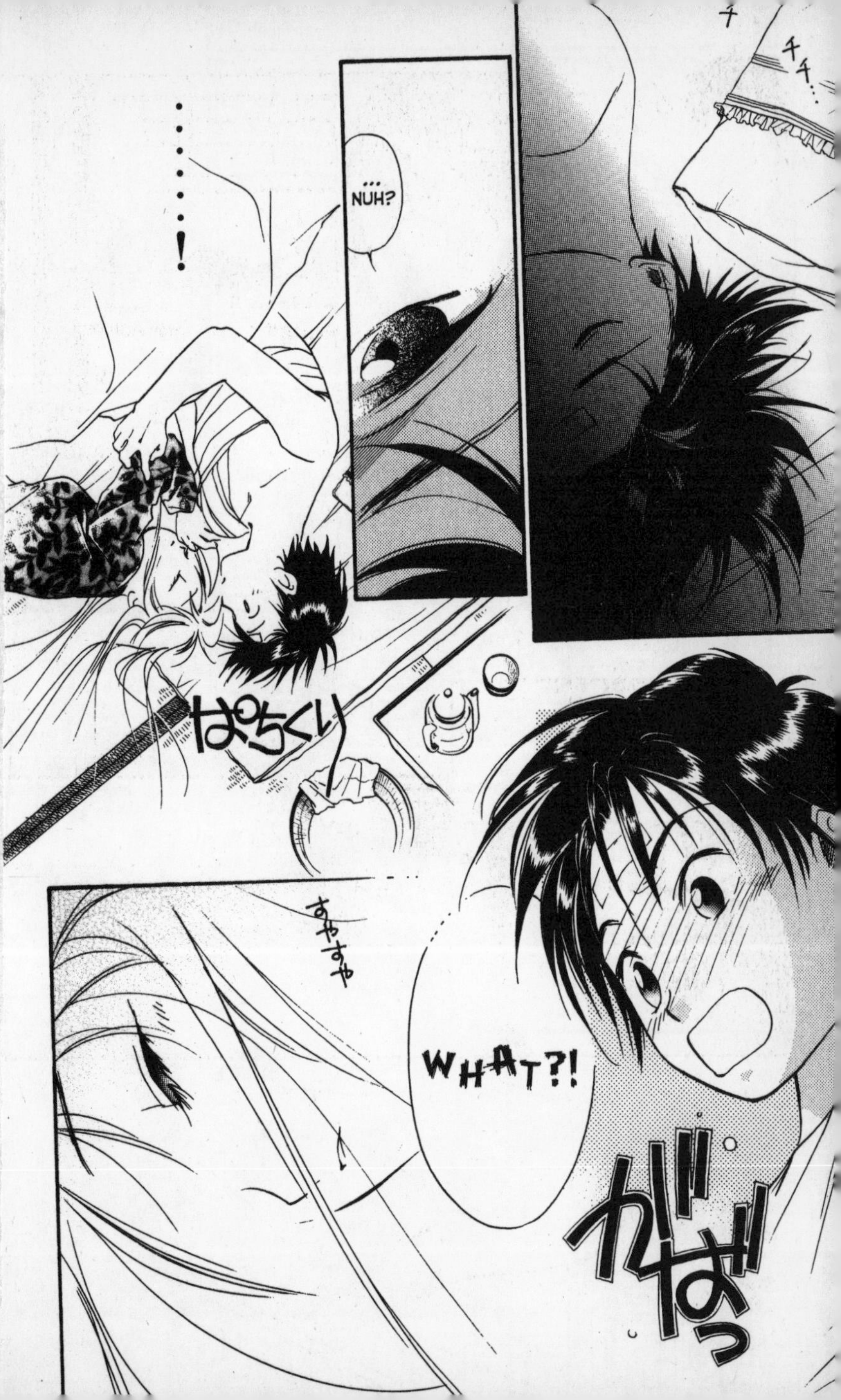

チ
チチ…
...NUH?
......!
ぱちくり
WHAT?!
がばっ
すやすや

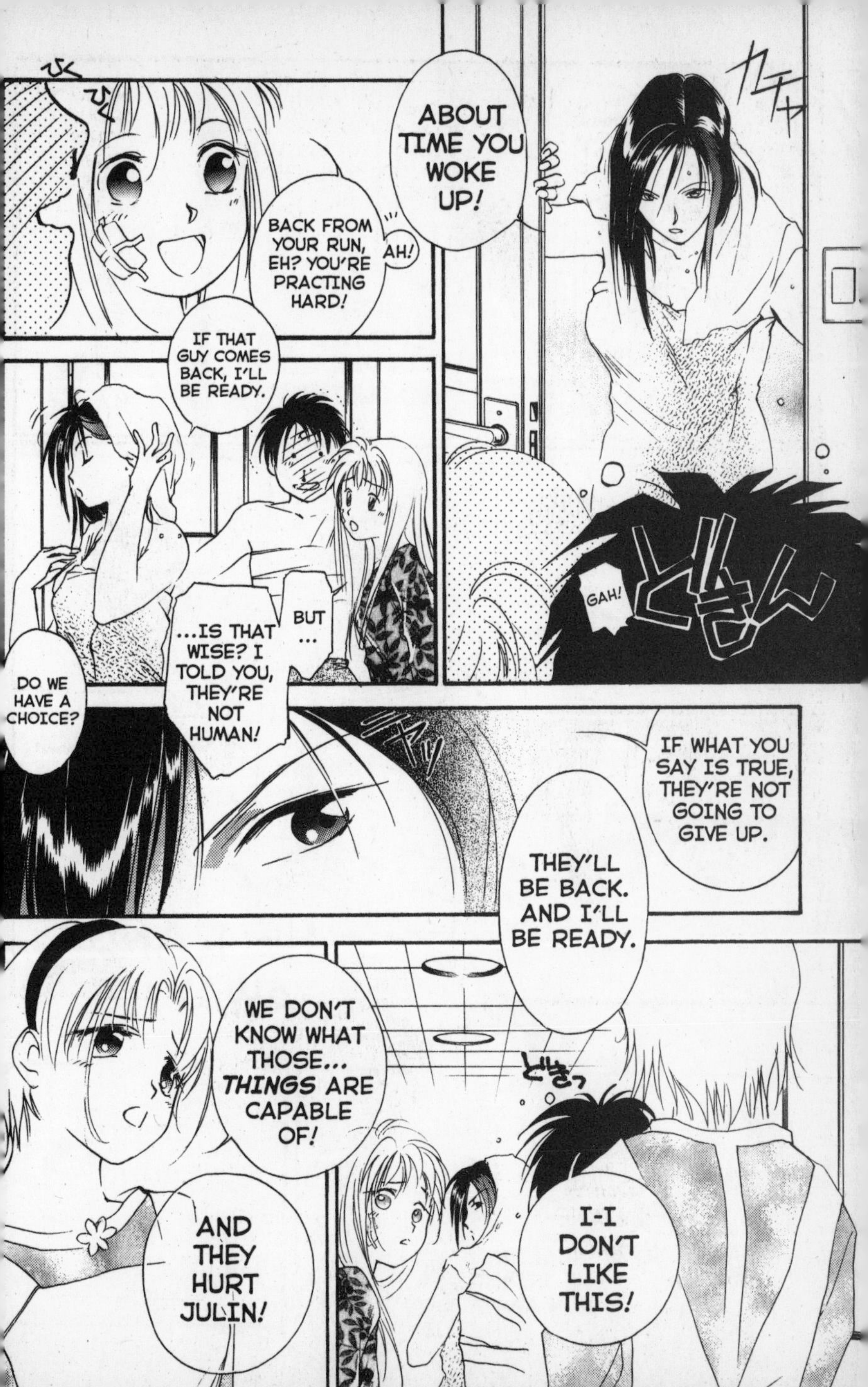
カチャ
ABOUT TIME YOU WOKE UP!
どきん
GAH!
ぴくぴく
AH!
BACK FROM YOUR RUN, EH? YOU'RE PRACTING HARD!
IF THAT GUY COMES BACK, I'LL BE READY.
BUT ...
...IS THAT WISE? I TOLD YOU, THEY'RE NOT HUMAN!
DO WE HAVE A CHOICE?
ニヤッ
IF WHAT YOU SAY IS TRUE, THEY'RE NOT GOING TO GIVE UP.
THEY'LL BE BACK. AND I'LL BE READY.
どきっ
I-I DON'T LIKE THIS!
WE DON'T KNOW WHAT THOSE... THINGS ARE CAPABLE OF!
AND THEY HURT JULIN!

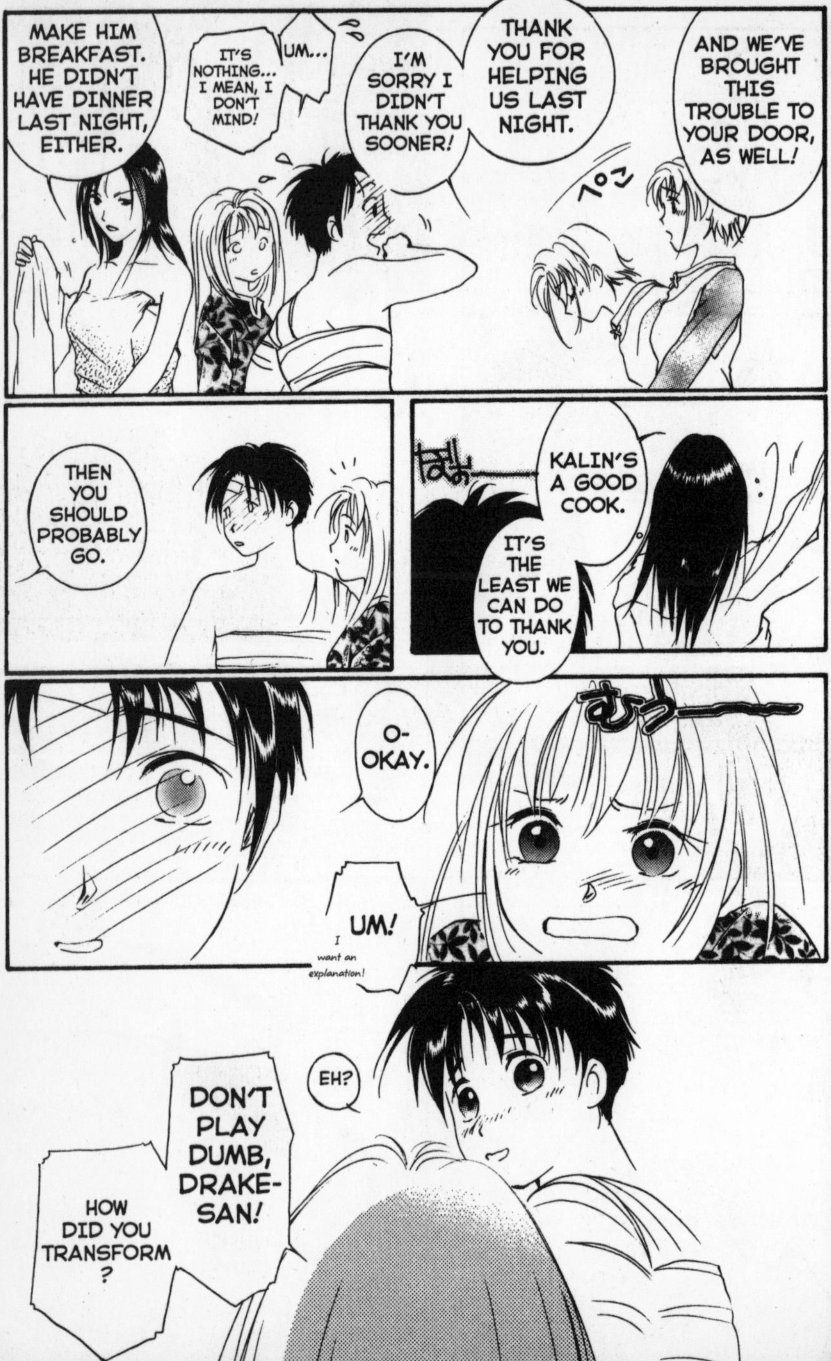
AND WE'VE BROUGHT THIS TROUBLE TO YOUR DOOR, AS WELL!
THANK YOU FOR HELPING US LAST NIGHT.
I'M SORRY I DIDN'T THANK YOU SOONER!
UM...
IT'S NOTHING... I MEAN, I DON'T MIND!
MAKE HIM BREAKFAST. HE DIDN'T HAVE DINNER LAST NIGHT, EITHER.
KALIN'S A GOOD COOK.
IT'S THE LEAST WE CAN DO TO THANK YOU.
THEN YOU SHOULD PROBABLY GO.
O-OKAY.
UM!
I want an explanation!
EH?
DON'T PLAY DUMB, DRAKE-SAN!
HOW DID YOU TRANSFORM?

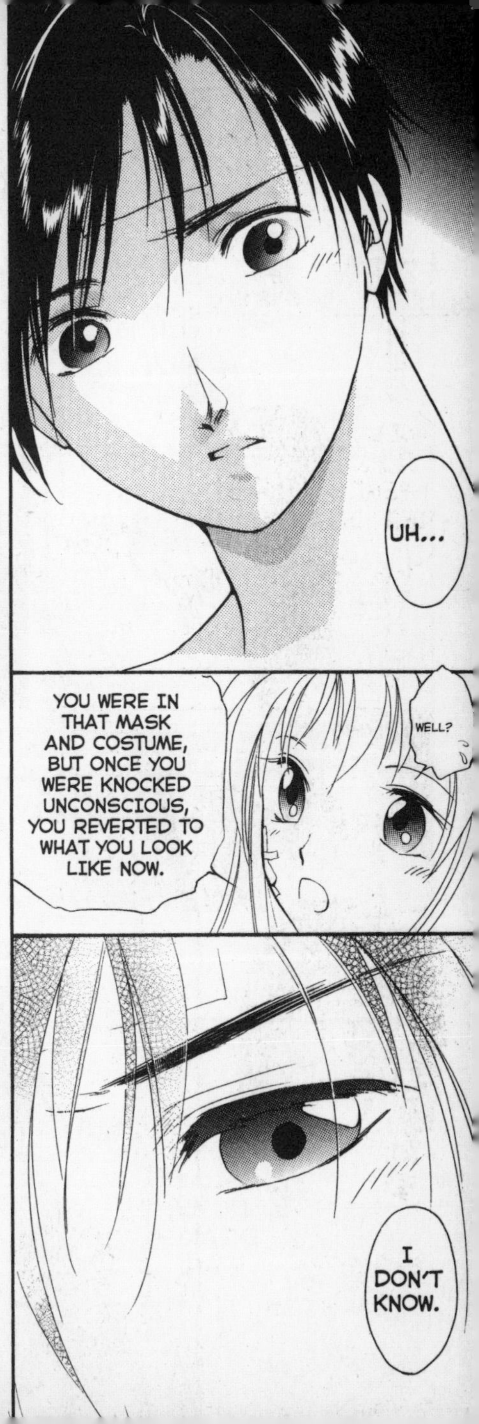
UH...
WELL?
YOU WERE IN THAT MASK AND COSTUME, BUT ONCE YOU WERE KNOCKED UNCONSCIOUS, YOU REVERTED TO WHAT YOU LOOK LIKE NOW.
I DON'T KNOW.

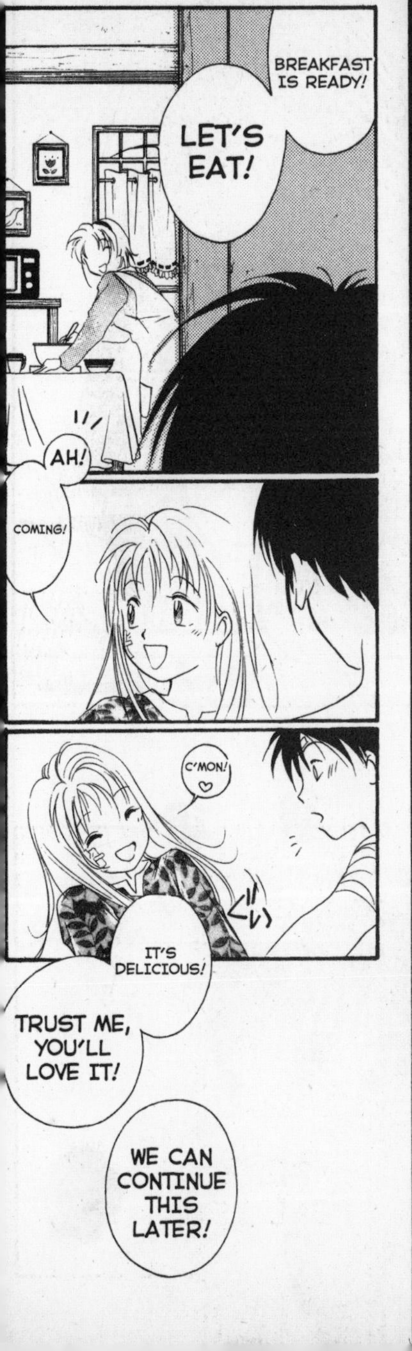
BREAKFAST IS READY!
LET'S EAT!
AH!
COMING!
C'MON!
IT'S DELICIOUS!
TRUST ME, YOU'LL LOVE IT!
WE CAN CONTINUE THIS LATER!

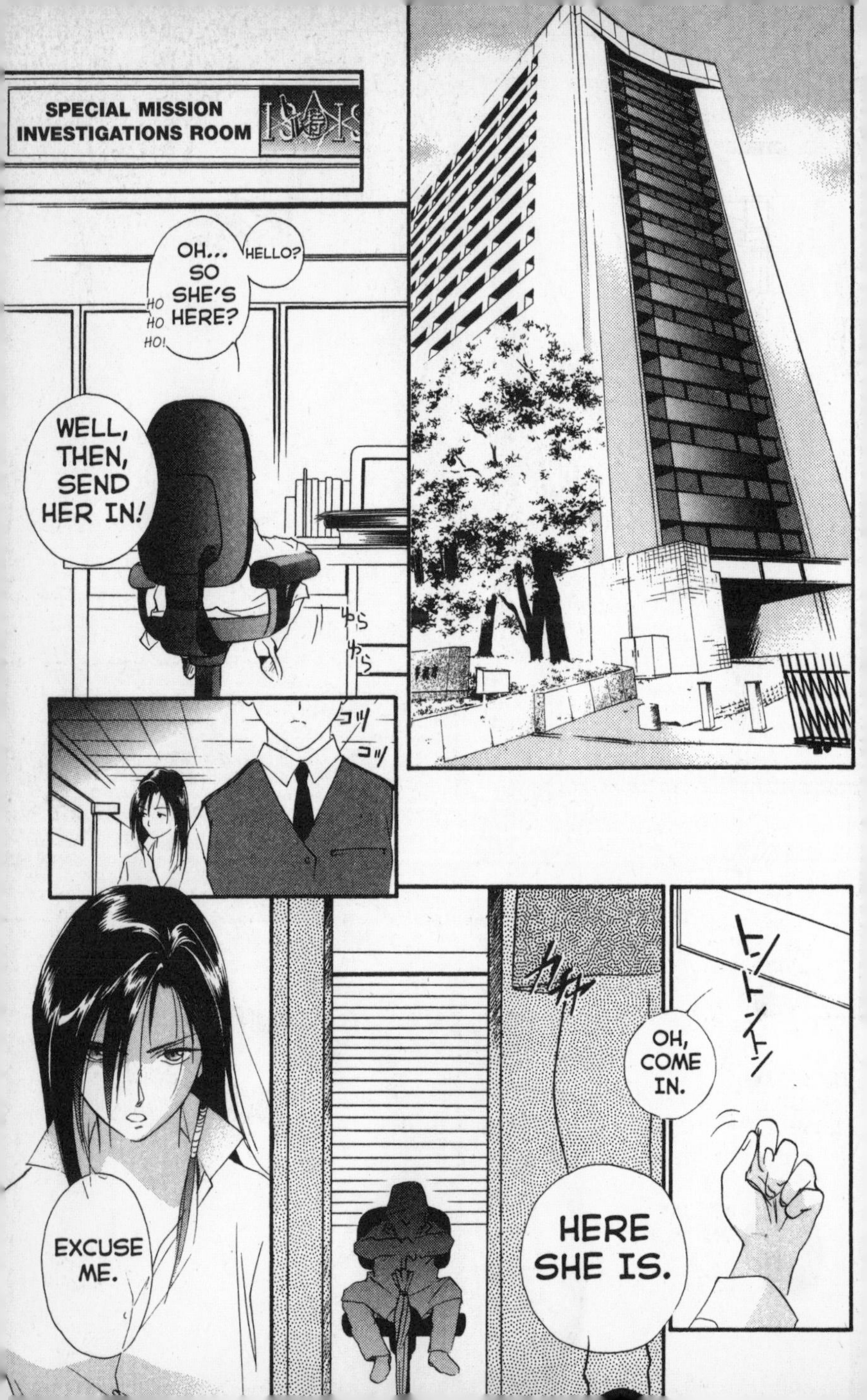
SPECIAL MISSION INVESTIGATIONS ROOM
HELLO?
OH... SO SHE'S HERE?
HO HO HO!
WELL, THEN, SEND HER IN!
ゆら ゆら
コツ コツ
トントン
OH, COME IN.
HERE SHE IS.
カチャ
EXCUSE ME.

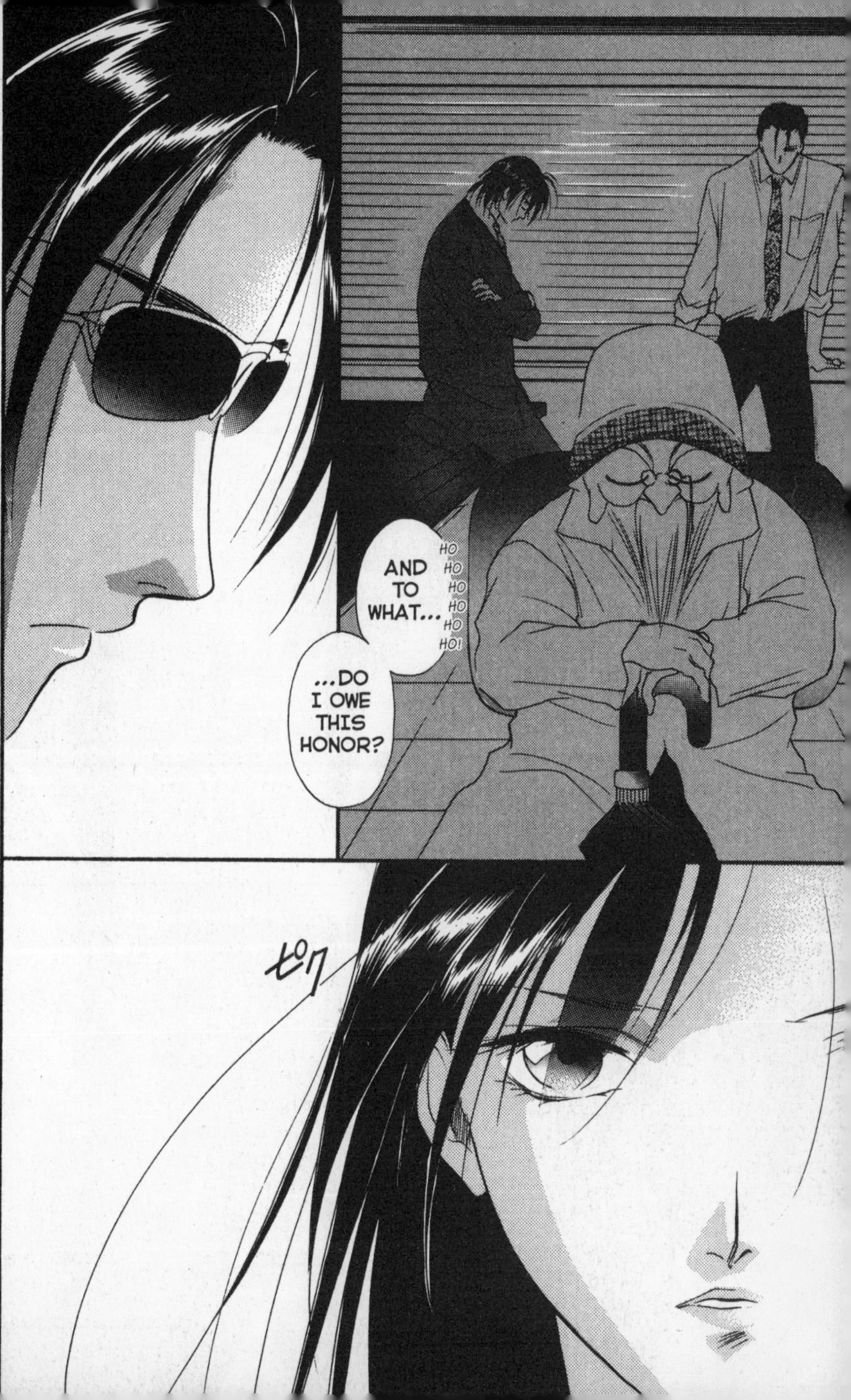
AND TO WHAT...
HO HO HO HO HO HO!
...DO I OWE THIS HONOR?
ピク

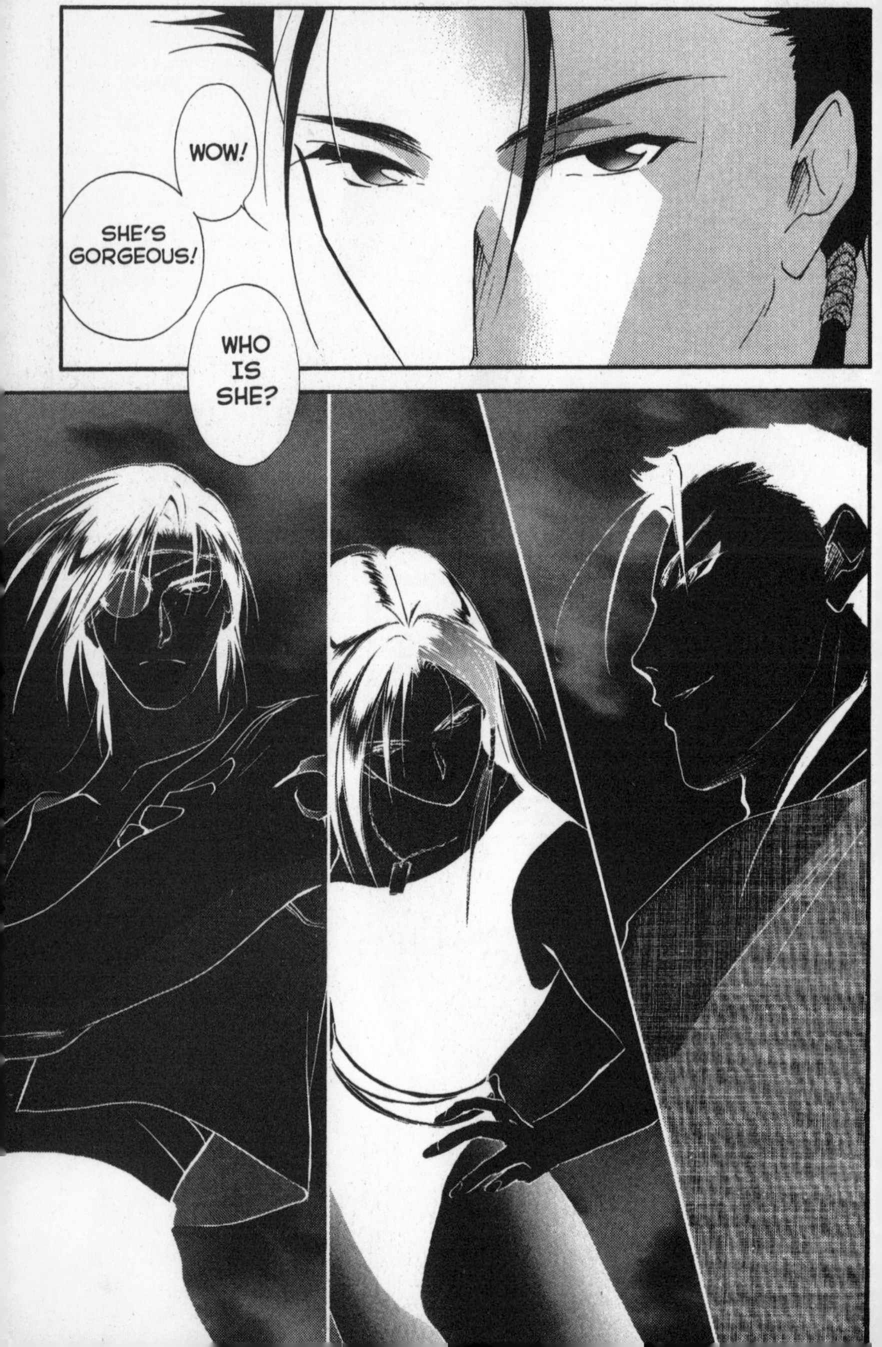
WOW!
SHE'S GORGEOUS!
WHO IS SHE?

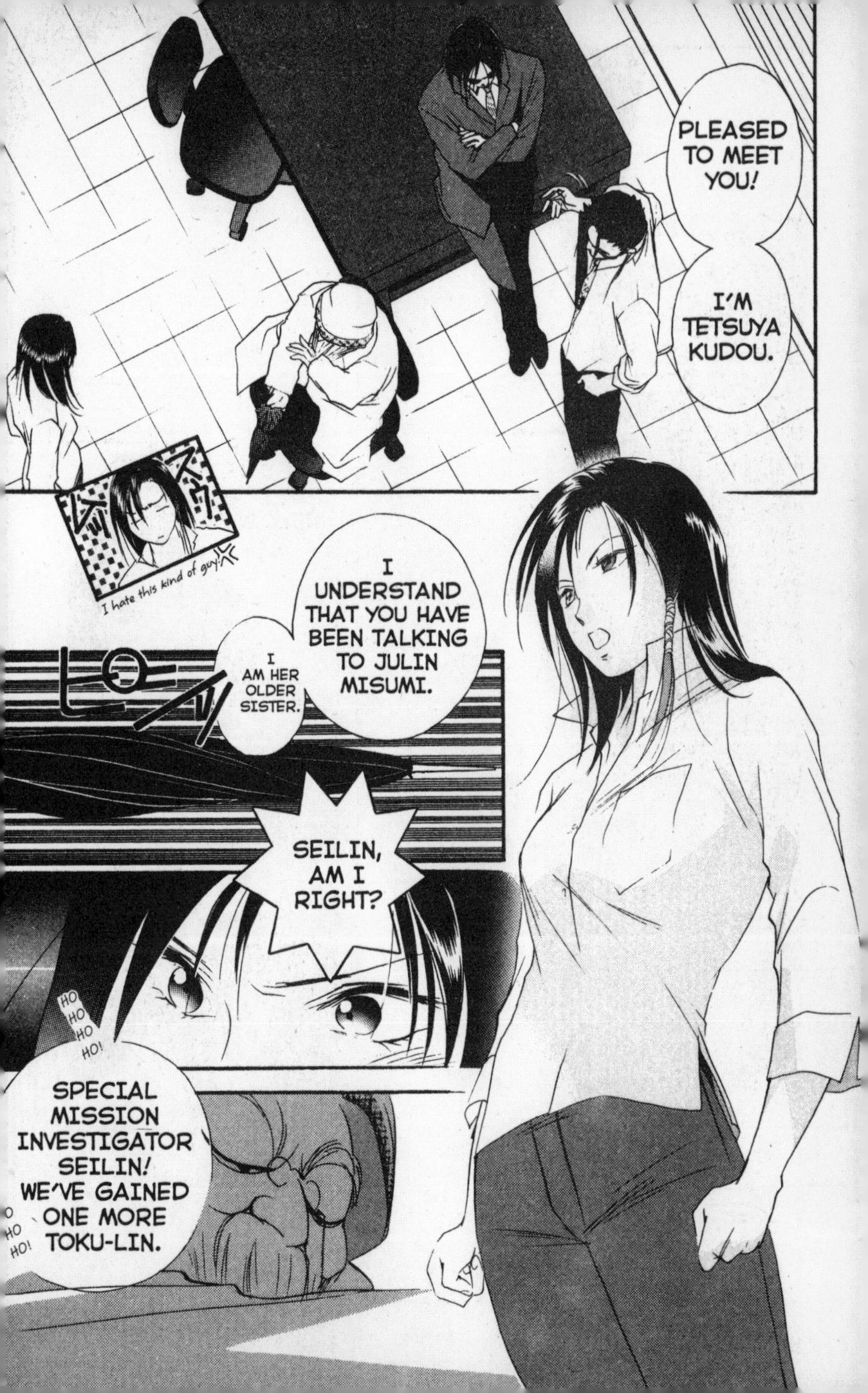

PLEASED TO MEET YOU!
I'M TETSUYA KUDOU.
I hate this kind of guy!
I UNDERSTAND THAT YOU HAVE BEEN TALKING TO JULIN MISUMI.
I AM HER OLDER SISTER.
SEILIN, AM I RIGHT?
HO HO HO HO!
SPECIAL MISSION INVESTIGATOR SEILIN! WE'VE GAINED ONE MORE TOKU-LIN.
O HO HO!

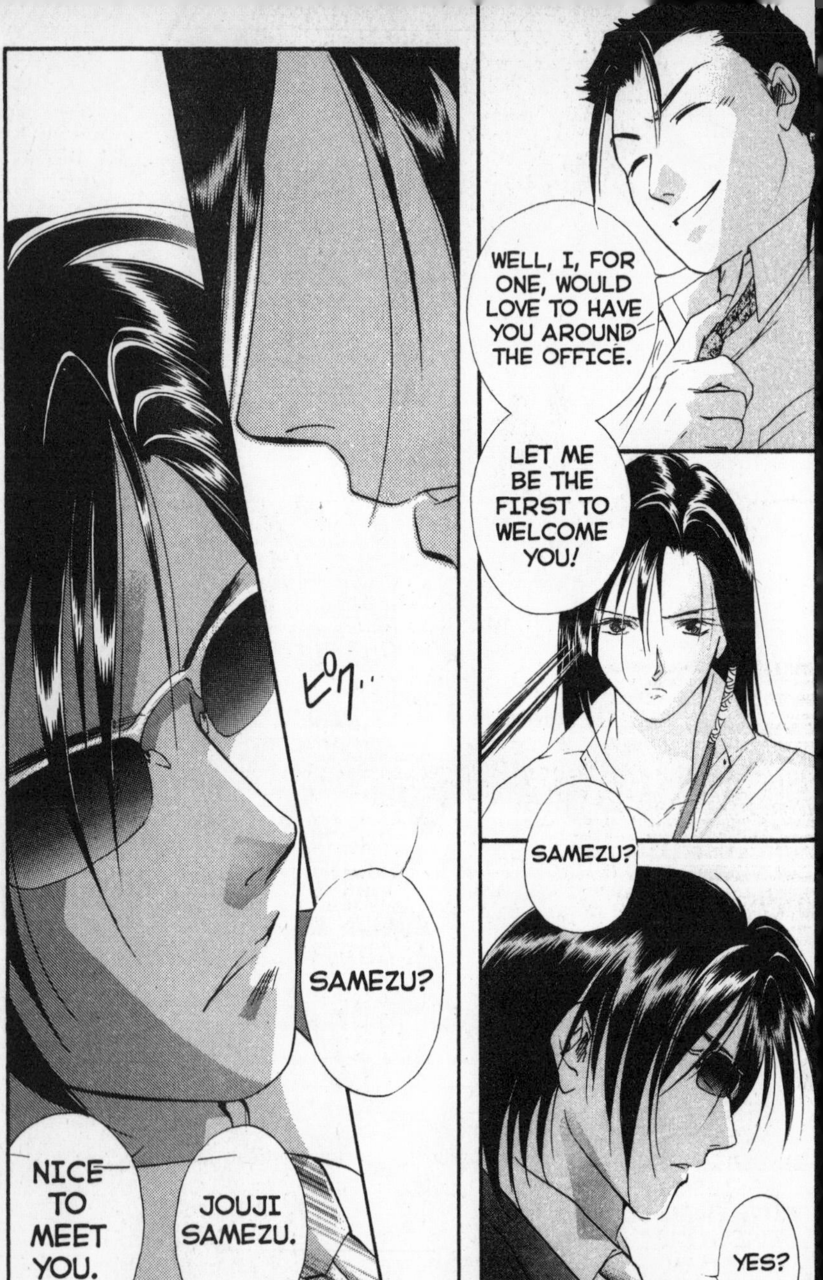
WELL, I, FOR ONE, WOULD LOVE TO HAVE YOU AROUND THE OFFICE.
LET ME BE THE FIRST TO WELCOME YOU!
SAMEZU?
YES?
ピク…
SAMEZU?
JOUJI SAMEZU.
NICE TO MEET YOU.

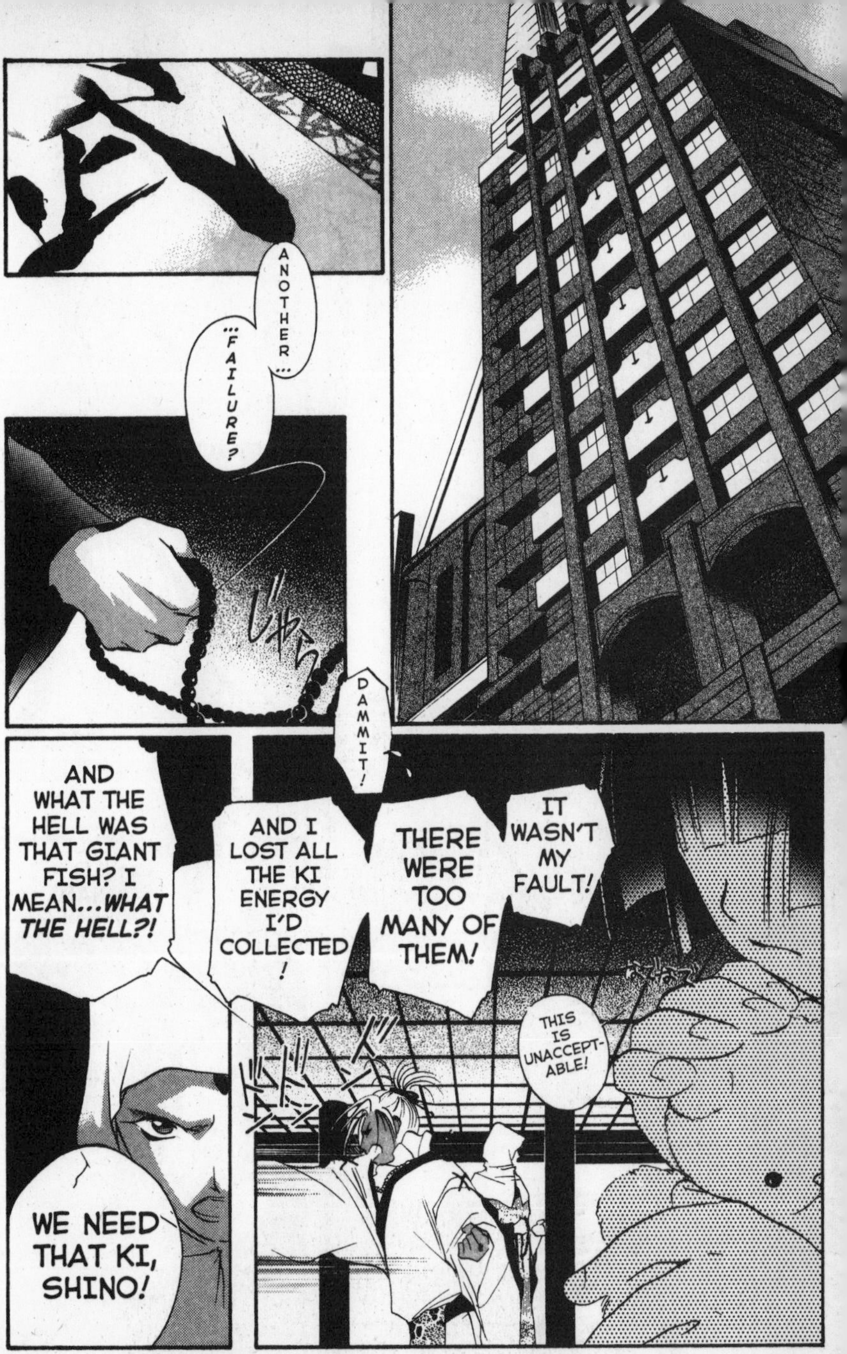

ANOTHER...
...FAILURE?
DAMMIT!
IT WASN'T MY FAULT!
THERE WERE TOO MANY OF THEM!
AND I LOST ALL THE KI ENERGY I'D COLLECTED!
THIS IS UNACCEPTABLE!
AND WHAT THE HELL WAS THAT GIANT FISH? I MEAN...*WHAT THE HELL?!*
WE NEED THAT KI, SHINO!

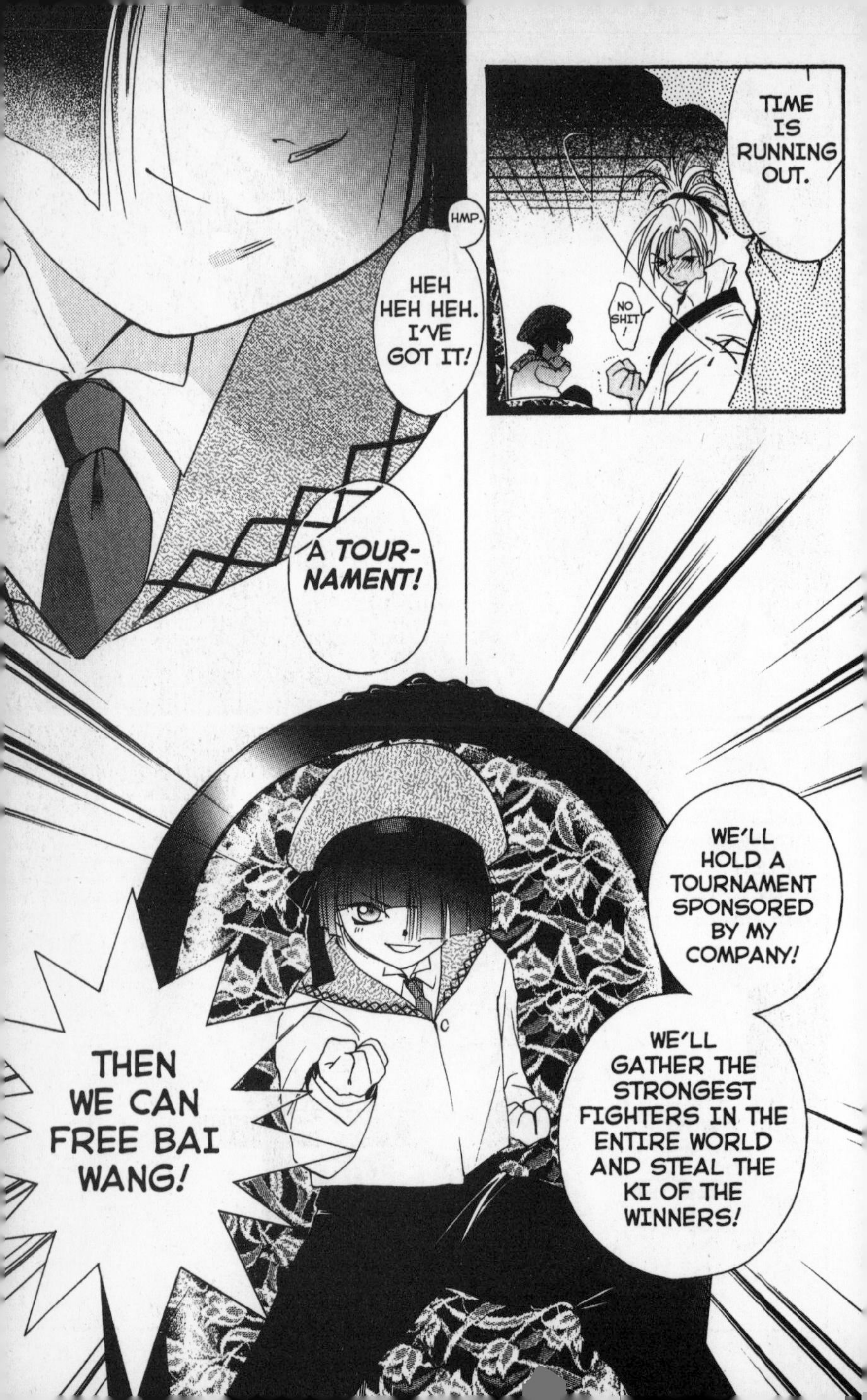
TIME IS RUNNING OUT.
NO SHIT!
HMP.
HEH HEH HEH. I'VE GOT IT!
A TOURNAMENT!
WE'LL HOLD A TOURNAMENT SPONSORED BY MY COMPANY!
WE'LL GATHER THE STRONGEST FIGHTERS IN THE ENTIRE WORLD AND STEAL THE KI OF THE WINNERS!
THEN WE CAN FREE BAI WANG!

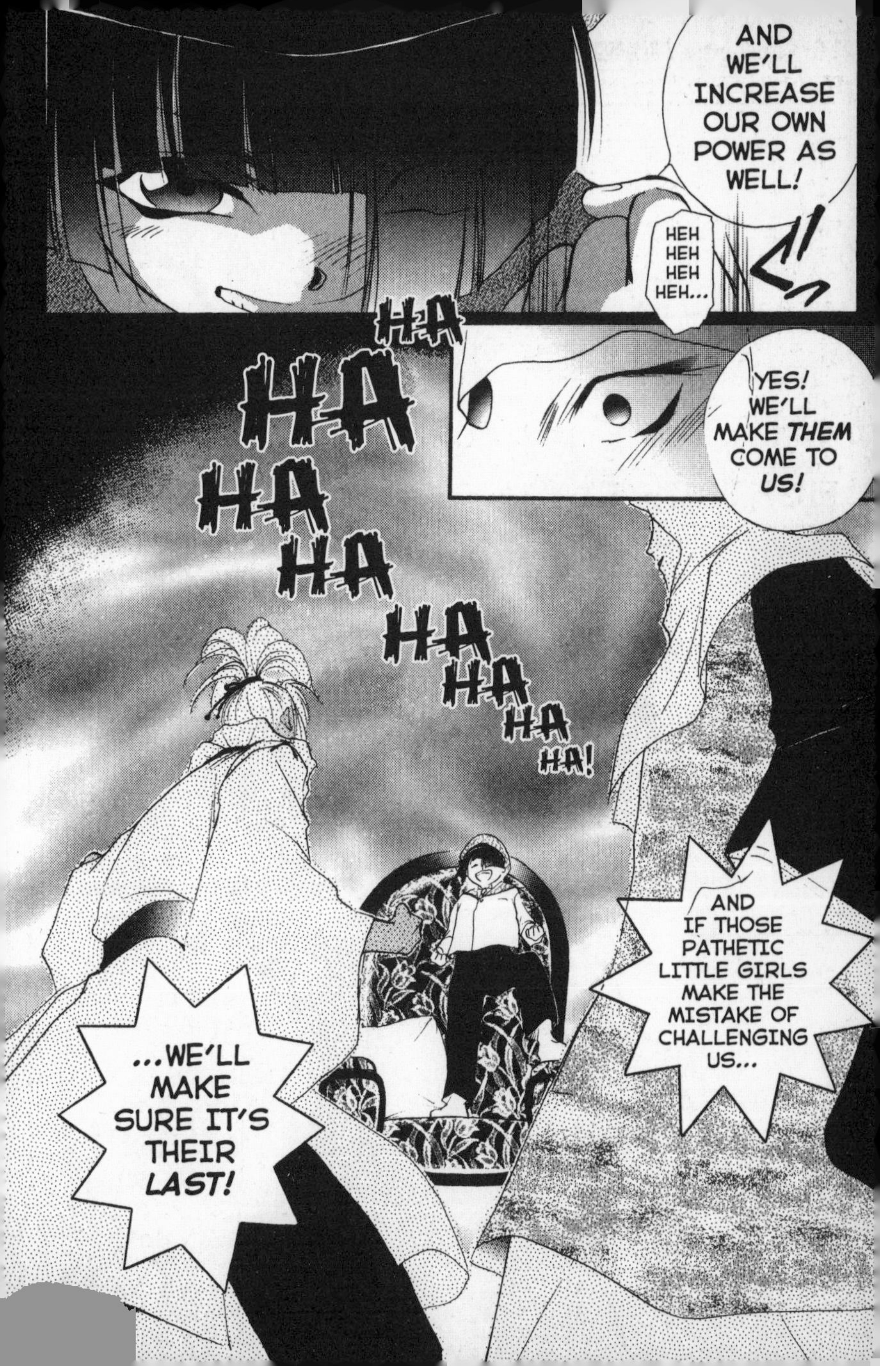
AND WE'LL INCREASE OUR OWN POWER AS WELL!
HEH HEH HEH HEH...
YES! WE'LL MAKE *THEM* COME TO *US!*
HA HA HA HA HA HA HA HA!
AND IF THOSE PATHETIC LITTLE GIRLS MAKE THE MISTAKE OF CHALLENGING US...
...WE'LL MAKE SURE IT'S THEIR *LAST!*

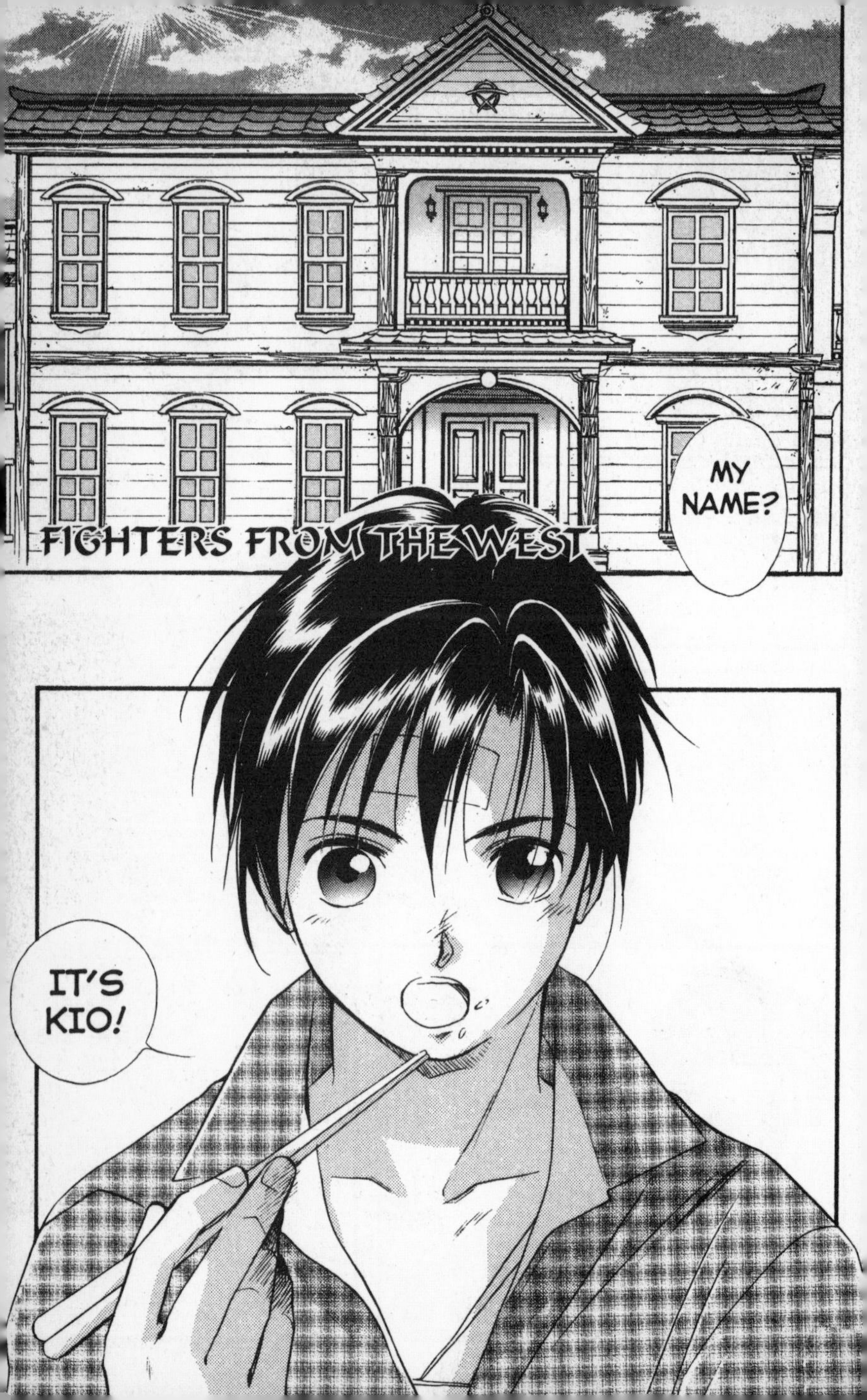
FIGHTERS FROM THE WEST
MY NAME?
IT'S KIO!

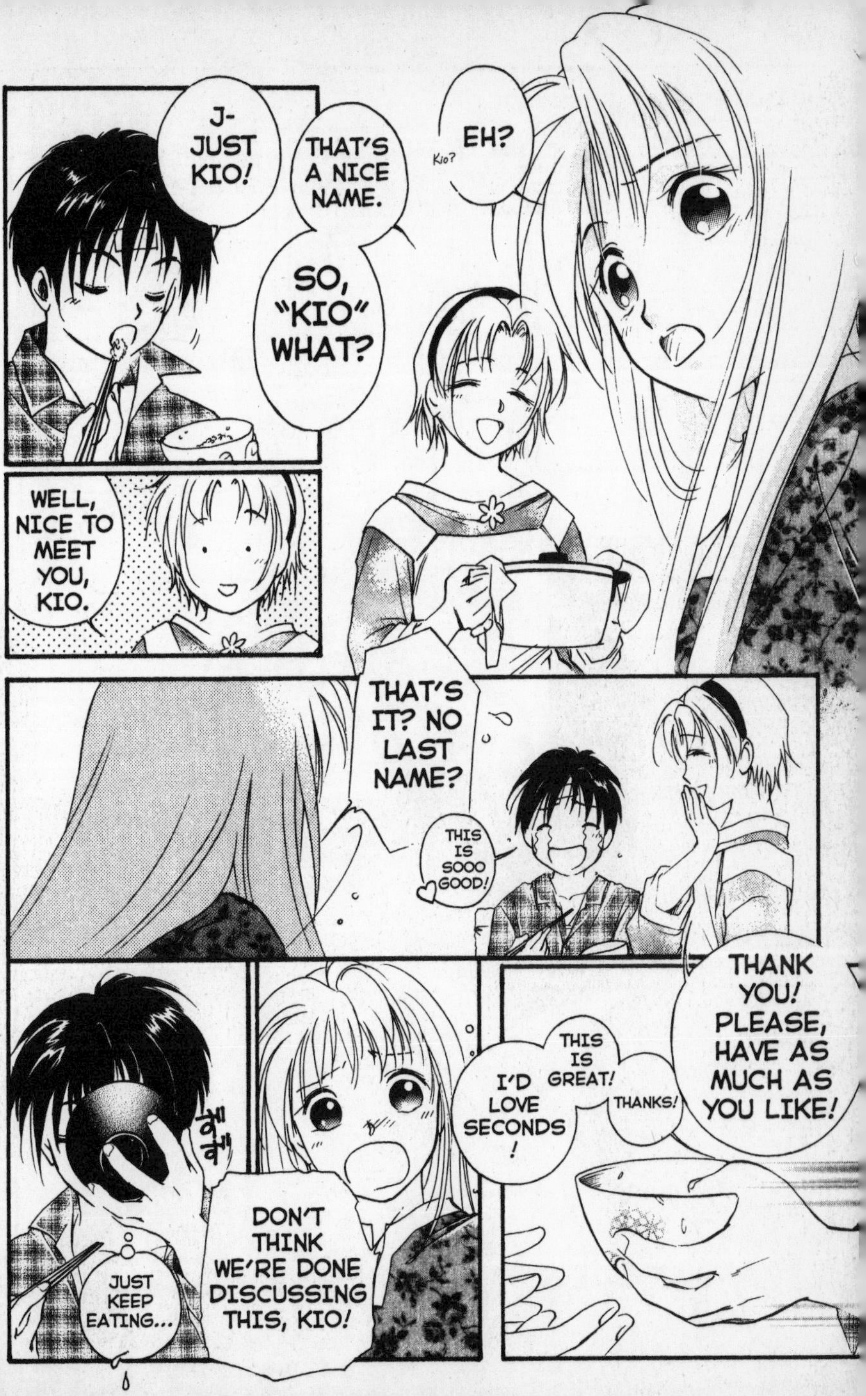
Kio?
EH?
THAT'S A NICE NAME.
SO, "KIO" WHAT?
J- JUST KIO!
WELL, NICE TO MEET YOU, KIO.
THAT'S IT? NO LAST NAME?
THIS IS SOOO GOOD!
THANK YOU! PLEASE, HAVE AS MUCH AS YOU LIKE!
THIS IS GREAT!
THANKS!
I'D LOVE SECONDS!
DON'T THINK WE'RE DONE DISCUSSING THIS, KIO!
ずず
JUST KEEP EATING...

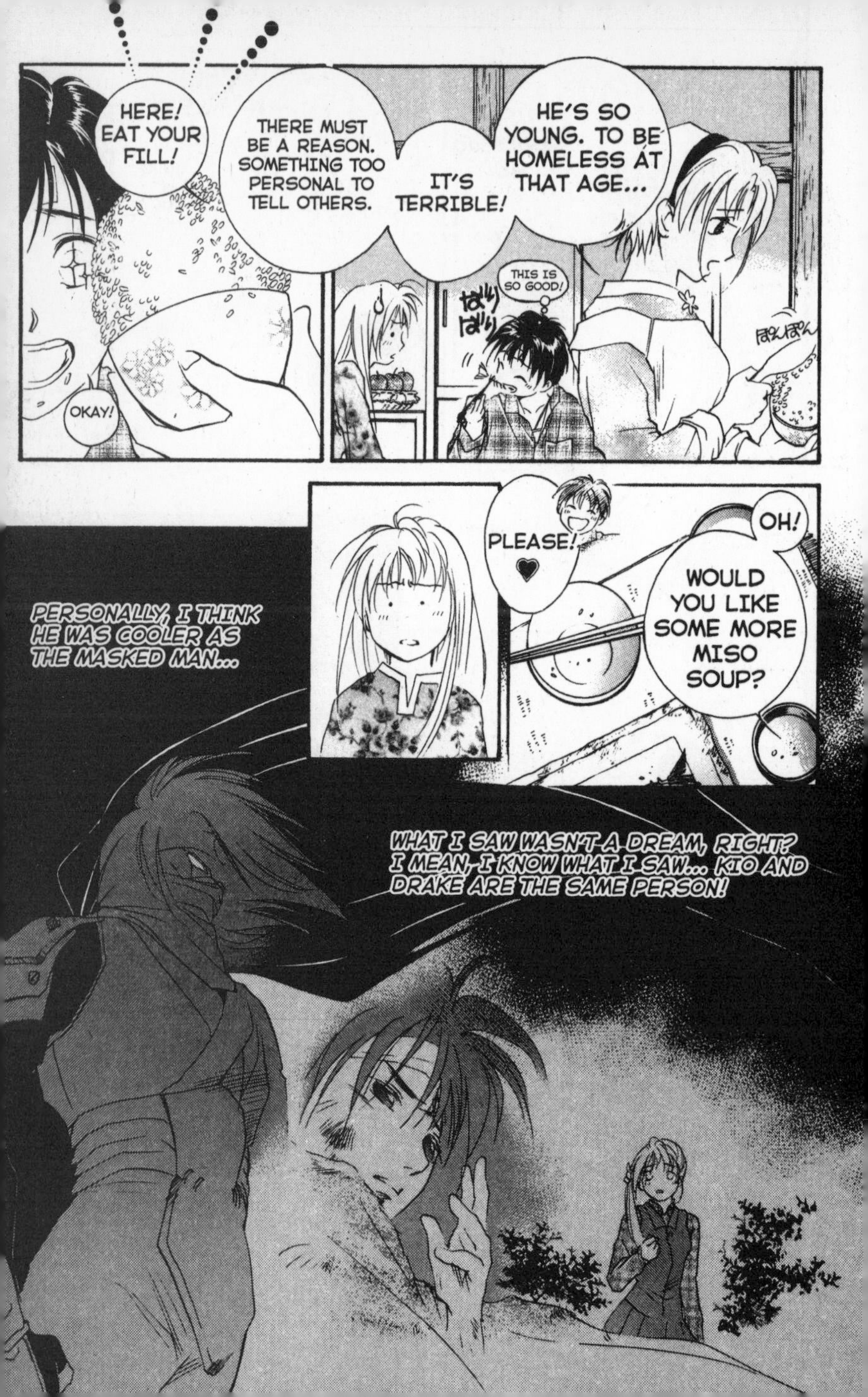
HE'S SO YOUNG. TO BE HOMELESS AT THAT AGE...
IT'S TERRIBLE!
THIS IS SO GOOD!
THERE MUST BE A REASON. SOMETHING TOO PERSONAL TO TELL OTHERS.
HERE! EAT YOUR FILL!
OKAY!
OH!
WOULD YOU LIKE SOME MORE MISO SOUP?
PLEASE! ♥
PERSONALLY, I THINK HE WAS COOLER AS THE MASKED MAN...
WHAT I SAW WASN'T A DREAM, RIGHT? I MEAN, I KNOW WHAT I SAW... KIO AND DRAKE ARE THE SAME PERSON!

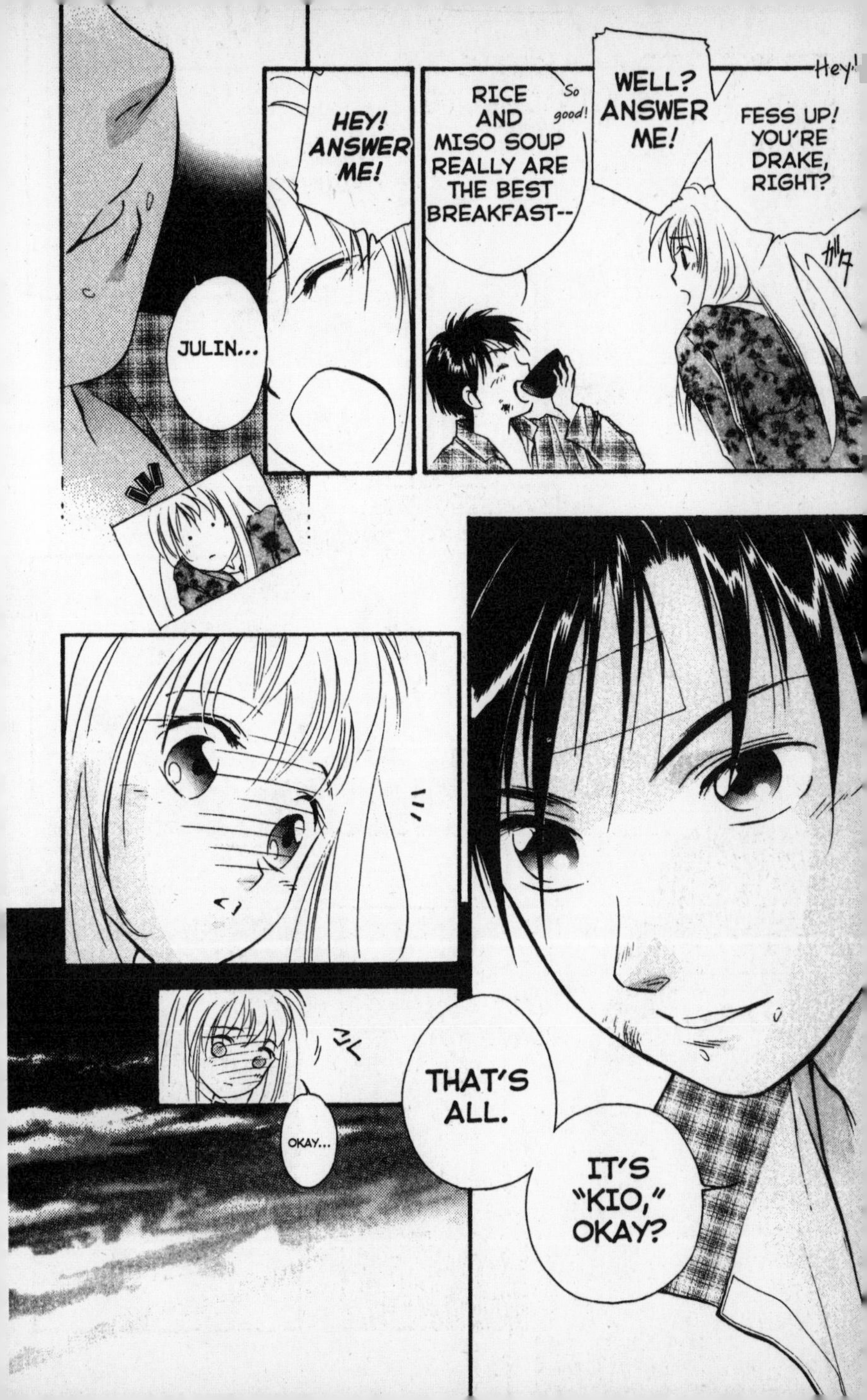
Hey!
FESS UP! YOU'RE DRAKE, RIGHT?
WELL? ANSWER ME!
So good!
RICE AND MISO SOUP REALLY ARE THE BEST BREAKFAST--
HEY! ANSWER ME!
JULIN...
THAT'S ALL.
IT'S "KIO," OKAY?
OKAY...

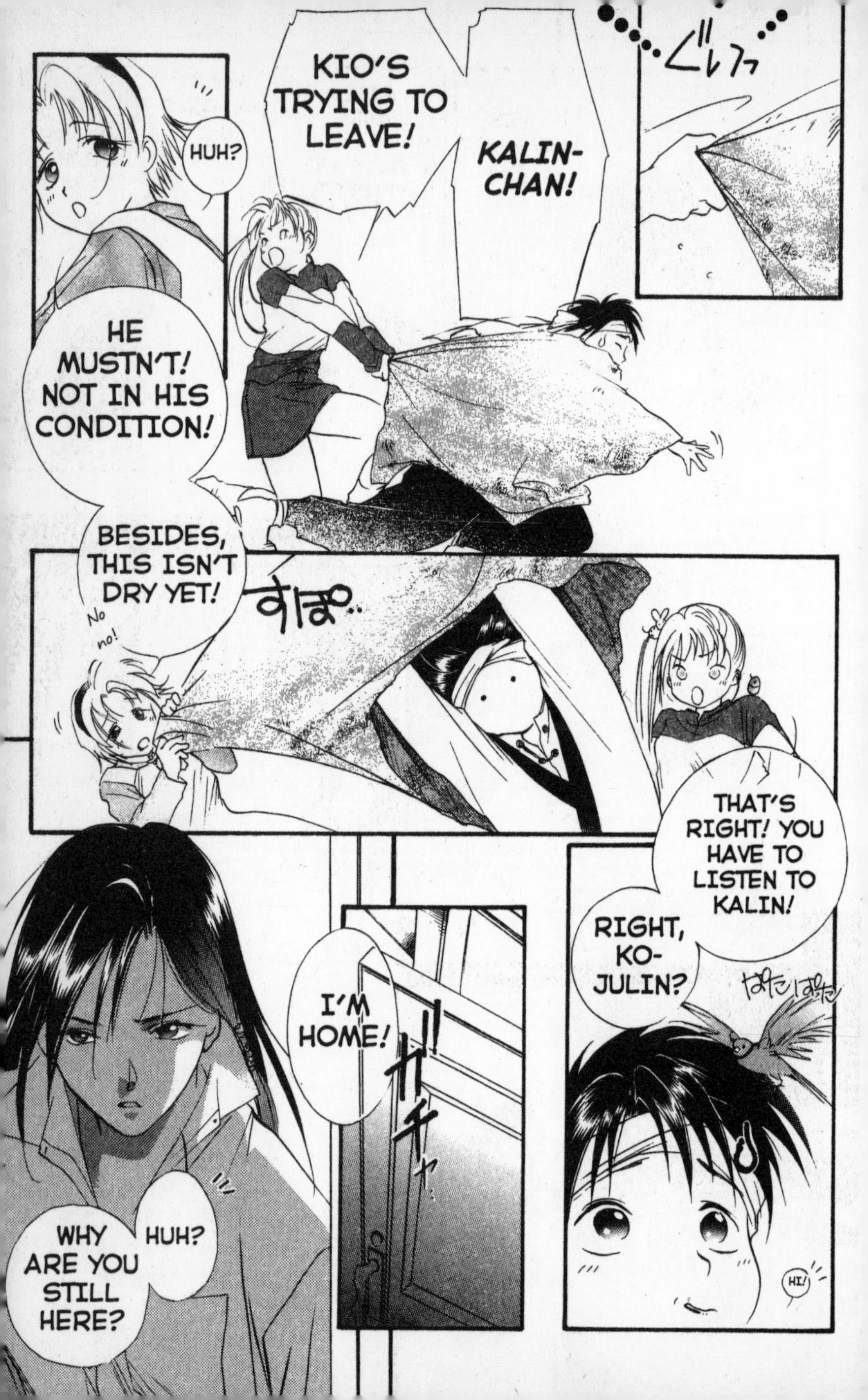
ぐいっ
KALIN-CHAN!
KIO'S TRYING TO LEAVE!
HUH?
HE MUSTN'T! NOT IN HIS CONDITION!
BESIDES, THIS ISN'T DRY YET!
すぽ..
No no!
THAT'S RIGHT! YOU HAVE TO LISTEN TO KALIN!
RIGHT, KO-JULIN?
ぱたぱた
HI!
I'M HOME!
ガチャ
HUH?
WHY ARE YOU STILL HERE?

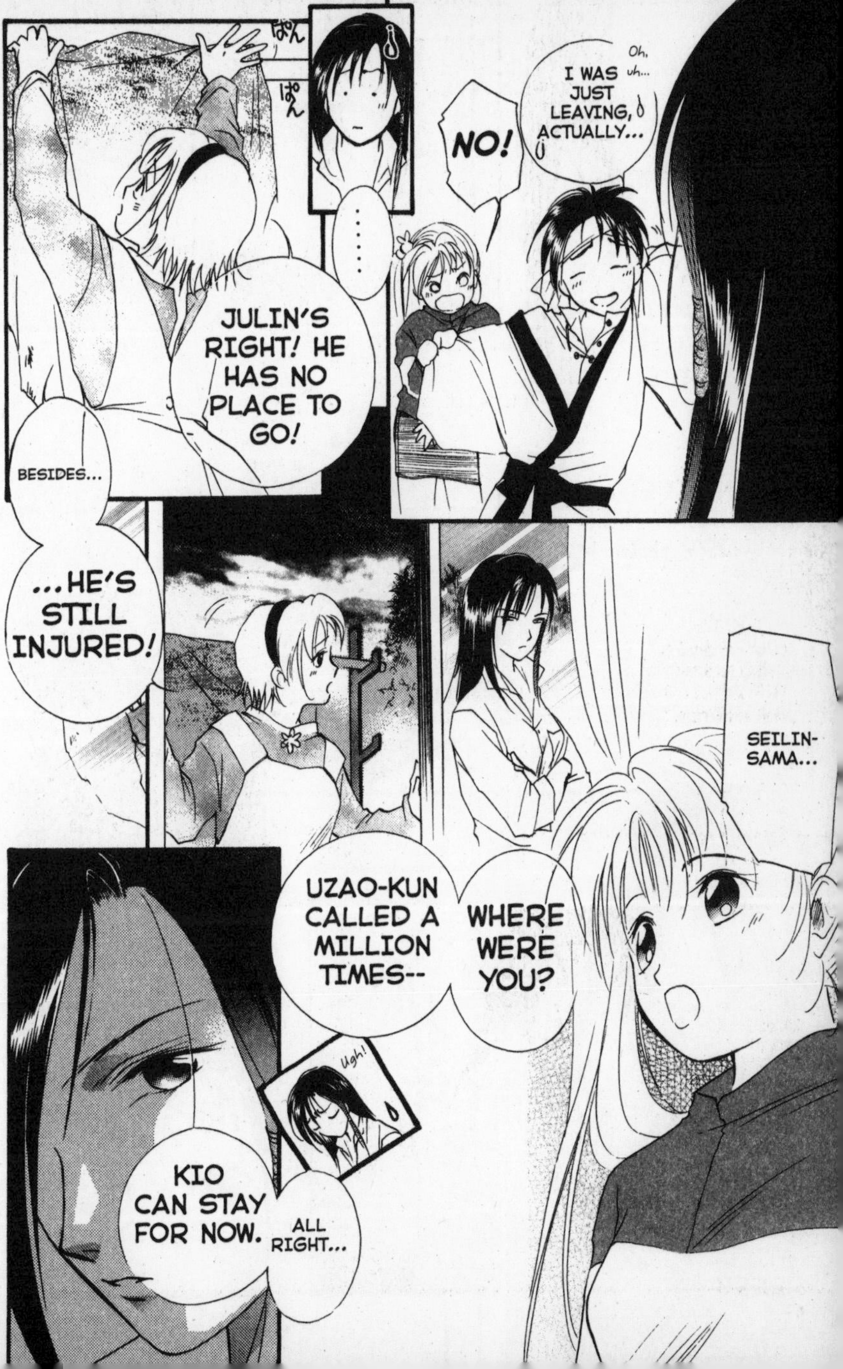
Oh, uh...
I WAS JUST LEAVING, ACTUALLY...
NO!
ぱん
ぱん
......
JULIN'S RIGHT! HE HAS NO PLACE TO GO!
BESIDES...
...HE'S STILL INJURED!
SEILIN-SAMA...
WHERE WERE YOU?
UZAO-KUN CALLED A MILLION TIMES--
Ugh!
ALL RIGHT...
KIO CAN STAY FOR NOW.

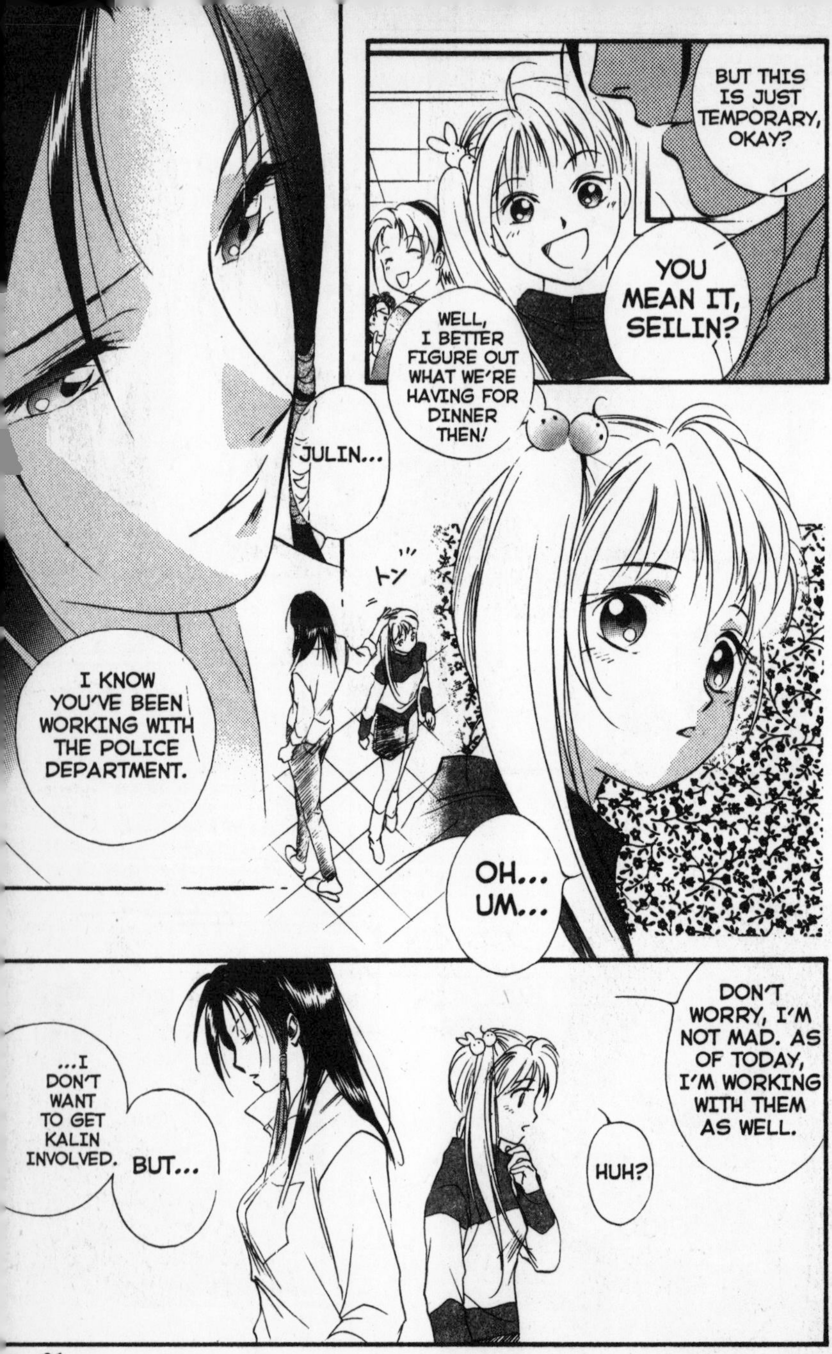

BUT THIS IS JUST TEMPORARY, OKAY?
YOU MEAN IT, SEILIN?
WELL, I BETTER FIGURE OUT WHAT WE'RE HAVING FOR DINNER THEN!
JULIN...
I KNOW YOU'VE BEEN WORKING WITH THE POLICE DEPARTMENT.
OH... UM...
DON'T WORRY, I'M NOT MAD. AS OF TODAY, I'M WORKING WITH THEM AS WELL.
HUH?
...I DON'T WANT TO GET KALIN INVOLVED.
BUT...

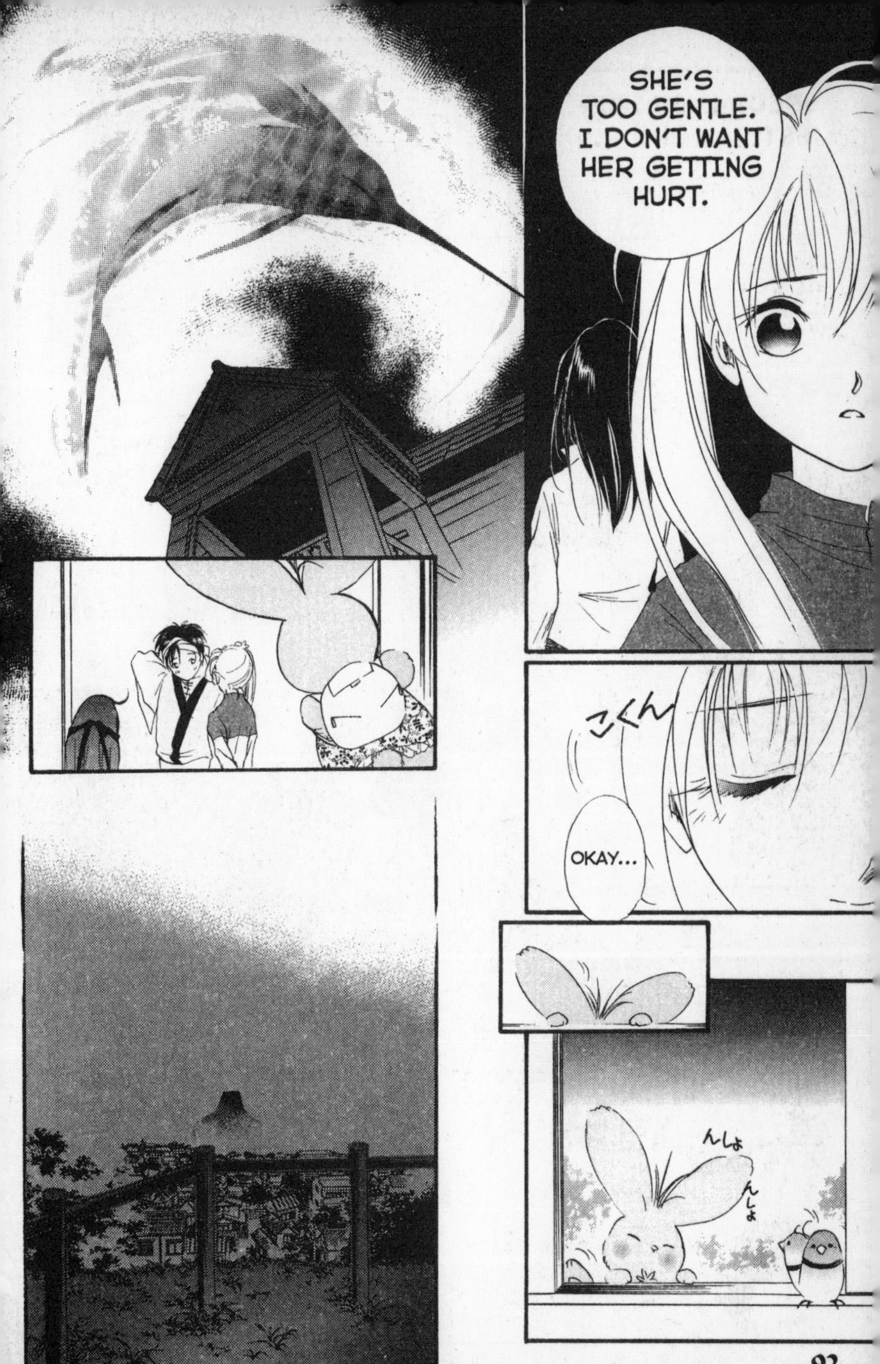
SHE'S TOO GENTLE. I DON'T WANT HER GETTING HURT.
こくん
OKAY...
んしょ
んしょ

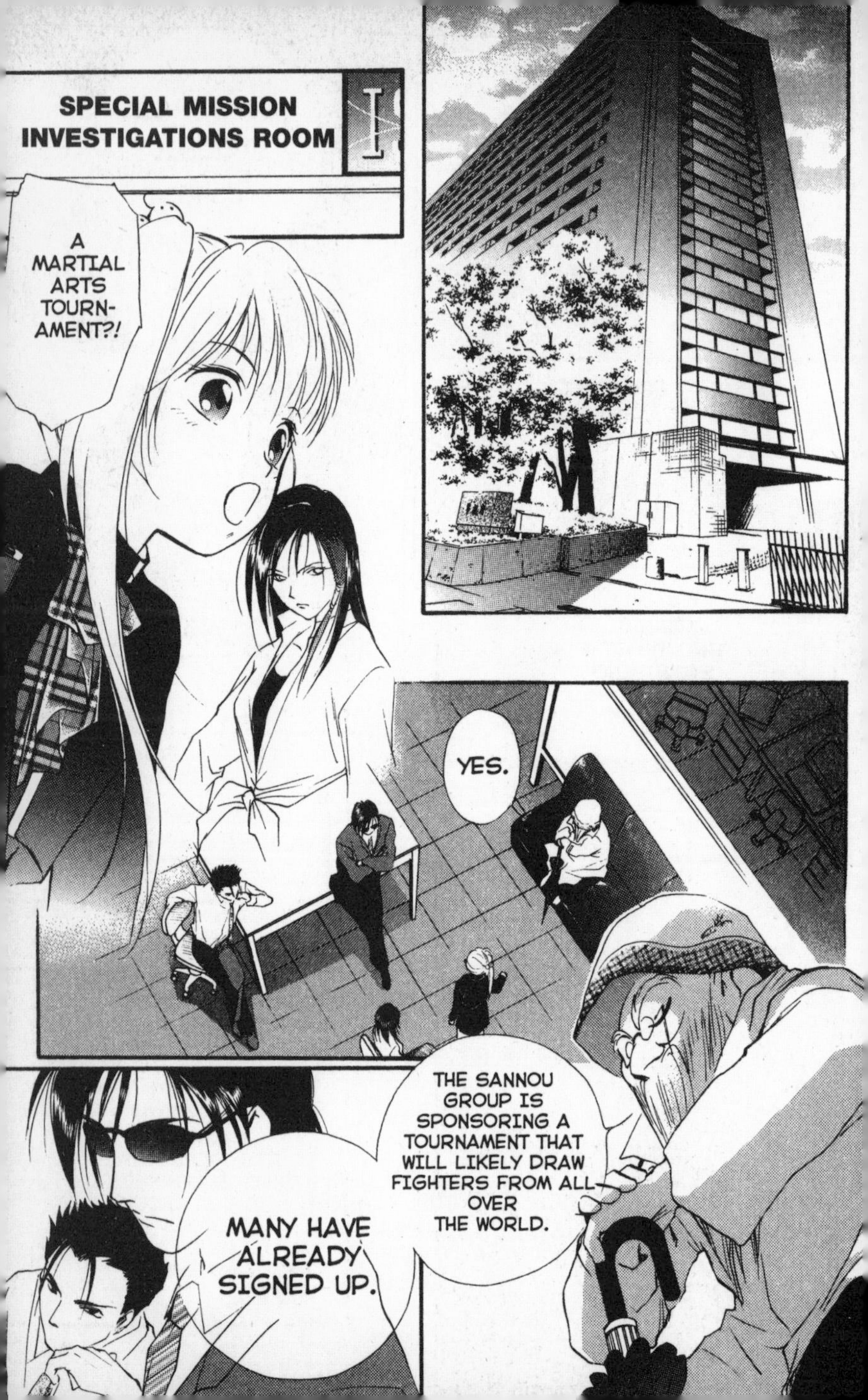
SPECIAL MISSION INVESTIGATIONS ROOM
A MARTIAL ARTS TOURN-AMENT?!
YES.
THE SANNOU GROUP IS SPONSORING A TOURNAMENT THAT WILL LIKELY DRAW FIGHTERS FROM ALL OVER THE WORLD.
MANY HAVE ALREADY SIGNED UP.

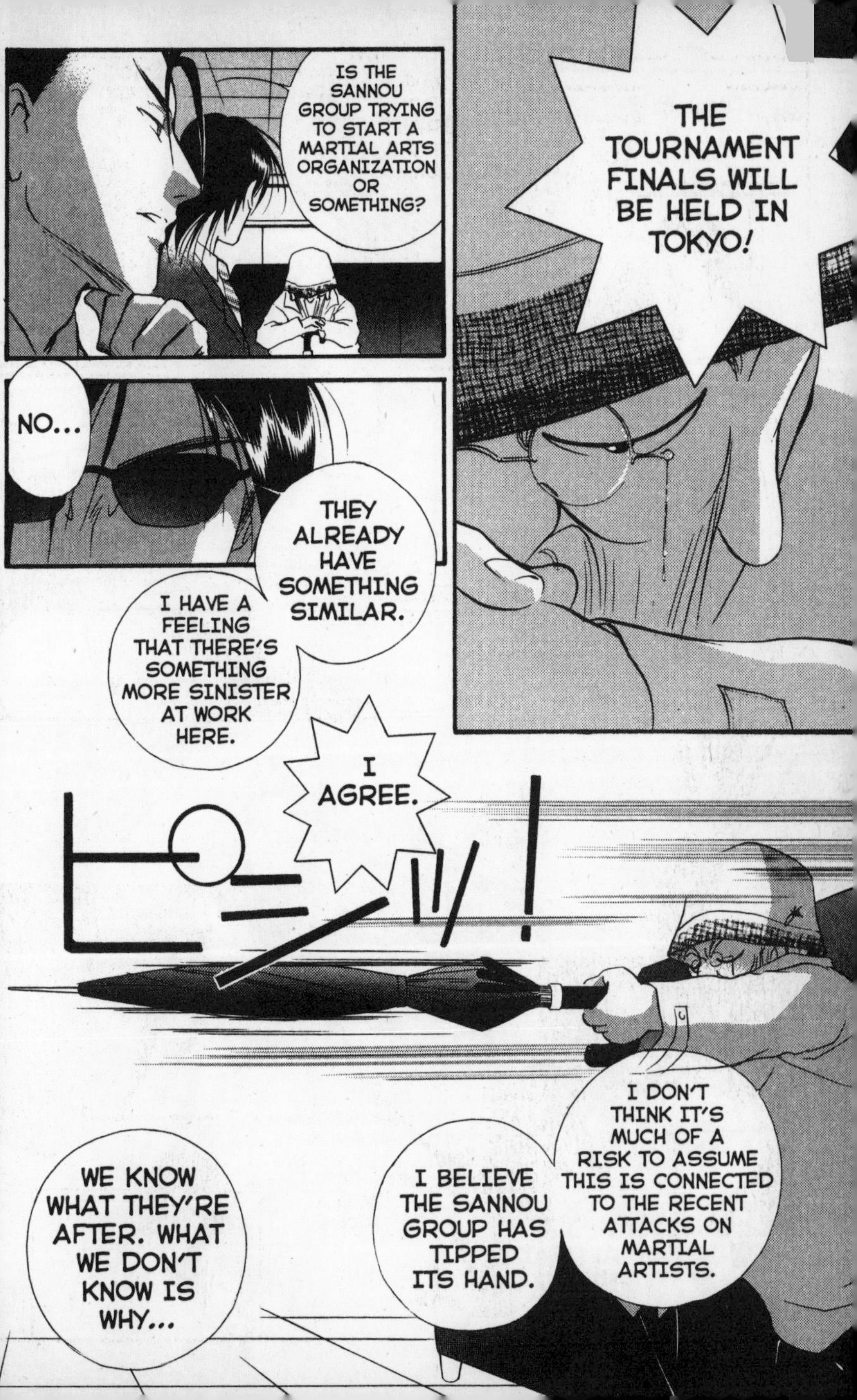
THE TOURNAMENT FINALS WILL BE HELD IN TOKYO!
IS THE SANNOU GROUP TRYING TO START A MARTIAL ARTS ORGANIZATION OR SOMETHING?
NO...
THEY ALREADY HAVE SOMETHING SIMILAR.
I HAVE A FEELING THAT THERE'S SOMETHING MORE SINISTER AT WORK HERE.
I AGREE.
I DON'T THINK IT'S MUCH OF A RISK TO ASSUME THIS IS CONNECTED TO THE RECENT ATTACKS ON MARTIAL ARTISTS.
I BELIEVE THE SANNOU GROUP HAS TIPPED ITS HAND.
WE KNOW WHAT THEY'RE AFTER. WHAT WE DON'T KNOW IS WHY...

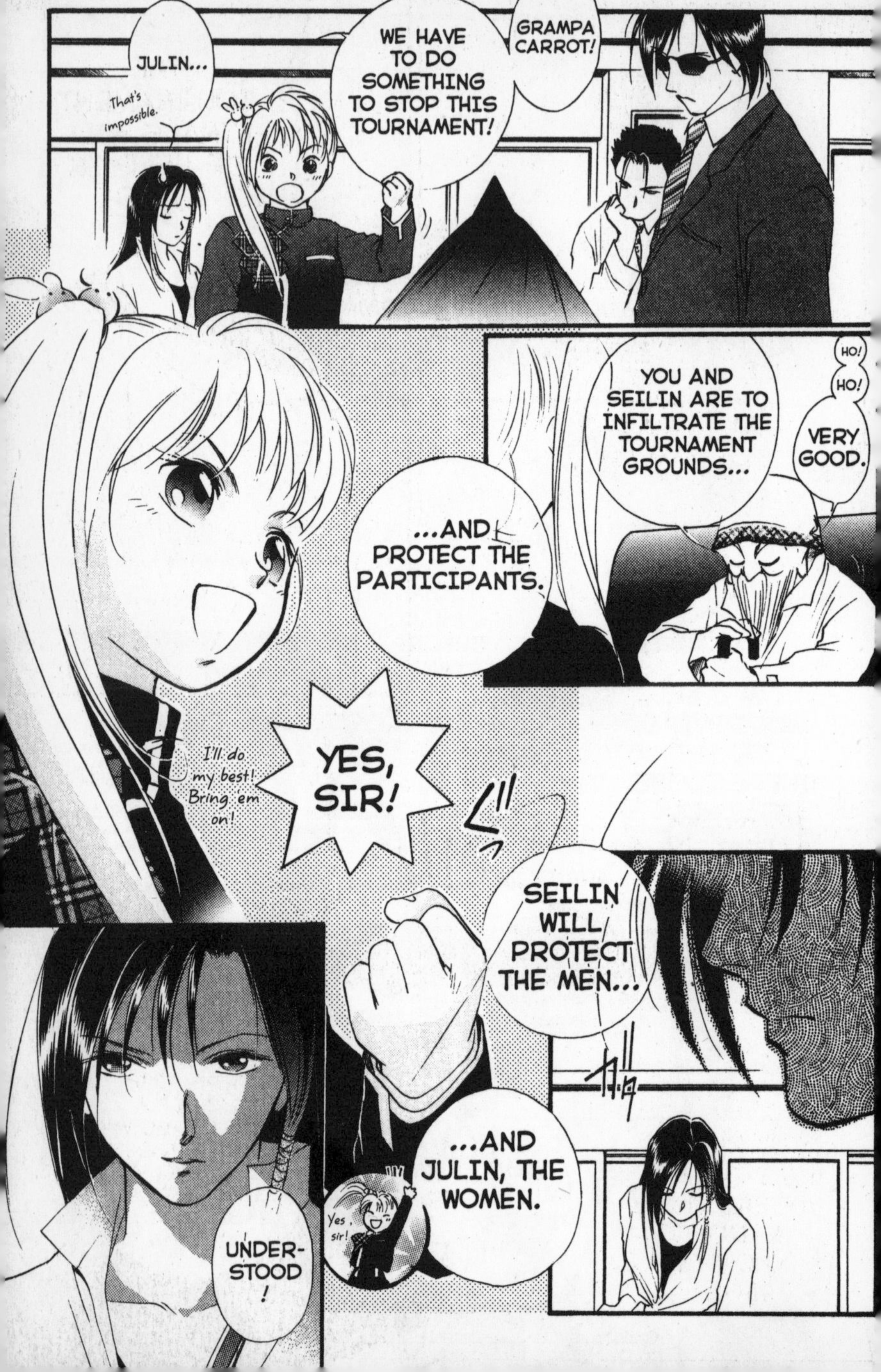

GRAMPA CARROT!
WE HAVE TO DO SOMETHING TO STOP THIS TOURNAMENT!
JULIN...
That's impossible.
HO! HO!
VERY GOOD.
YOU AND SEILIN ARE TO INFILTRATE THE TOURNAMENT GROUNDS...
...AND PROTECT THE PARTICIPANTS.
YES, SIR!
I'll do my best! Bring 'em on!
SEILIN WILL PROTECT THE MEN...
...AND JULIN, THE WOMEN.
Yes, sir!
UNDER-STOOD!

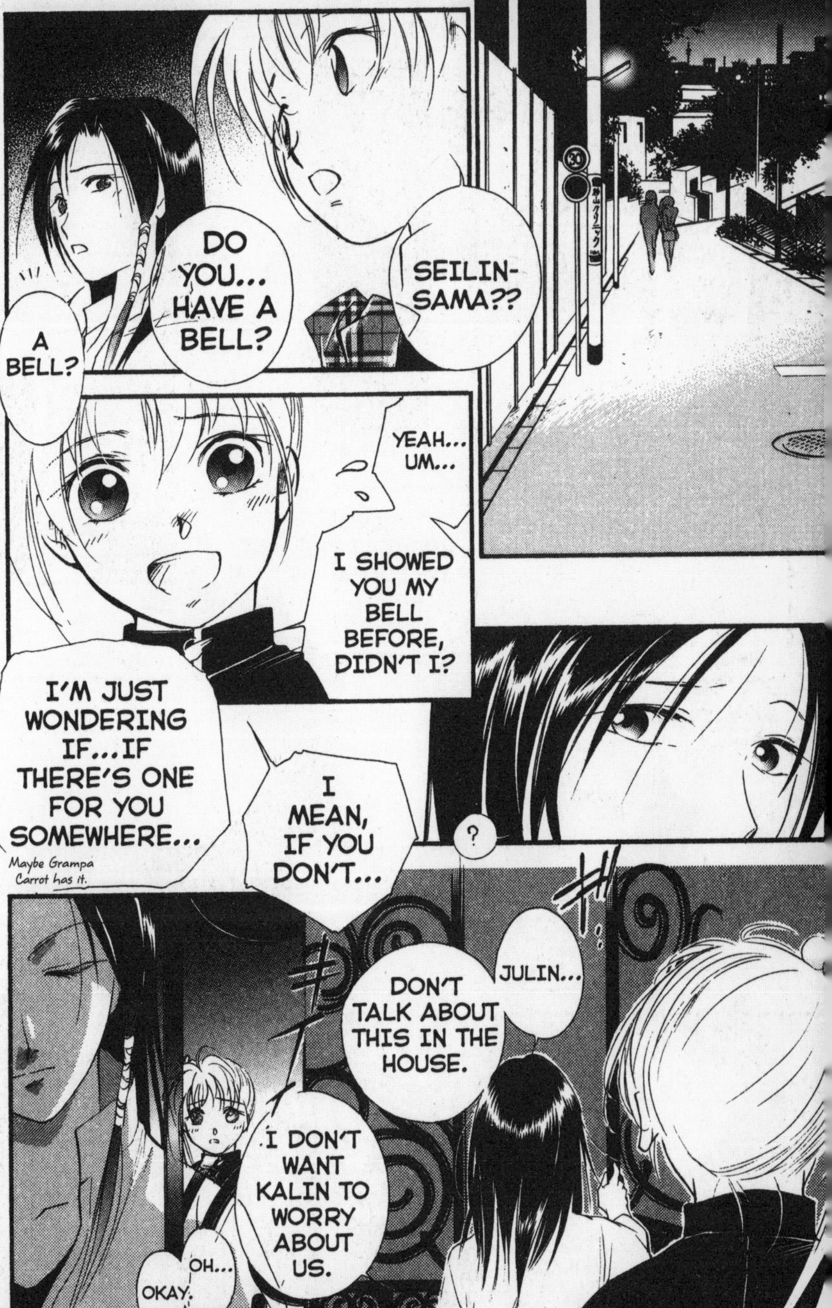
SEILIN-SAMA??
DO YOU... HAVE A BELL?
A BELL?
YEAH... UM...
I SHOWED YOU MY BELL BEFORE, DIDN'T I?
I'M JUST WONDERING IF... IF THERE'S ONE FOR YOU SOMEWHERE...
I MEAN, IF YOU DON'T...
?
Maybe Grampa Carrot has it.
JULIN...
DON'T TALK ABOUT THIS IN THE HOUSE.
I DON'T WANT KALIN TO WORRY ABOUT US.
OH... OKAY.

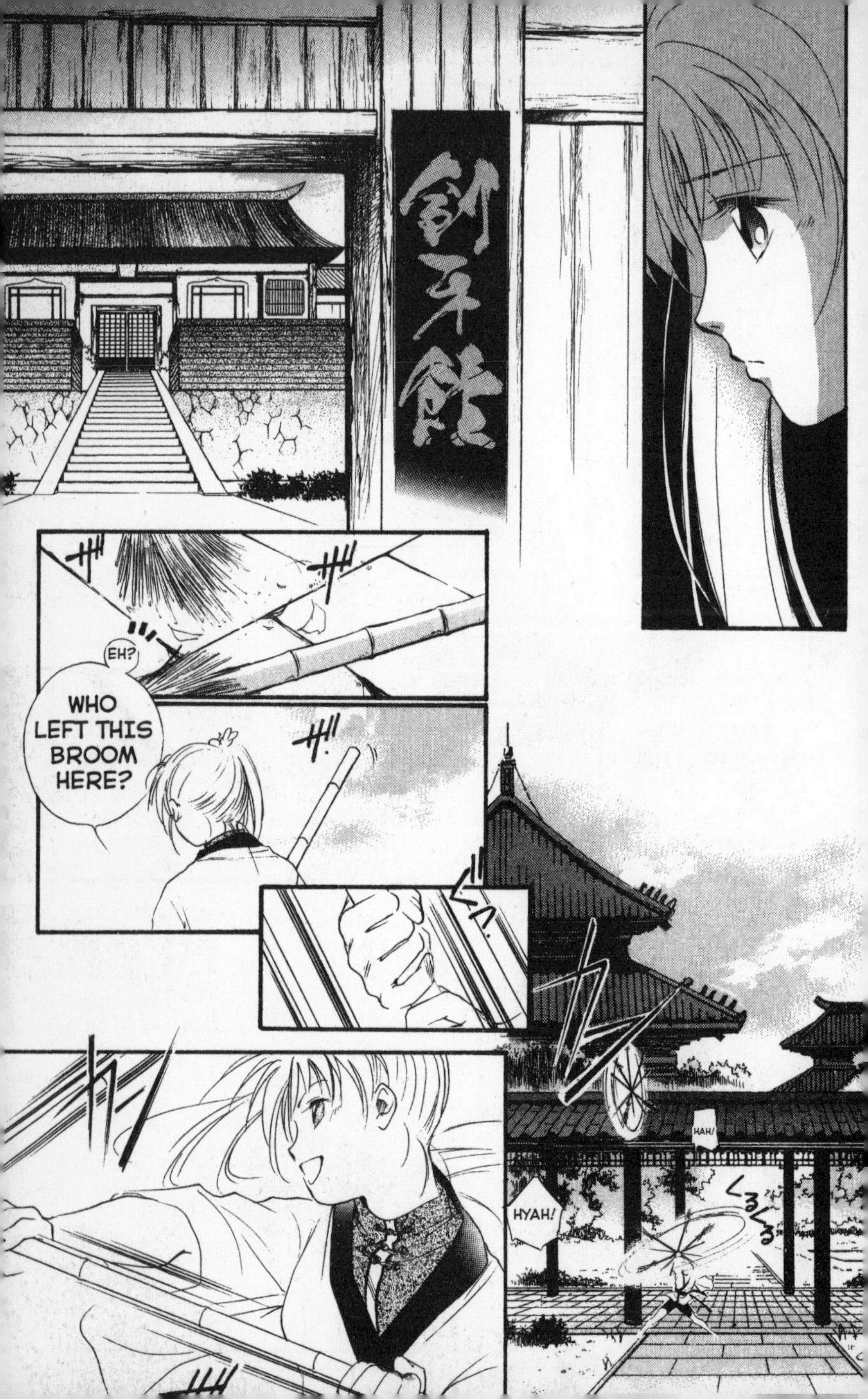
EH?
WHO LEFT THIS BROOM HERE?
HAH!
HYAH!
くるくる

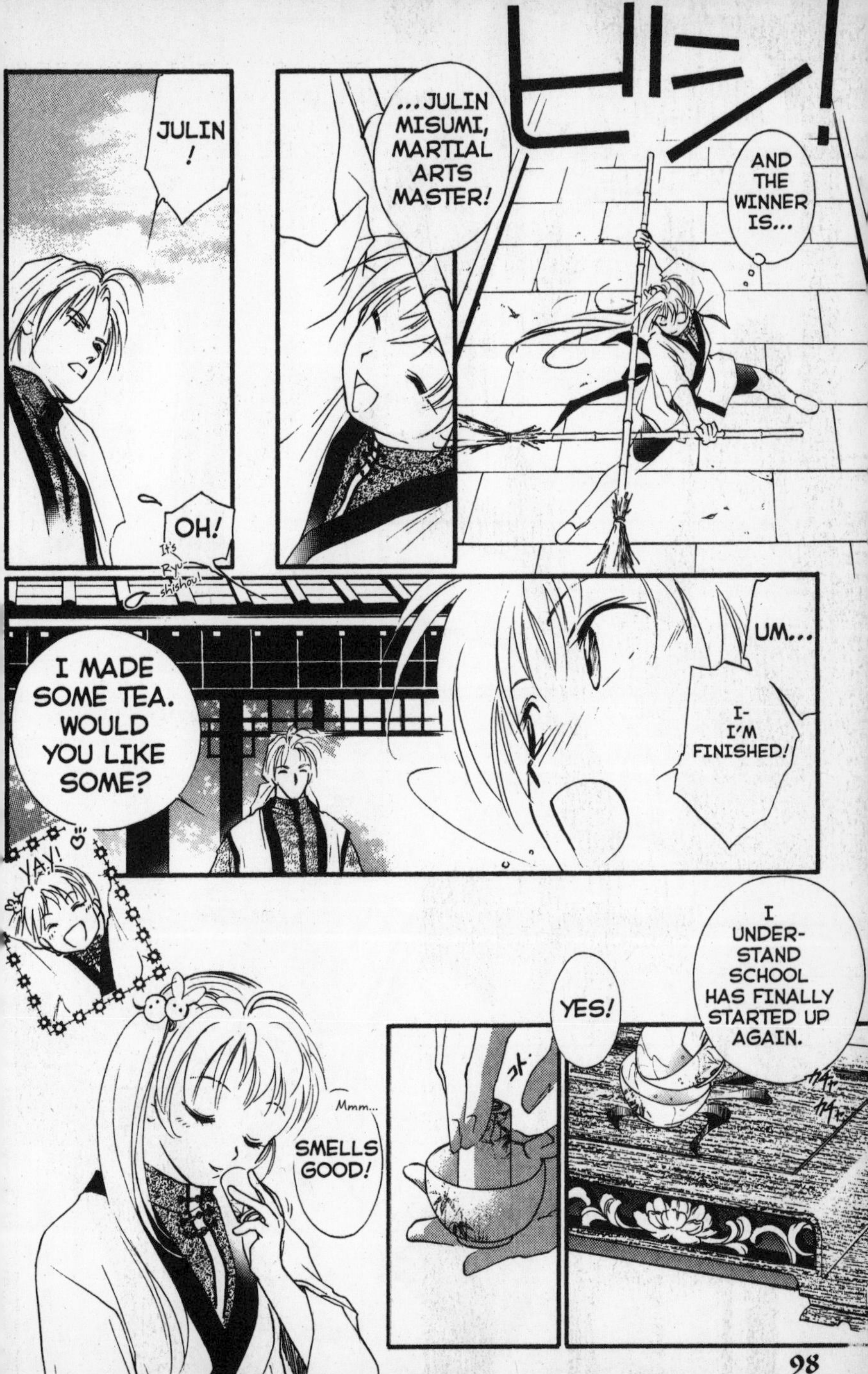
AND THE WINNER IS...
...JULIN MISUMI, MARTIAL ARTS MASTER!
JULIN!
OH!
It's Ryu-shishou!
UM...
I- I'M FINISHED!
I MADE SOME TEA. WOULD YOU LIKE SOME?
YAY!
I UNDERSTAND SCHOOL HAS FINALLY STARTED UP AGAIN.
YES!
Mmm...
SMELLS GOOD!

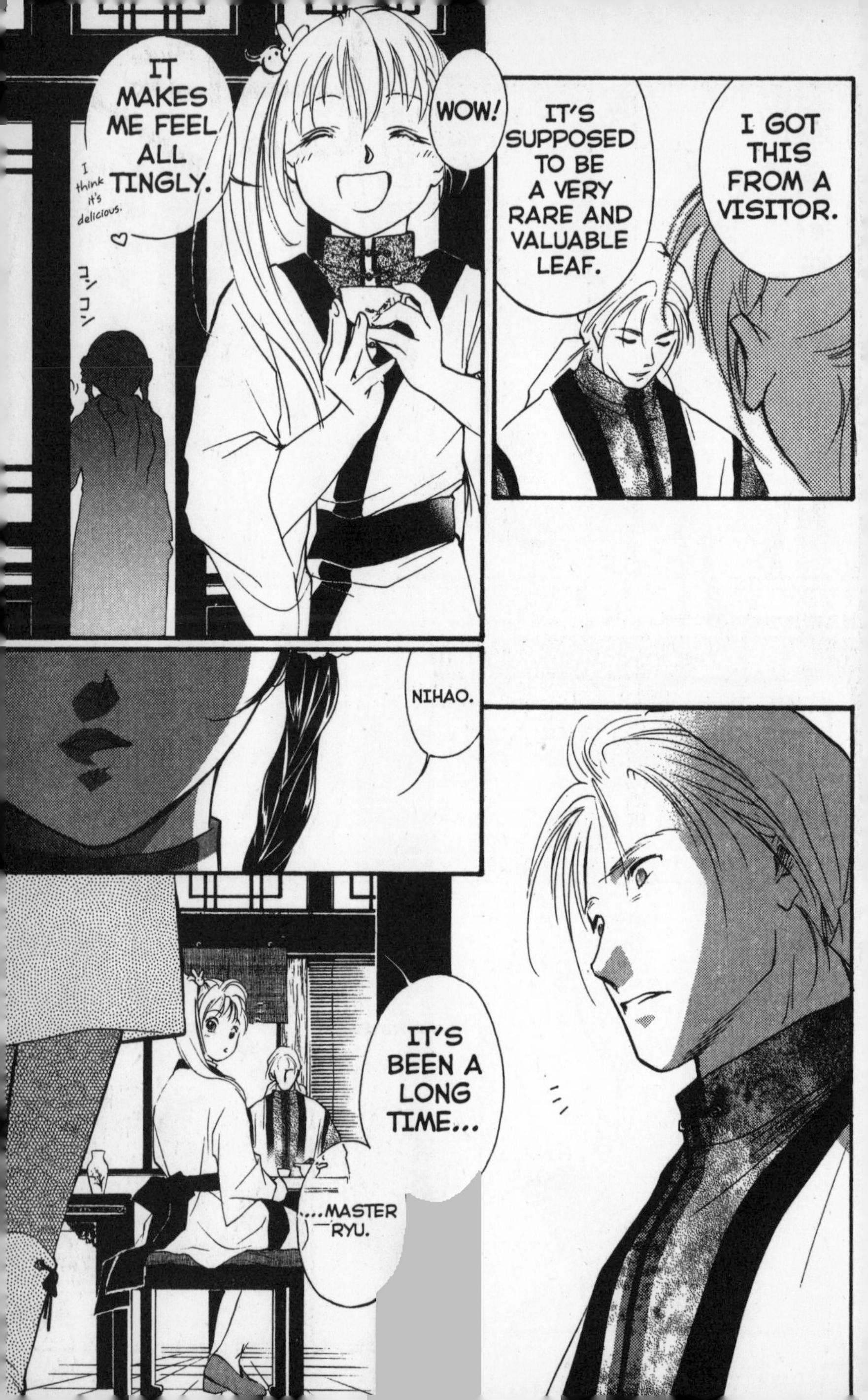
I GOT THIS FROM A VISITOR.
IT'S SUPPOSED TO BE A VERY RARE AND VALUABLE LEAF.
WOW!
IT MAKES ME FEEL ALL TINGLY.
I think it's delicious.
コンコン
NIHAO.
IT'S BEEN A LONG TIME...
....MASTER RYU.

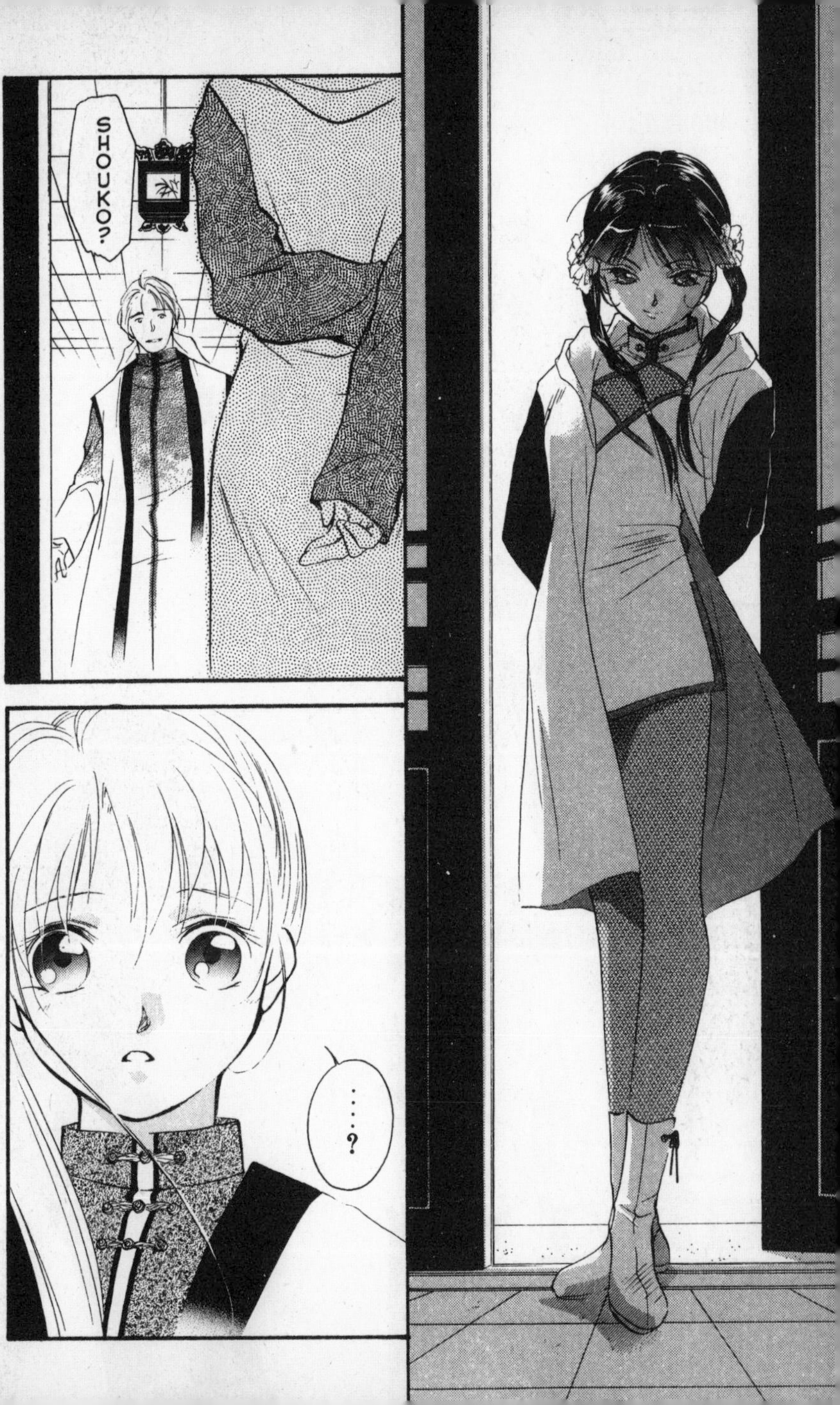
SHOUKO?
....?

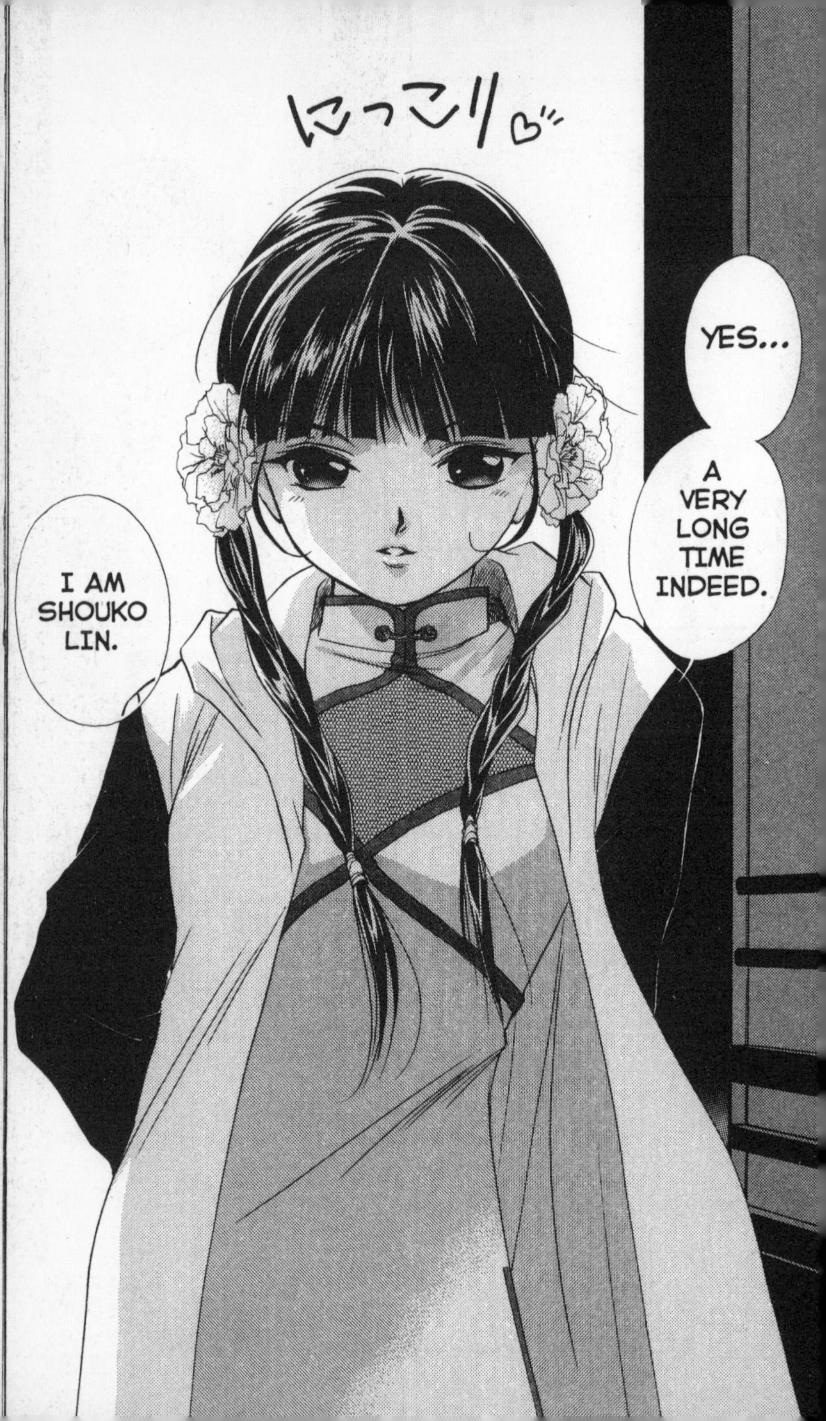
にっこり
YES...
A VERY LONG TIME INDEED.
I AM SHOUKO LIN.

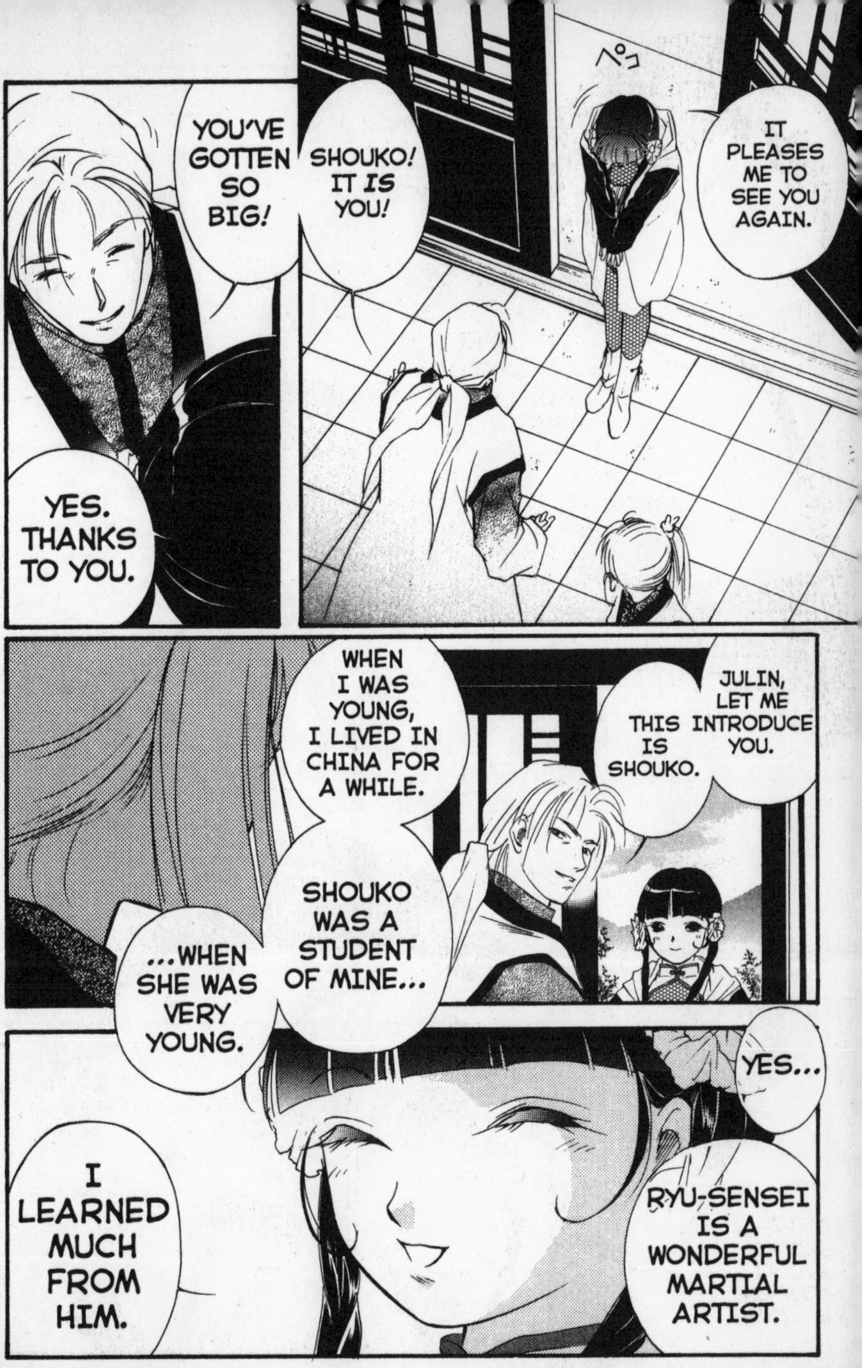
ペコ
IT PLEASES ME TO SEE YOU AGAIN.
SHOUKO! IT *IS* YOU!
YOU'VE GOTTEN SO BIG!
YES. THANKS TO YOU.
JULIN, LET ME INTRODUCE YOU.
THIS IS SHOUKO.
WHEN I WAS YOUNG, I LIVED IN CHINA FOR A WHILE.
SHOUKO WAS A STUDENT OF MINE...
...WHEN SHE WAS VERY YOUNG.
YES...
RYU-SENSEI IS A WONDERFUL MARTIAL ARTIST.
I LEARNED MUCH FROM HIM.

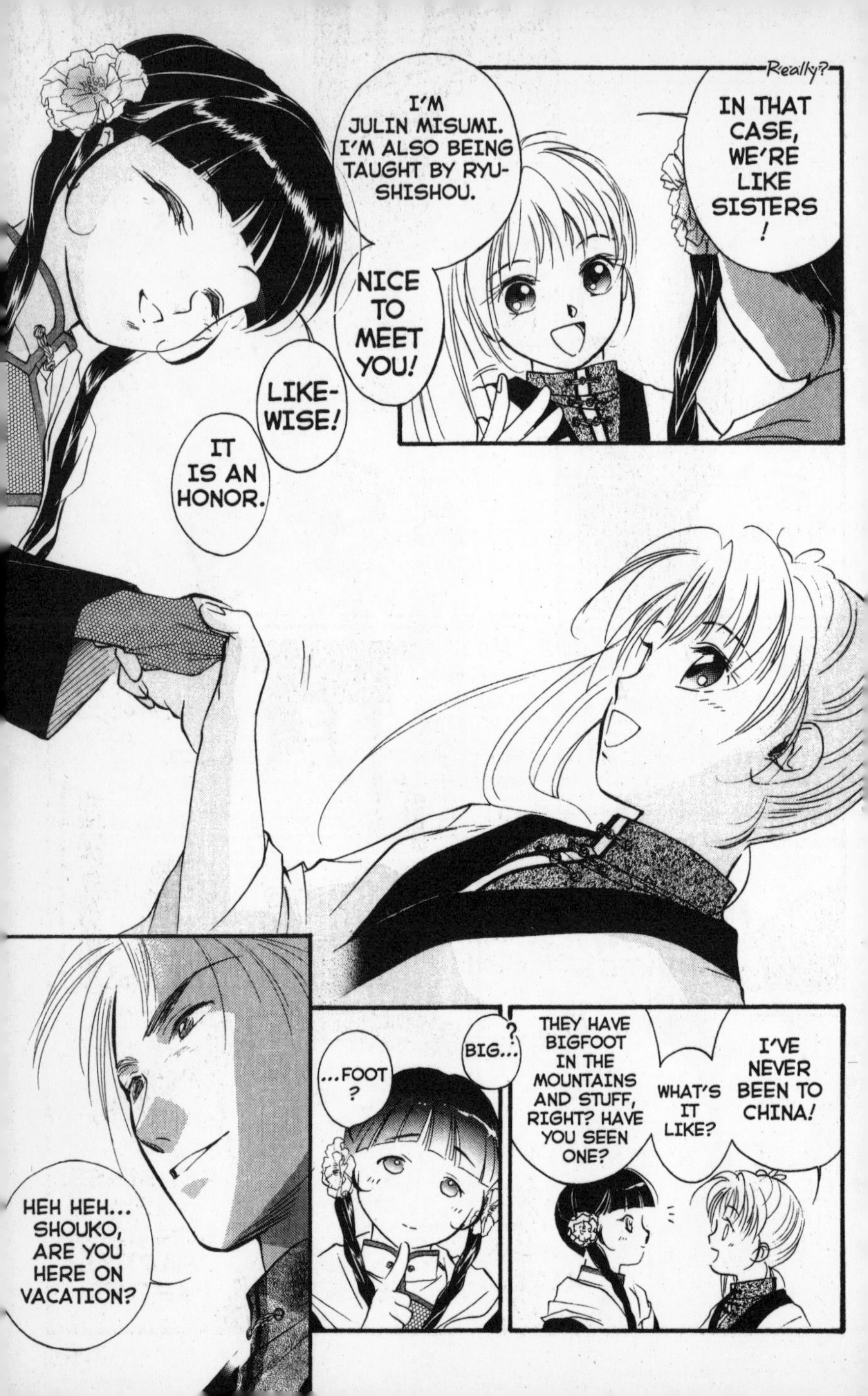
I'M JULIN MISUMI. I'M ALSO BEING TAUGHT BY RYU-SHISHOU.
NICE TO MEET YOU!
LIKE-WISE!
IT IS AN HONOR.
Really?
IN THAT CASE, WE'RE LIKE SISTERS!
I'VE NEVER BEEN TO CHINA!
WHAT'S IT LIKE?
THEY HAVE BIGFOOT IN THE MOUNTAINS AND STUFF, RIGHT? HAVE YOU SEEN ONE?
BIG...?
...FOOT?
HEH HEH... SHOUKO, ARE YOU HERE ON VACATION?

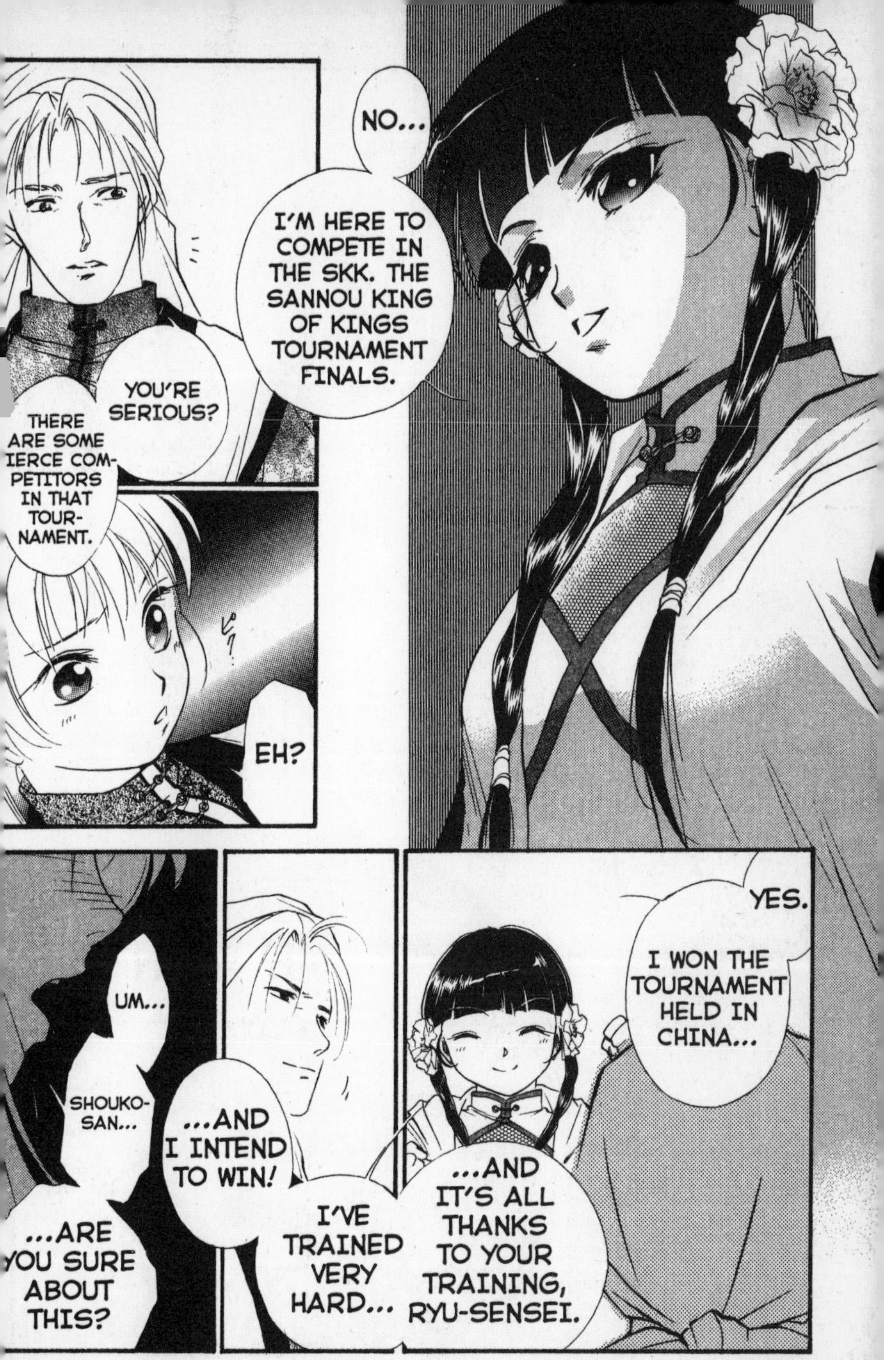
NO...
I'M HERE TO COMPETE IN THE SKK. THE SANNOU KING OF KINGS TOURNAMENT FINALS.
YOU'RE SERIOUS?
THERE ARE SOME IERCE COMPETITORS IN THAT TOURNAMENT.
ピク
EH?
YES.
I WON THE TOURNAMENT HELD IN CHINA...
...AND IT'S ALL THANKS TO YOUR TRAINING, RYU-SENSEI.
I'VE TRAINED VERY HARD...
...AND I INTEND TO WIN!
UM...
SHOUKO-SAN...
...ARE YOU SURE ABOUT THIS?

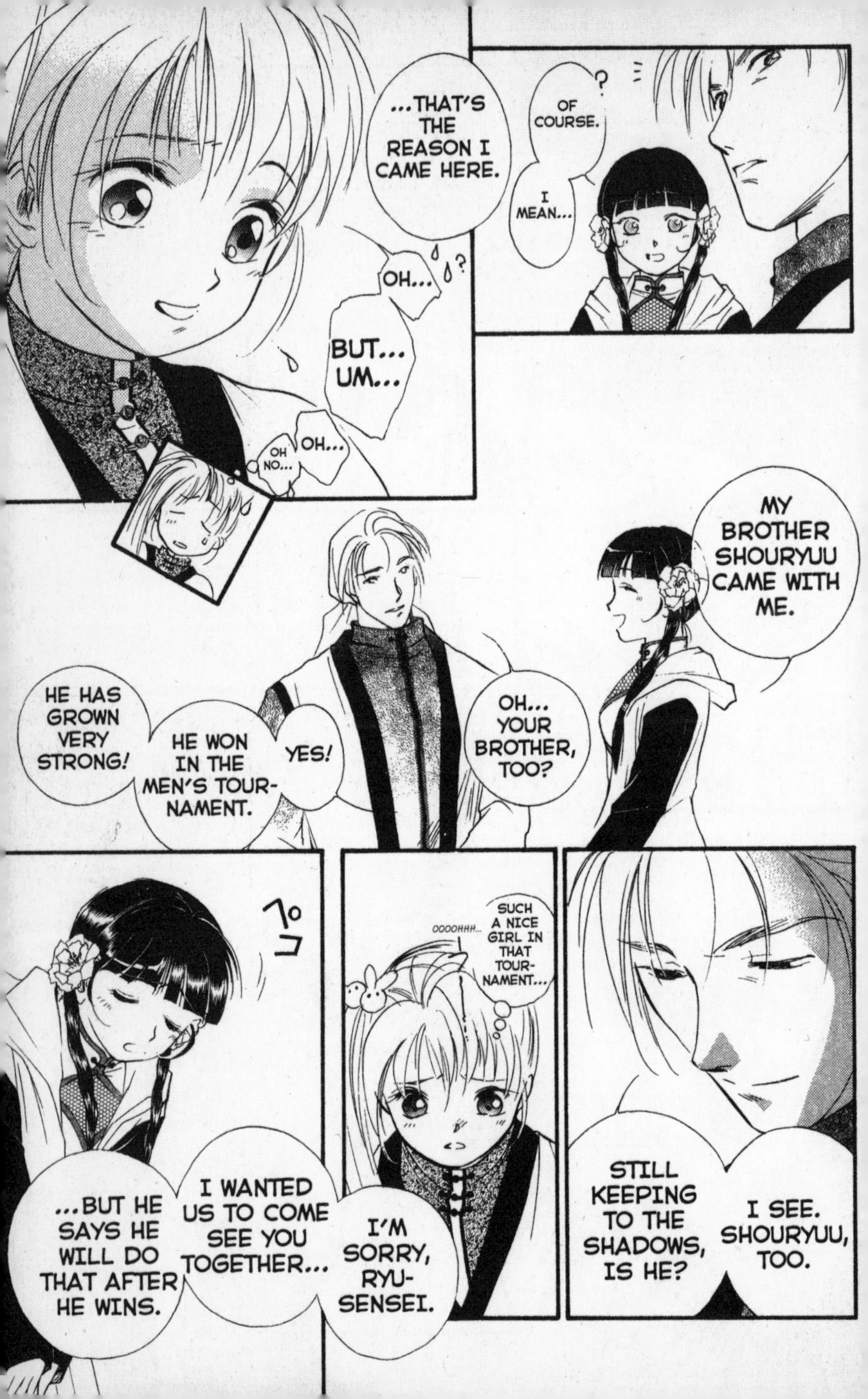
?
OF COURSE.
I MEAN...
...THAT'S THE REASON I CAME HERE.
OH...
?
BUT... UM...
OH...
OH NO...
MY BROTHER SHOURYUU CAME WITH ME.
OH... YOUR BROTHER, TOO?
YES!
HE WON IN THE MEN'S TOURNAMENT.
HE HAS GROWN VERY STRONG!
I SEE. SHOURYUU, TOO.
STILL KEEPING TO THE SHADOWS, IS HE?
SUCH A NICE GIRL IN THAT TOURNAMENT...
OOOOHHH...
ペコ
I'M SORRY, RYU-SENSEI.
I WANTED US TO COME SEE YOU TOGETHER...
...BUT HE SAYS HE WILL DO THAT AFTER HE WINS.

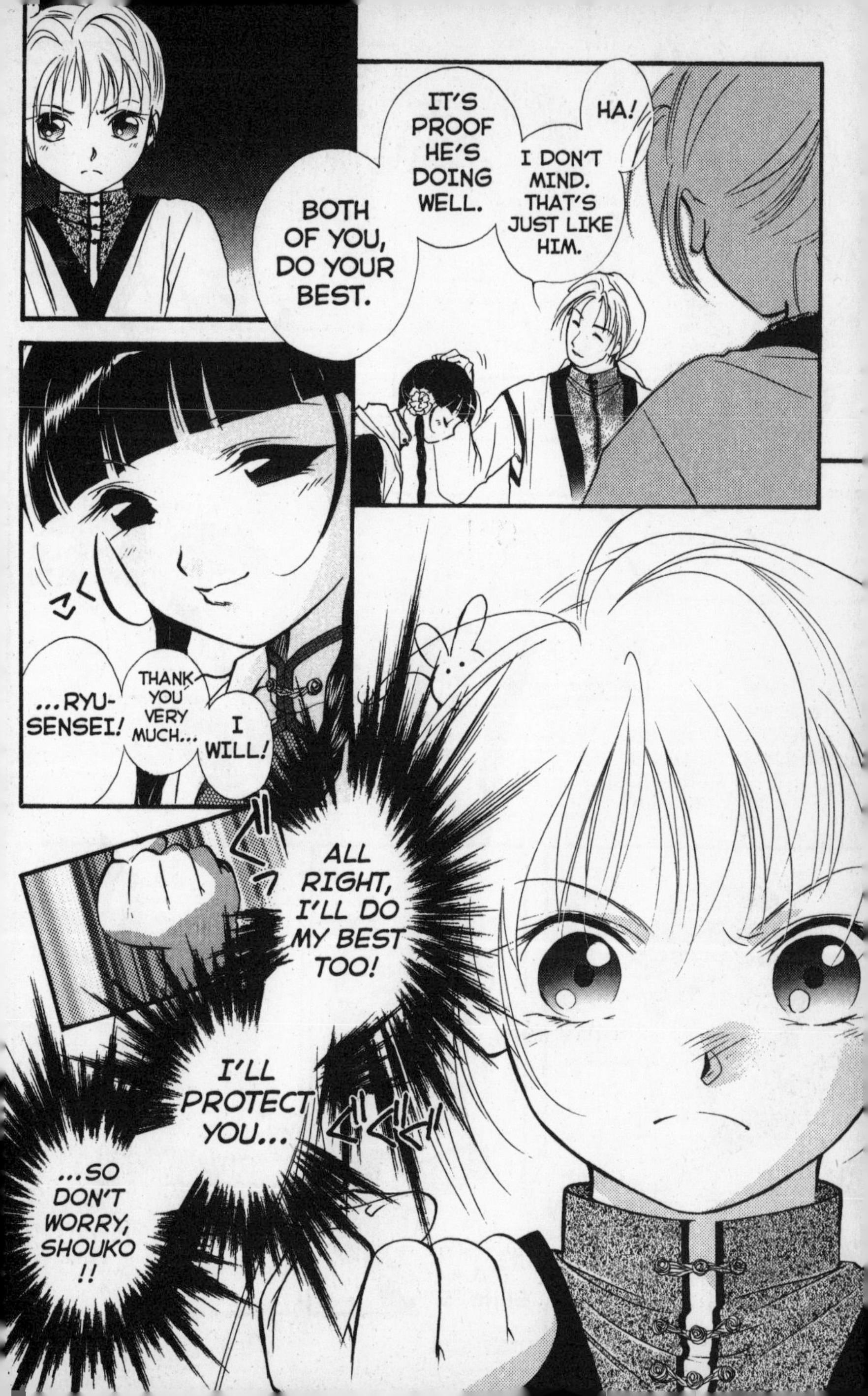
HA!
I DON'T MIND. THAT'S JUST LIKE HIM.
IT'S PROOF HE'S DOING WELL.
BOTH OF YOU, DO YOUR BEST.
I WILL!
THANK YOU VERY MUCH...
...RYU-SENSEI!
ALL RIGHT, I'LL DO MY BEST TOO!
I'LL PROTECT YOU...
...SO DON'T WORRY, SHOUKO !!

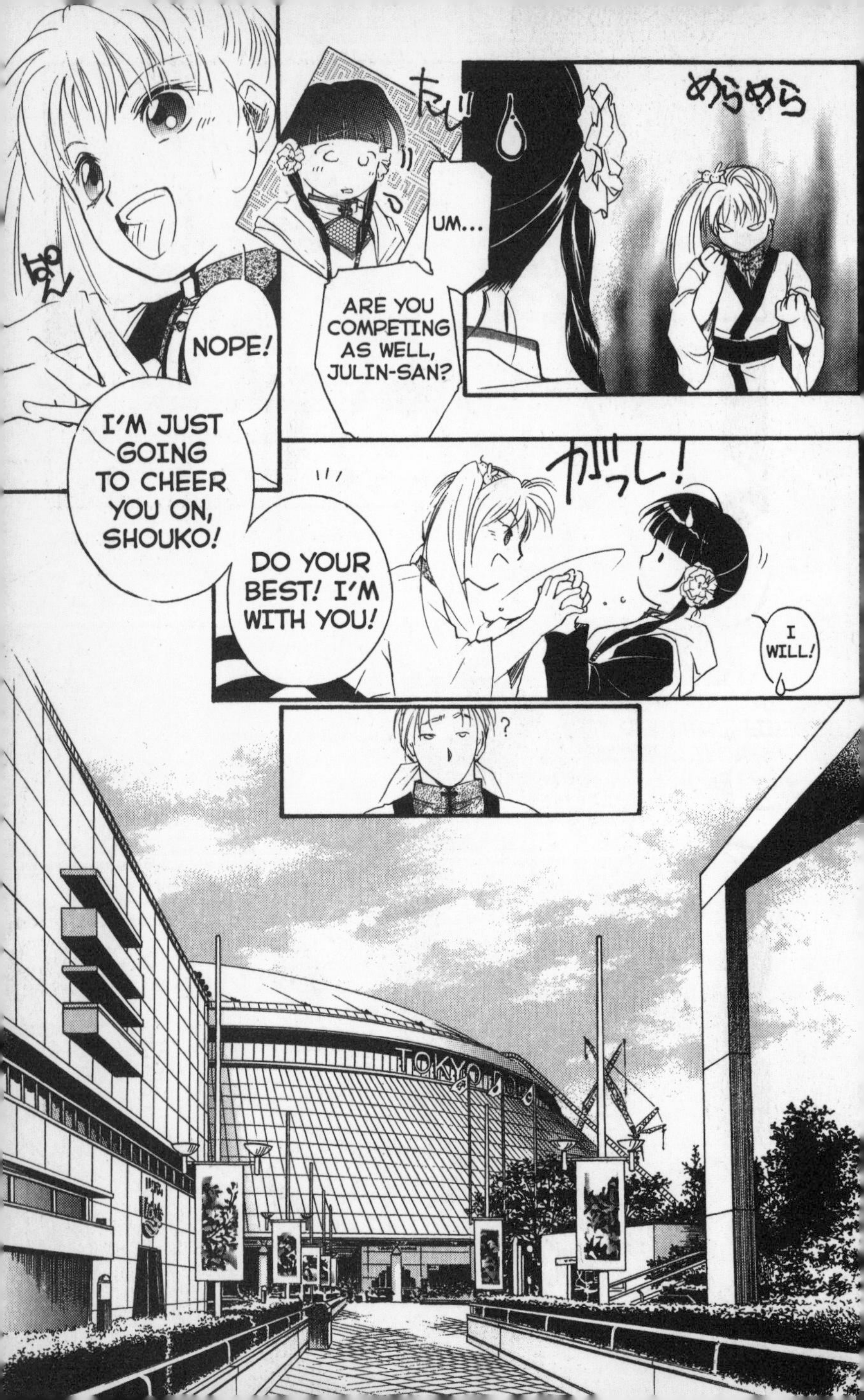
めらめら
たじ
UM...
ARE YOU COMPETING AS WELL, JULIN-SAN?
ぱん
NOPE!
I'M JUST GOING TO CHEER YOU ON, SHOUKO!
がっし!
DO YOUR BEST! I'M WITH YOU!
I WILL!
?
TOKYO

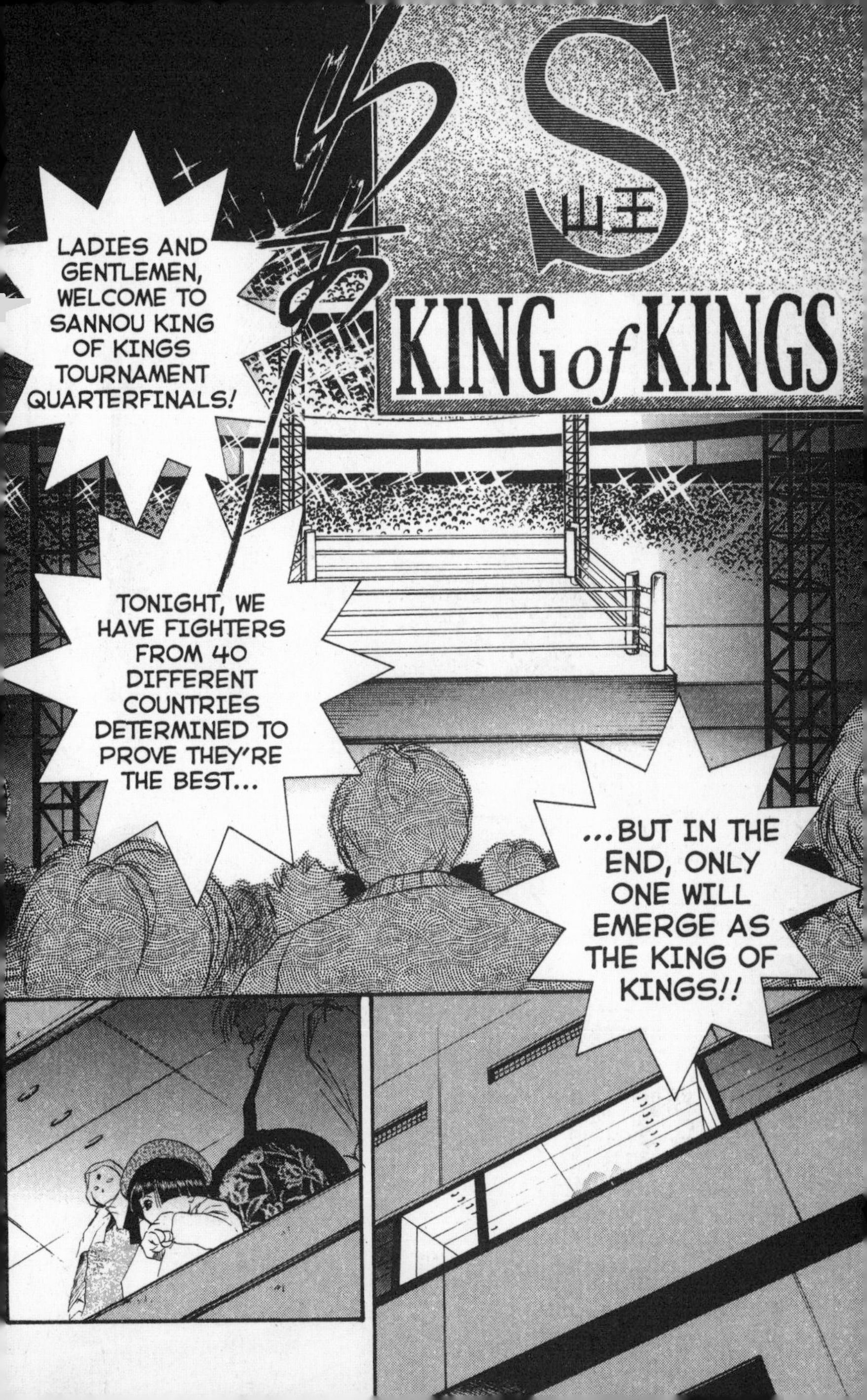
KING of KINGS
LADIES AND GENTLEMEN, WELCOME TO SANNOU KING OF KINGS TOURNAMENT QUARTERFINALS!
TONIGHT, WE HAVE FIGHTERS FROM 40 DIFFERENT COUNTRIES DETERMINED TO PROVE THEY'RE THE BEST...
...BUT IN THE END, ONLY ONE WILL EMERGE AS THE KING OF KINGS!!

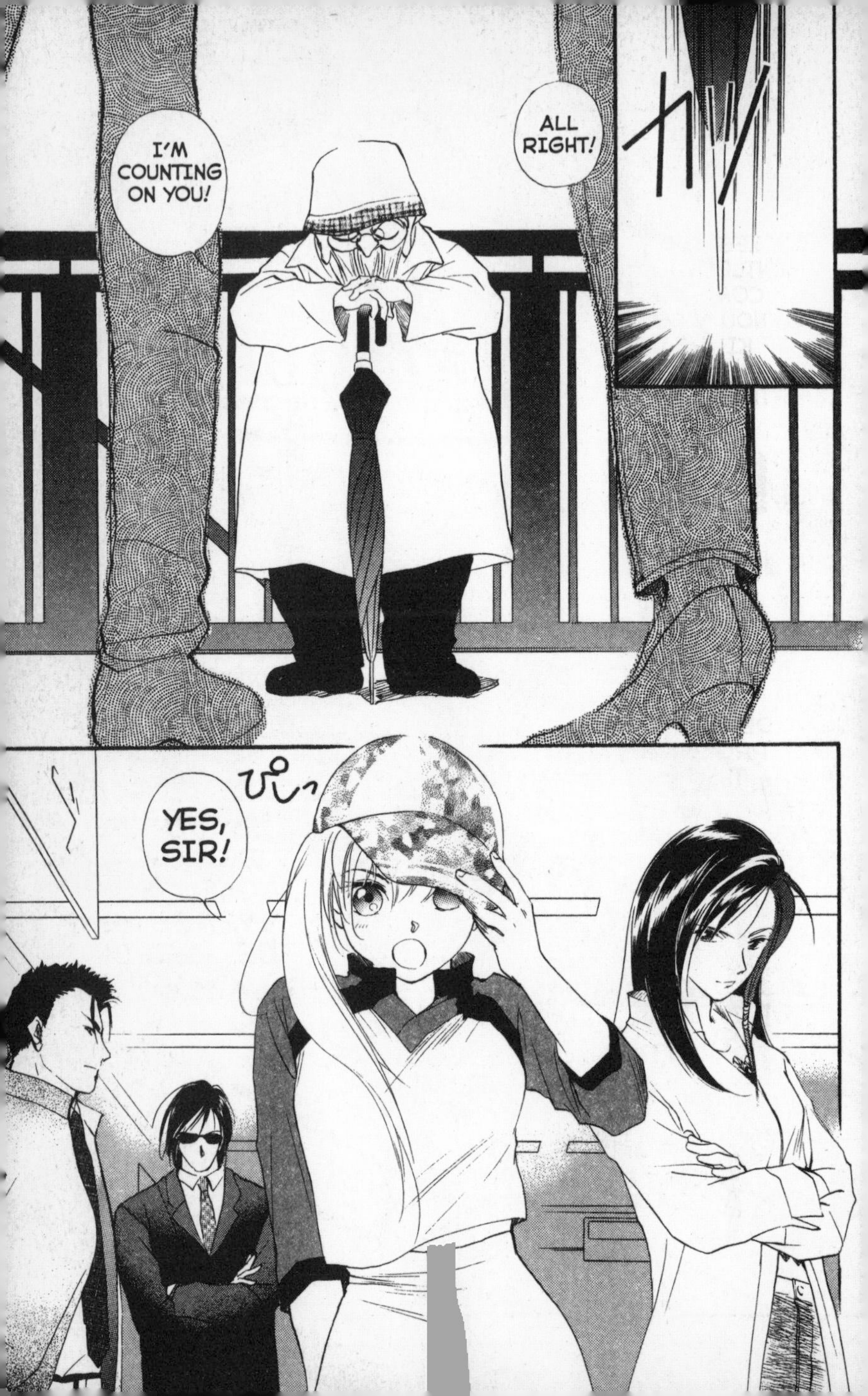
カッ
ALL RIGHT!
I'M COUNTING ON YOU!
ぴしっ
YES, SIR!

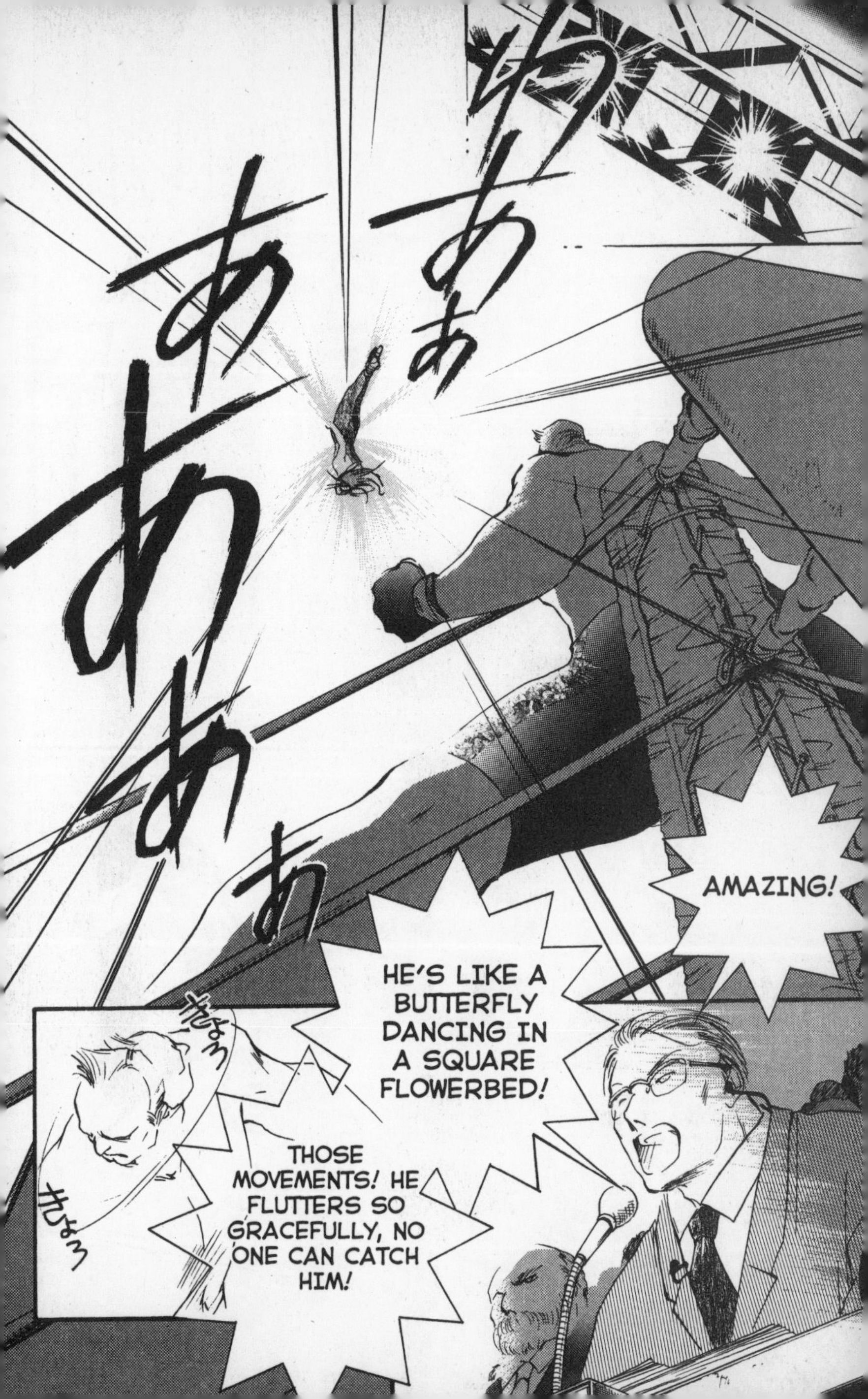
わあぁ〜
あああぁ
AMAZING!
HE'S LIKE A BUTTERFLY DANCING IN A SQUARE FLOWERBED!
THOSE MOVEMENTS! HE FLUTTERS SO GRACEFULLY, NO ONE CAN CATCH HIM!
きょろ
きょろ

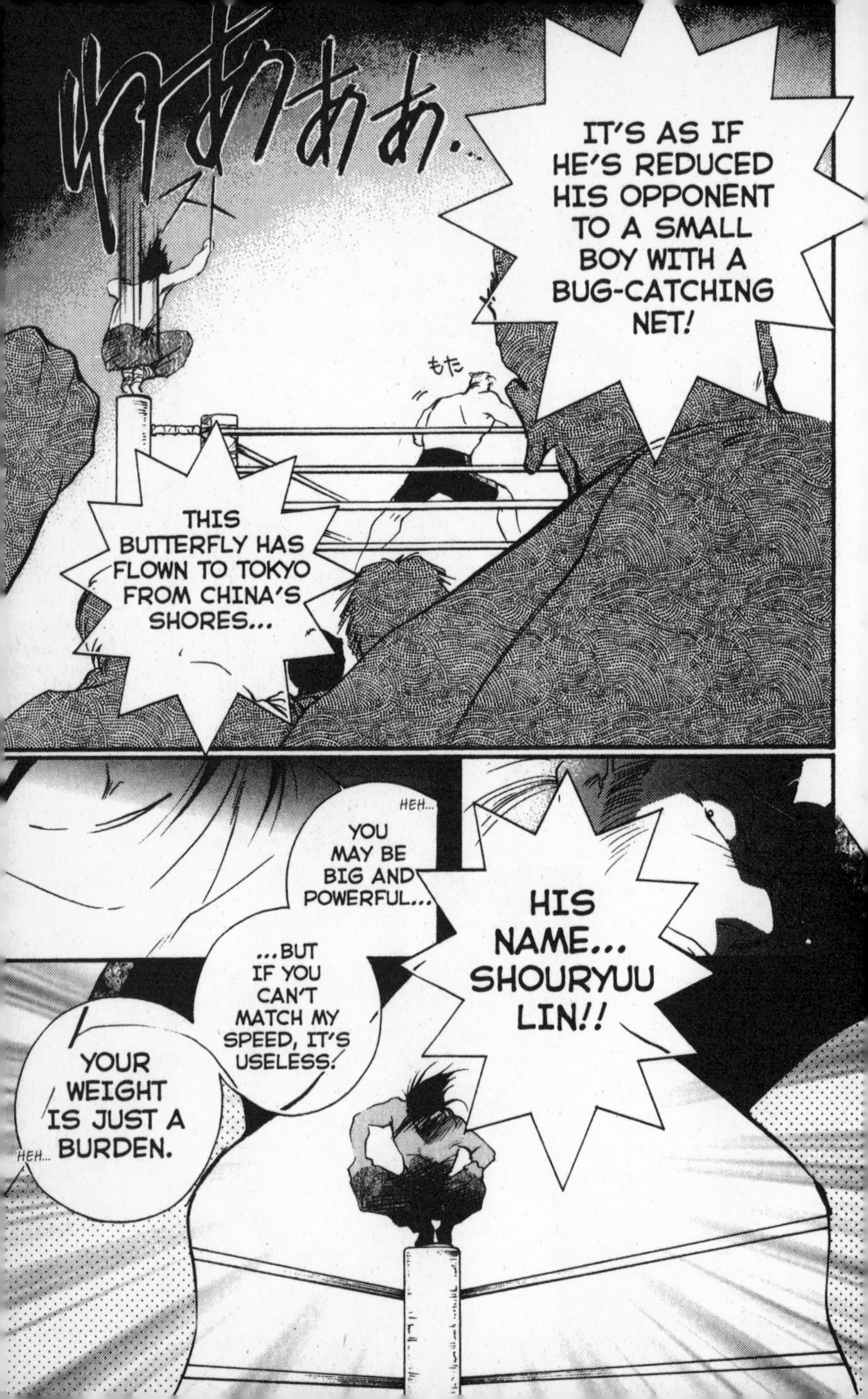
IT'S AS IF HE'S REDUCED HIS OPPONENT TO A SMALL BOY WITH A BUG-CATCHING NET!
もた
THIS BUTTERFLY HAS FLOWN TO TOKYO FROM CHINA'S SHORES...
HIS NAME... SHOURYUU LIN!!
HEH...
YOU MAY BE BIG AND POWERFUL...
...BUT IF YOU CAN'T MATCH MY SPEED, IT'S USELESS.
YOUR WEIGHT IS JUST A BURDEN.
HEH...

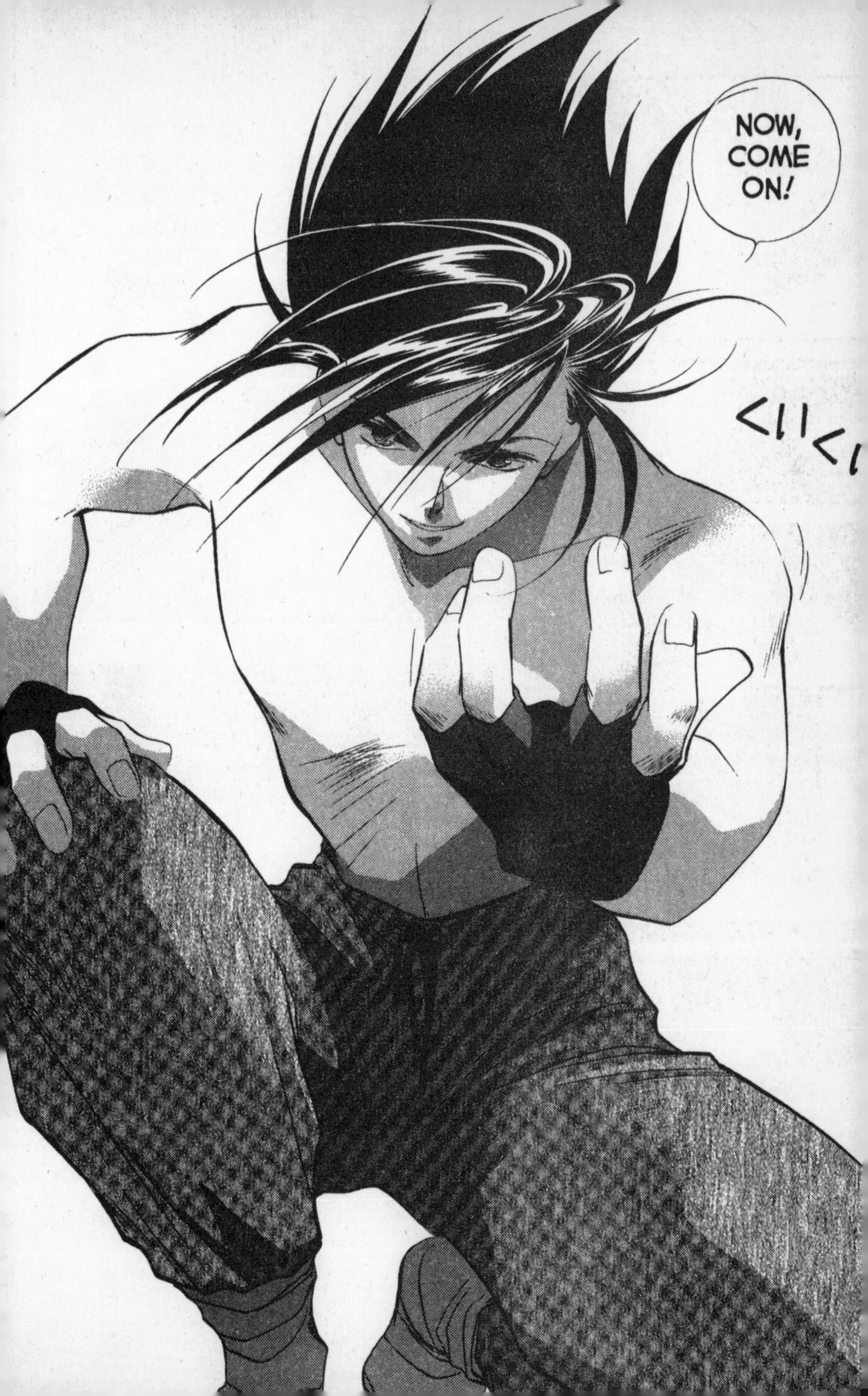
NOW, COME ON!
くいくい

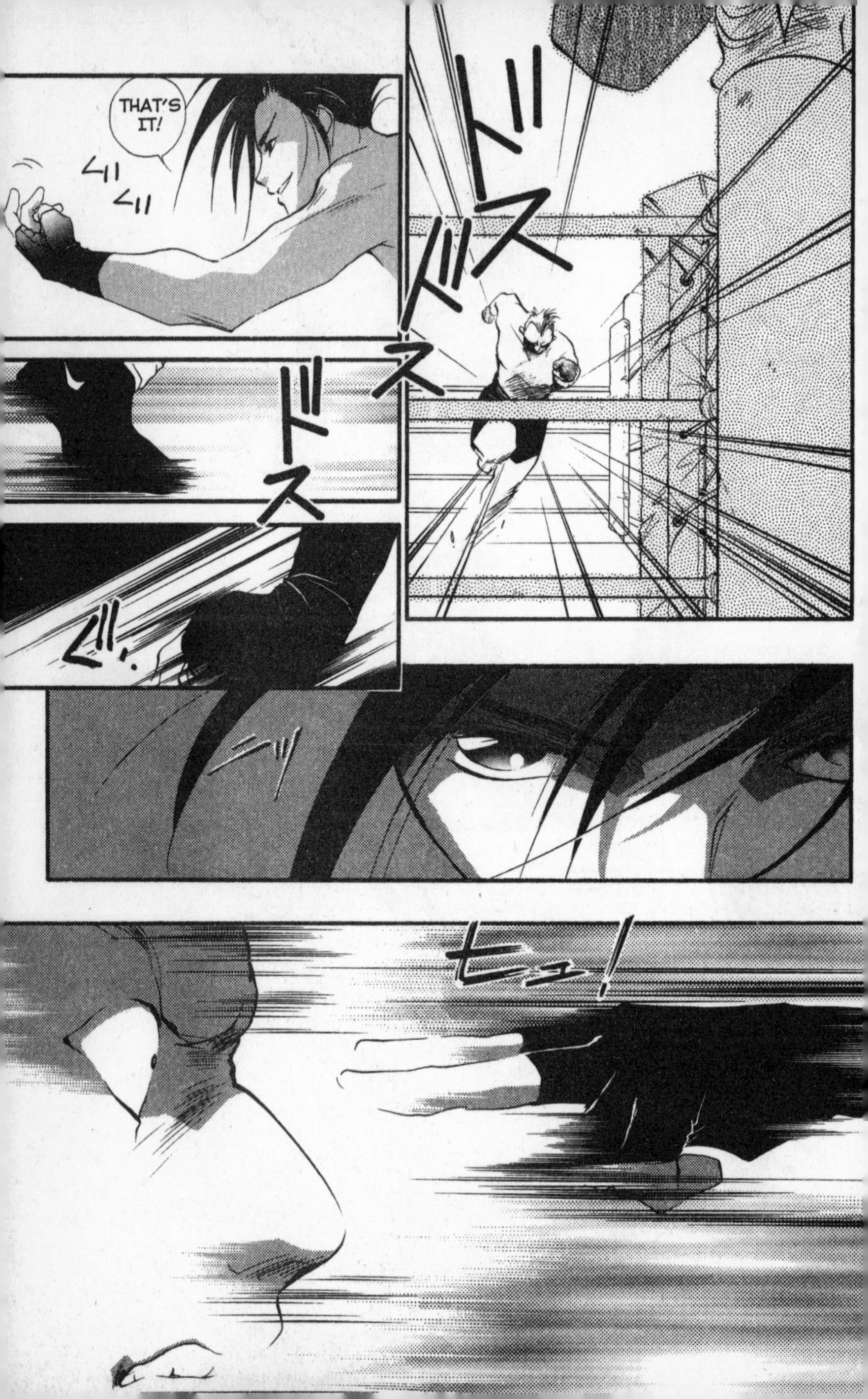
ドス
ドス
ドス
THAT'S IT!
ぐい ぐい
ぐ!
ニッ
ヒュ!

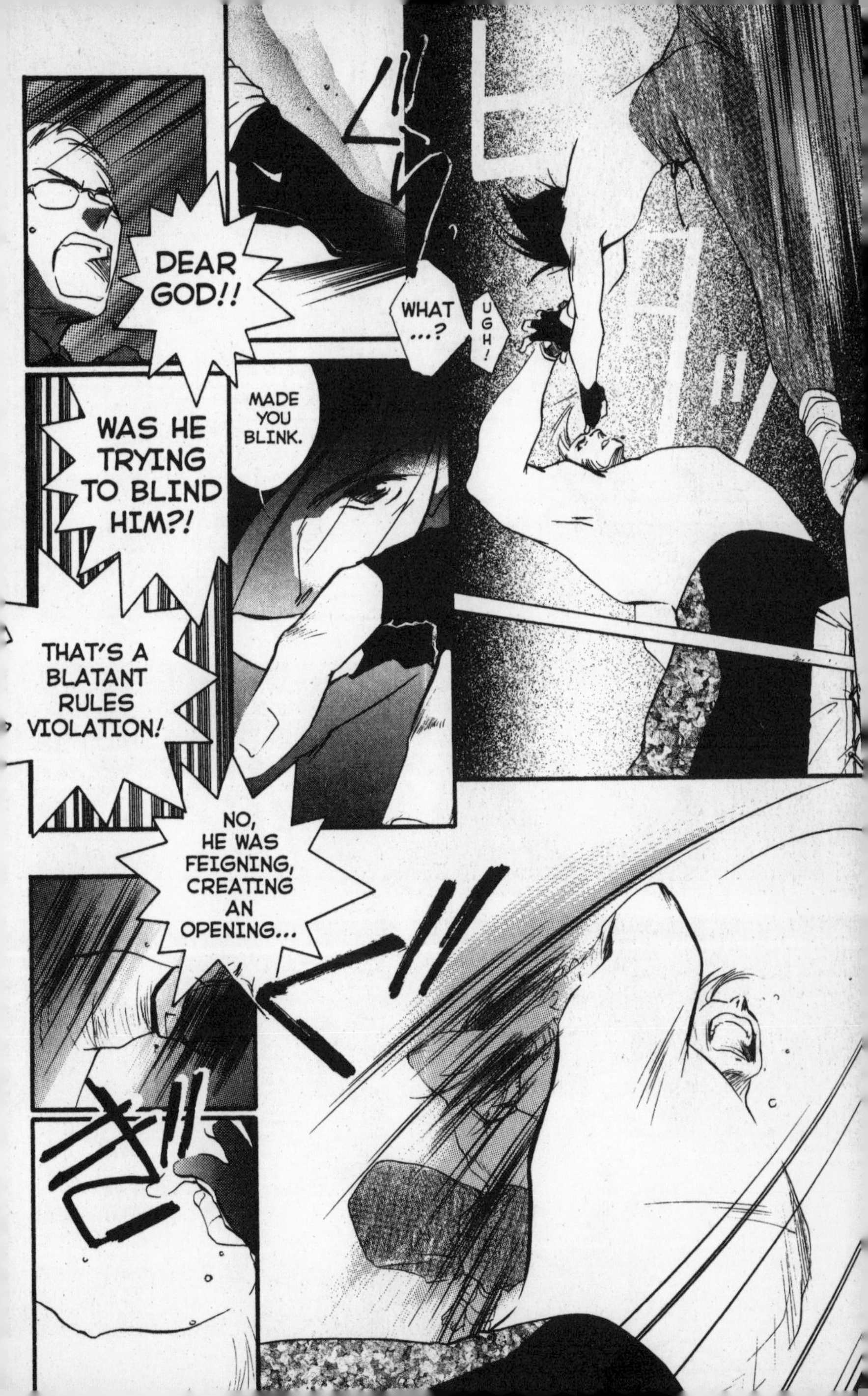
WHAT ...?
UGH!
DEAR GOD!!
MADE YOU BLINK.
WAS HE TRYING TO BLIND HIM?!
THAT'S A BLATANT RULES VIOLATION!
NO, HE WAS FEIGNING, CREATING AN OPENING...

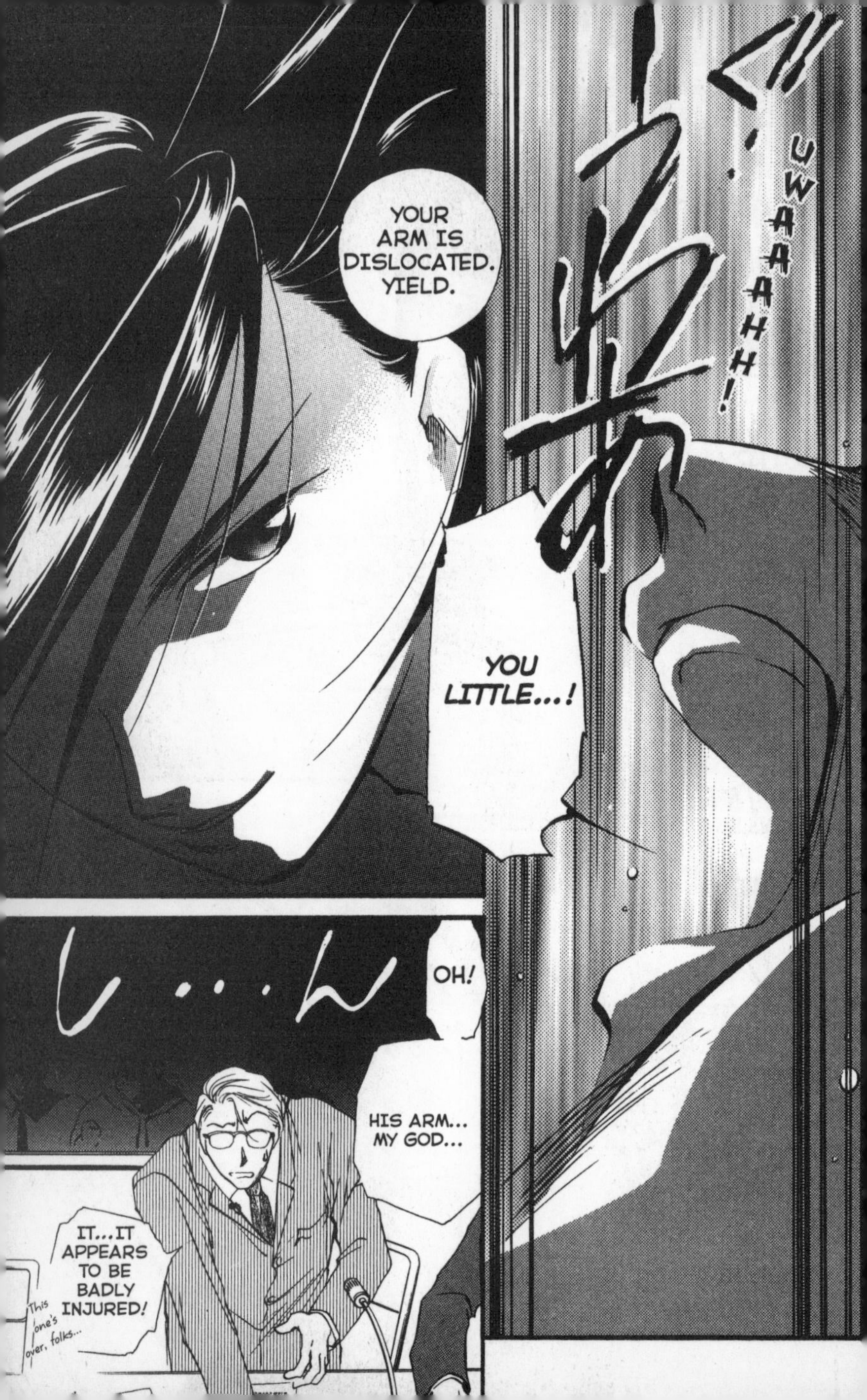
ぐうわあ
UWAAAHH!
YOUR ARM IS DISLOCATED. YIELD.
YOU LITTLE...!
し…ん
OH!
HIS ARM... MY GOD...
IT...IT APPEARS TO BE BADLY INJURED!
This one's over, folks...

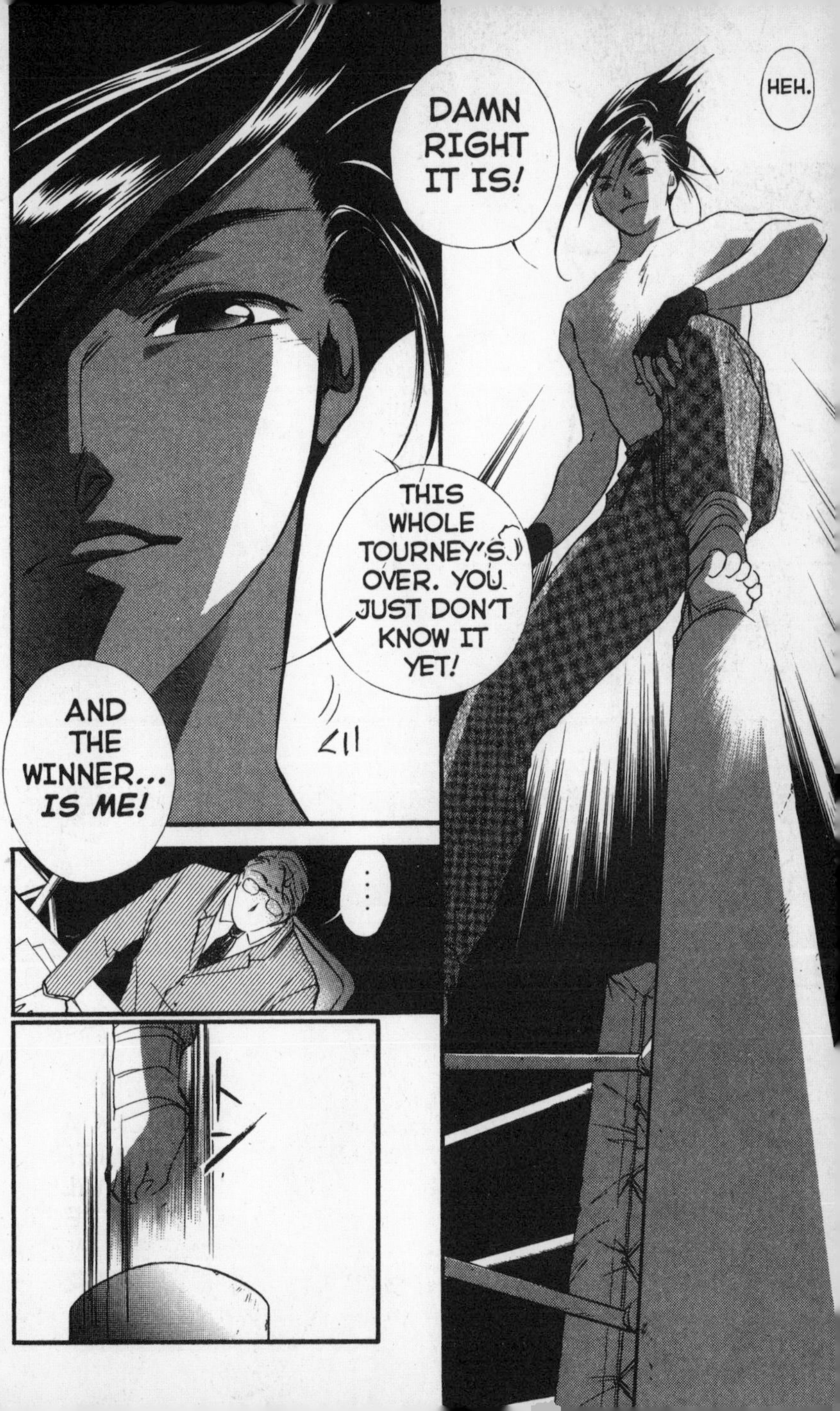
HEH.
DAMN RIGHT IT IS!
THIS WHOLE TOURNEY'S OVER. YOU JUST DON'T KNOW IT YET!
AND THE WINNER... IS ME!
....

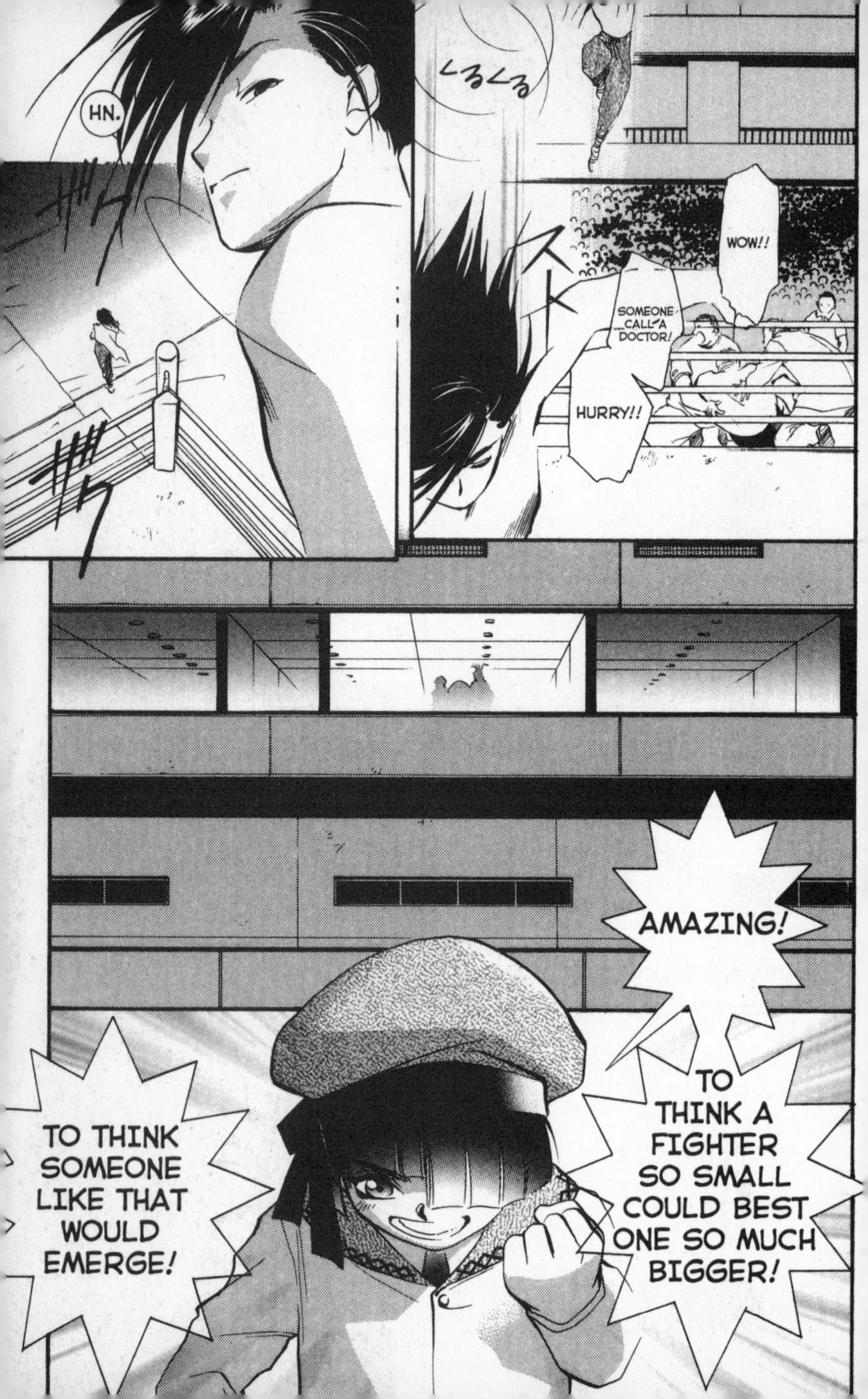
くるくる
WOW!!
SOMEONE CALL A DOCTOR!
HURRY!!
HN.
AMAZING!
TO THINK A FIGHTER SO SMALL COULD BEST ONE SO MUCH BIGGER!
TO THINK SOMEONE LIKE THAT WOULD EMERGE!

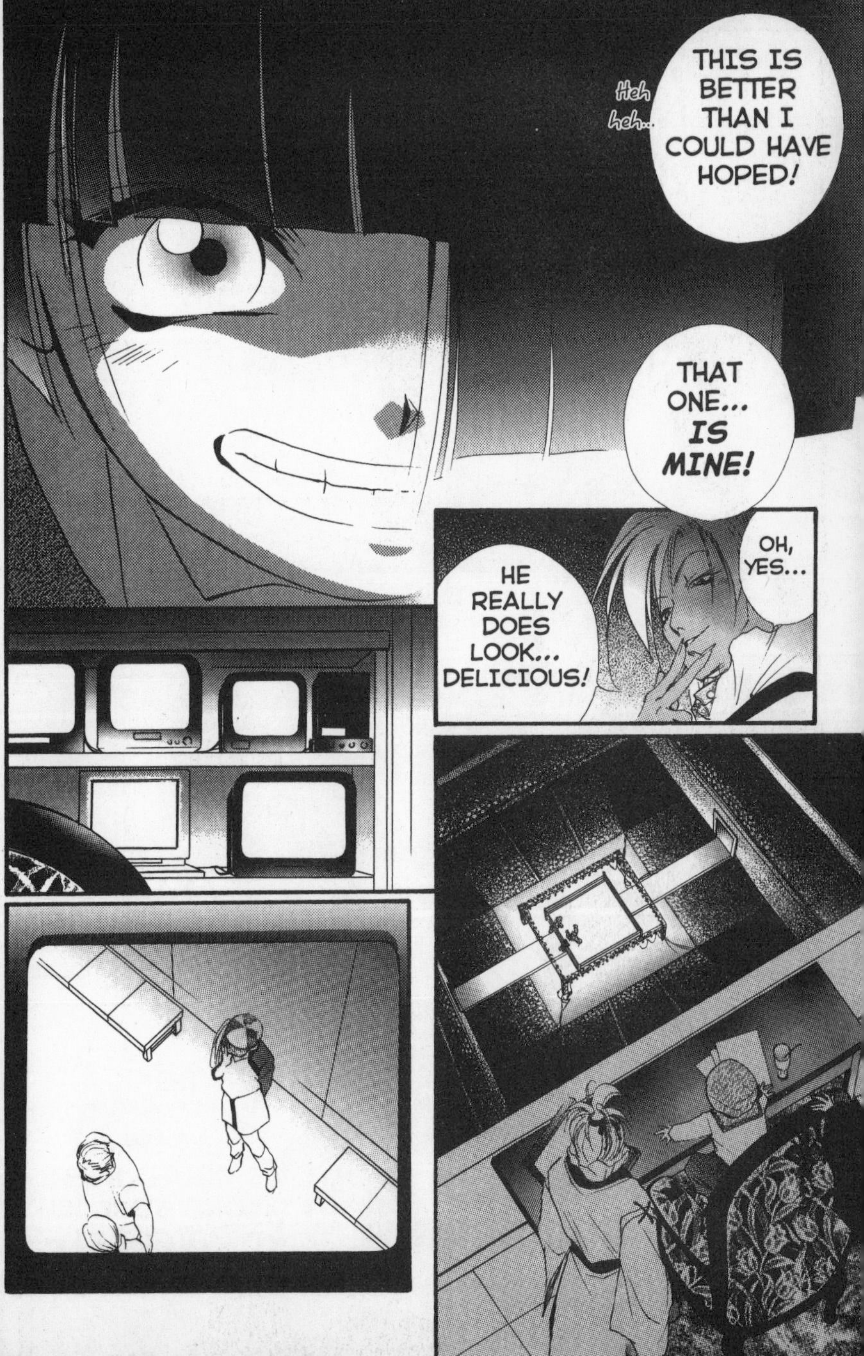
THIS IS BETTER THAN I COULD HAVE HOPED!
Heh heh...
THAT ONE... IS MINE!
OH, YES...
HE REALLY DOES LOOK... DELICIOUS!

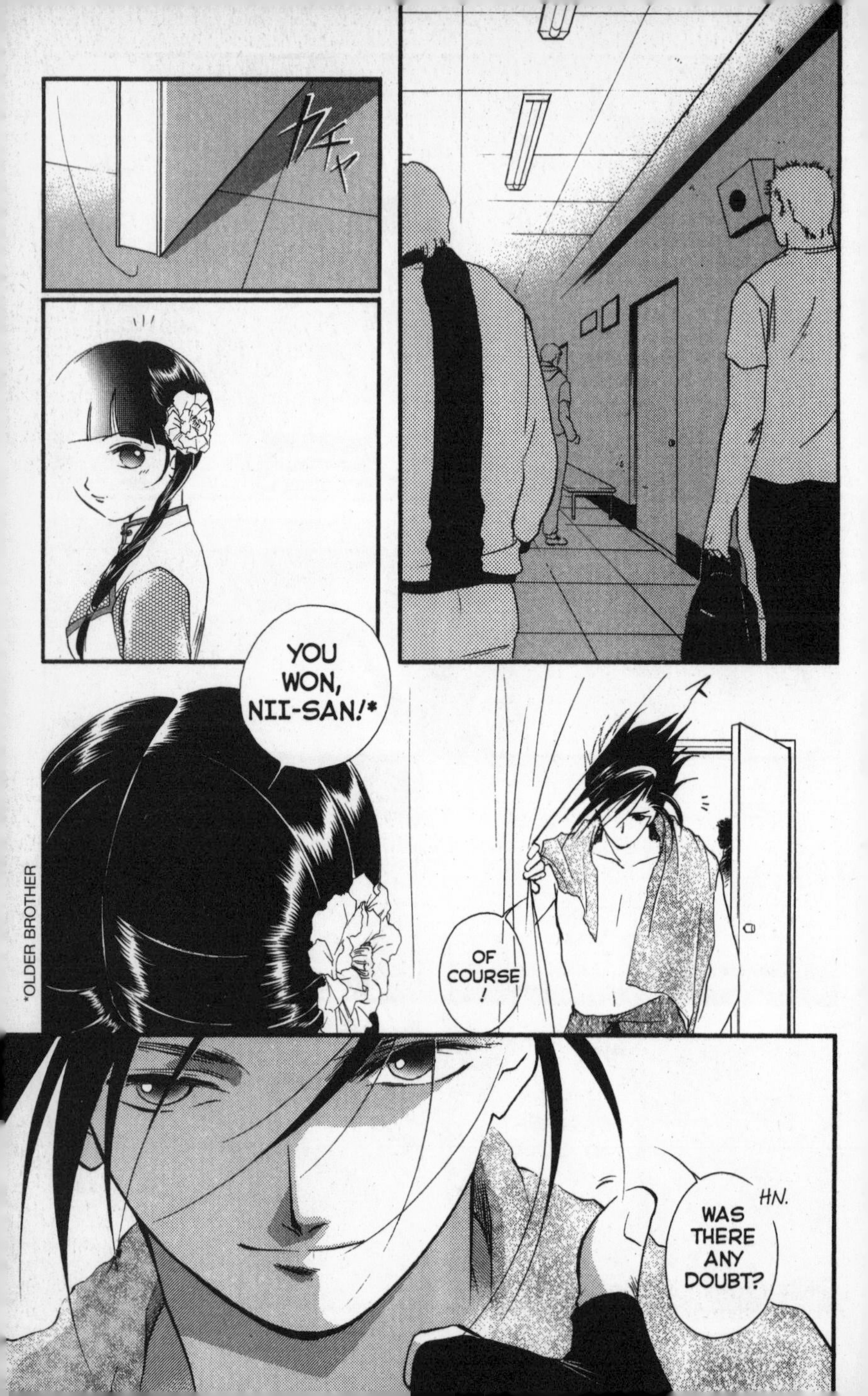
カチャ
YOU WON, NII-SAN!*
OF COURSE!
HN.
WAS THERE ANY DOUBT?

*OLDER BROTHER

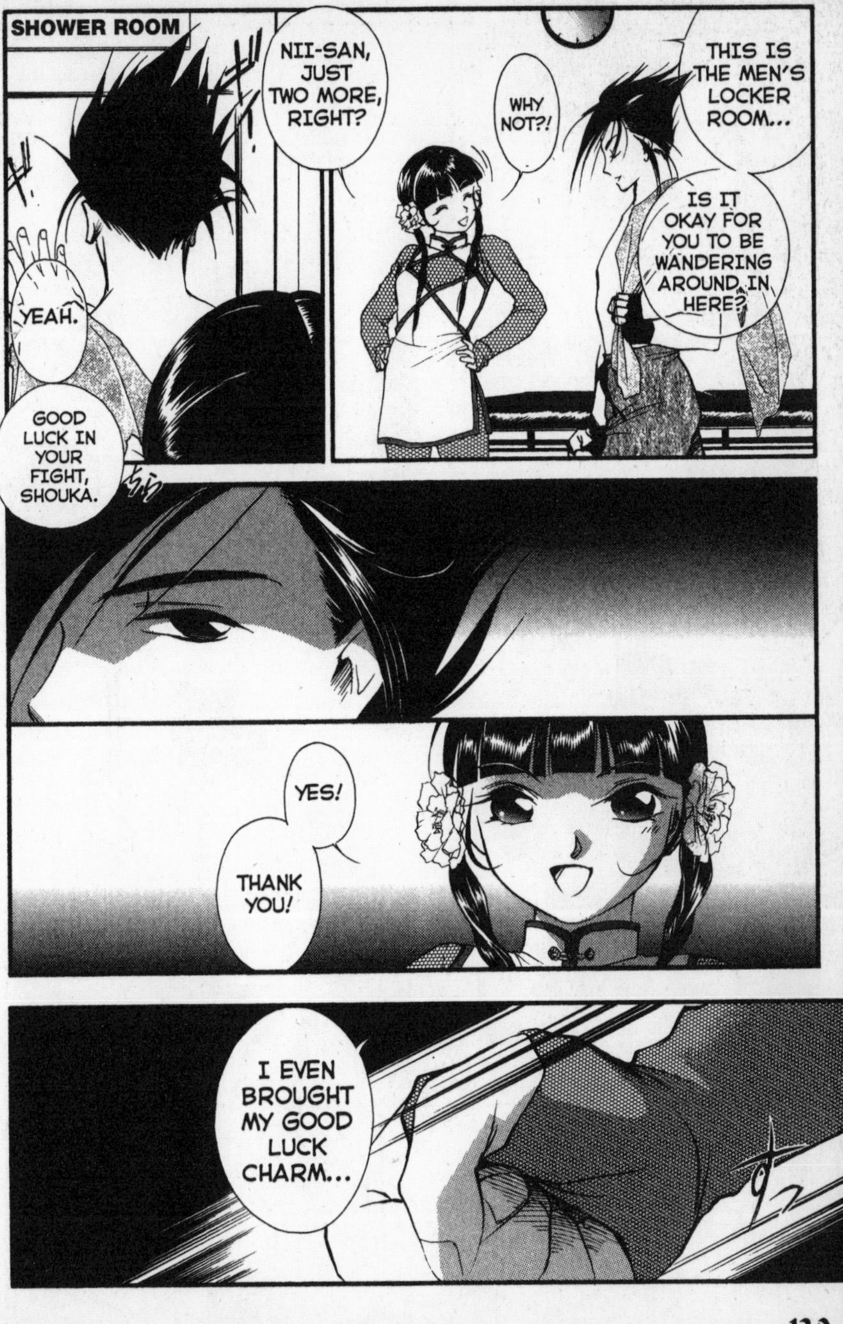
THIS IS THE MEN'S LOCKER ROOM...
IS IT OKAY FOR YOU TO BE WANDERING AROUND IN HERE?
WHY NOT?!
SHOWER ROOM
NII-SAN, JUST TWO MORE, RIGHT?
YEAH.
GOOD LUCK IN YOUR FIGHT, SHOUKA.
YES!
THANK YOU!
I EVEN BROUGHT MY GOOD LUCK CHARM...

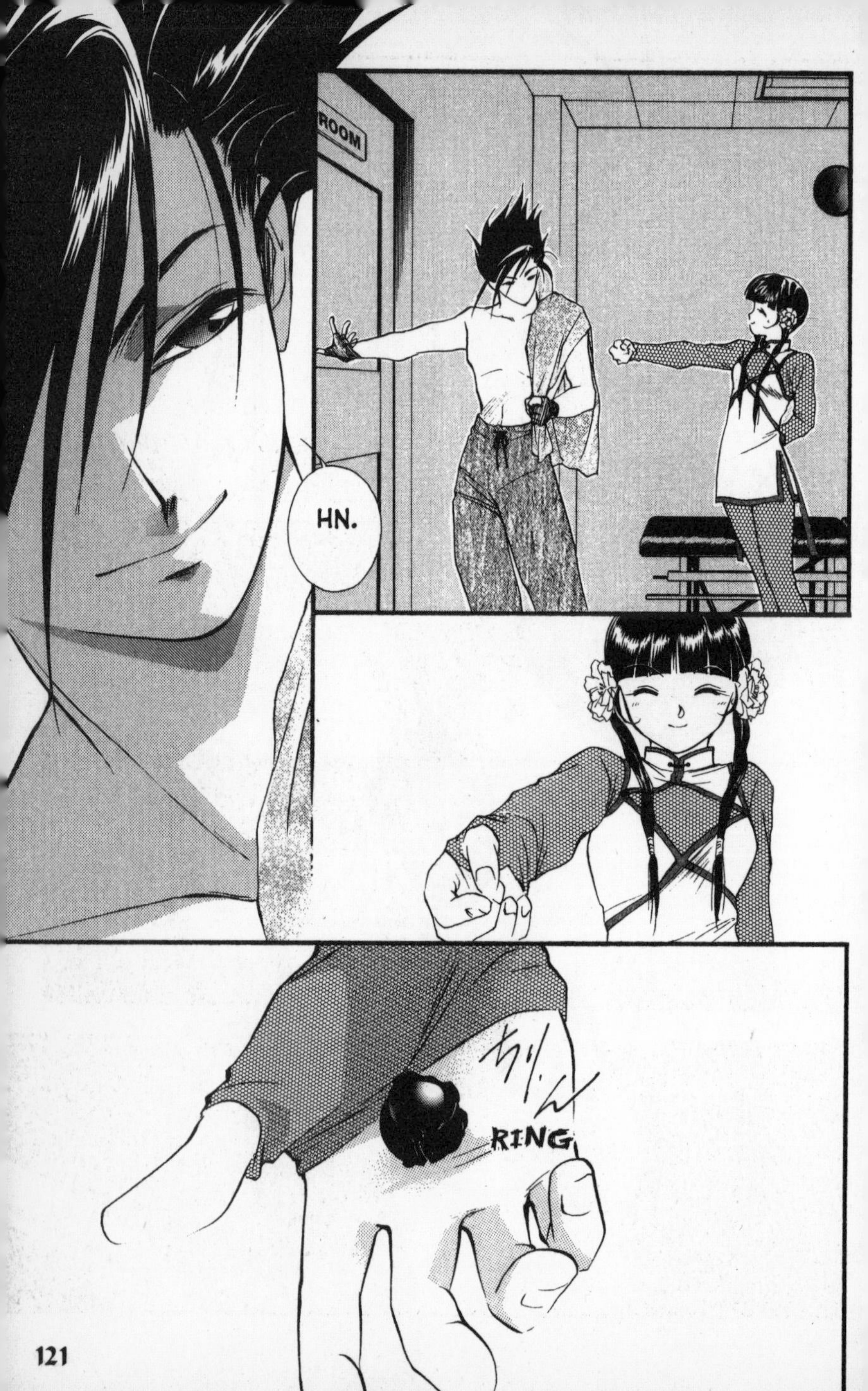
ROOM
HN.
ちりん
RING

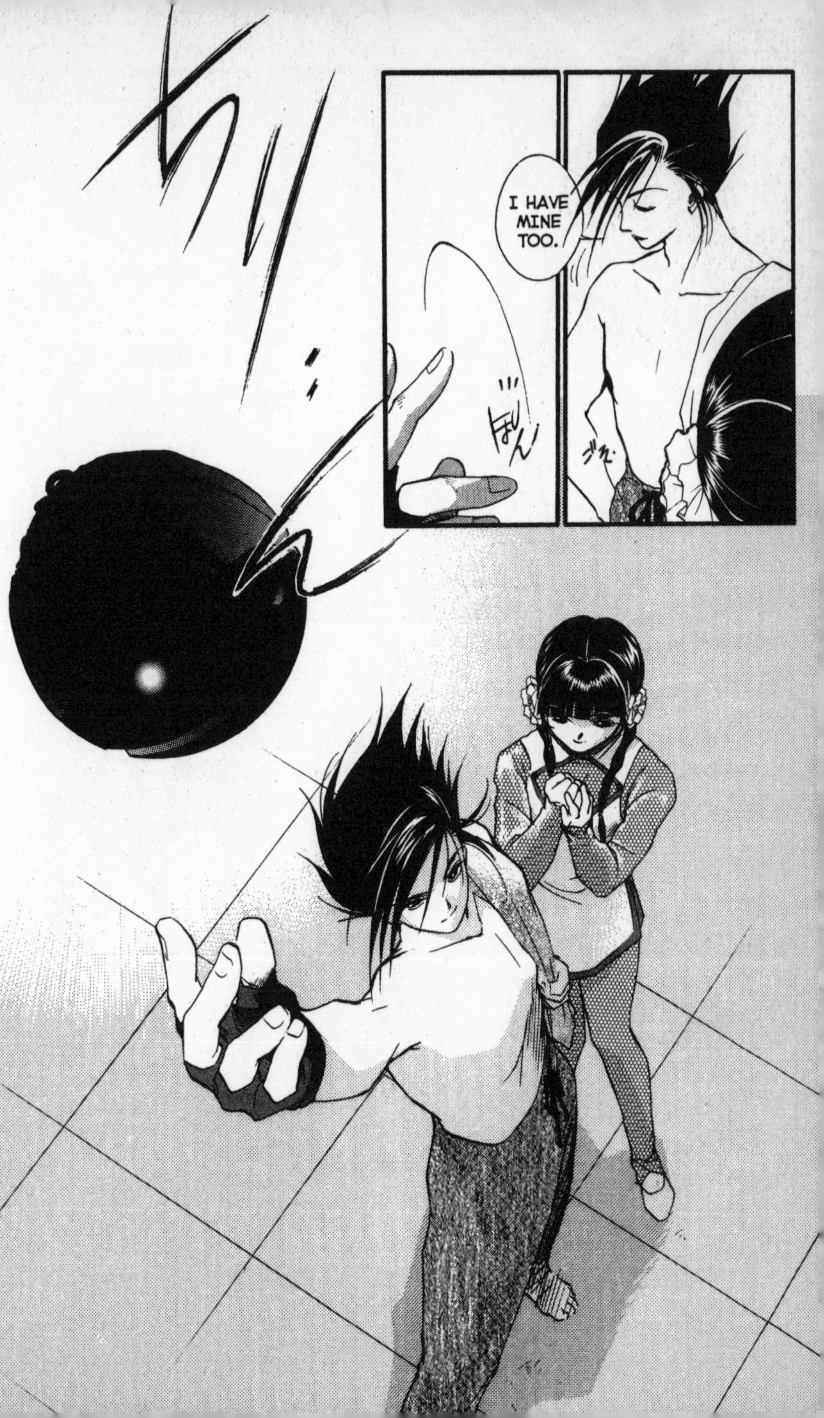
I HAVE MINE TOO.

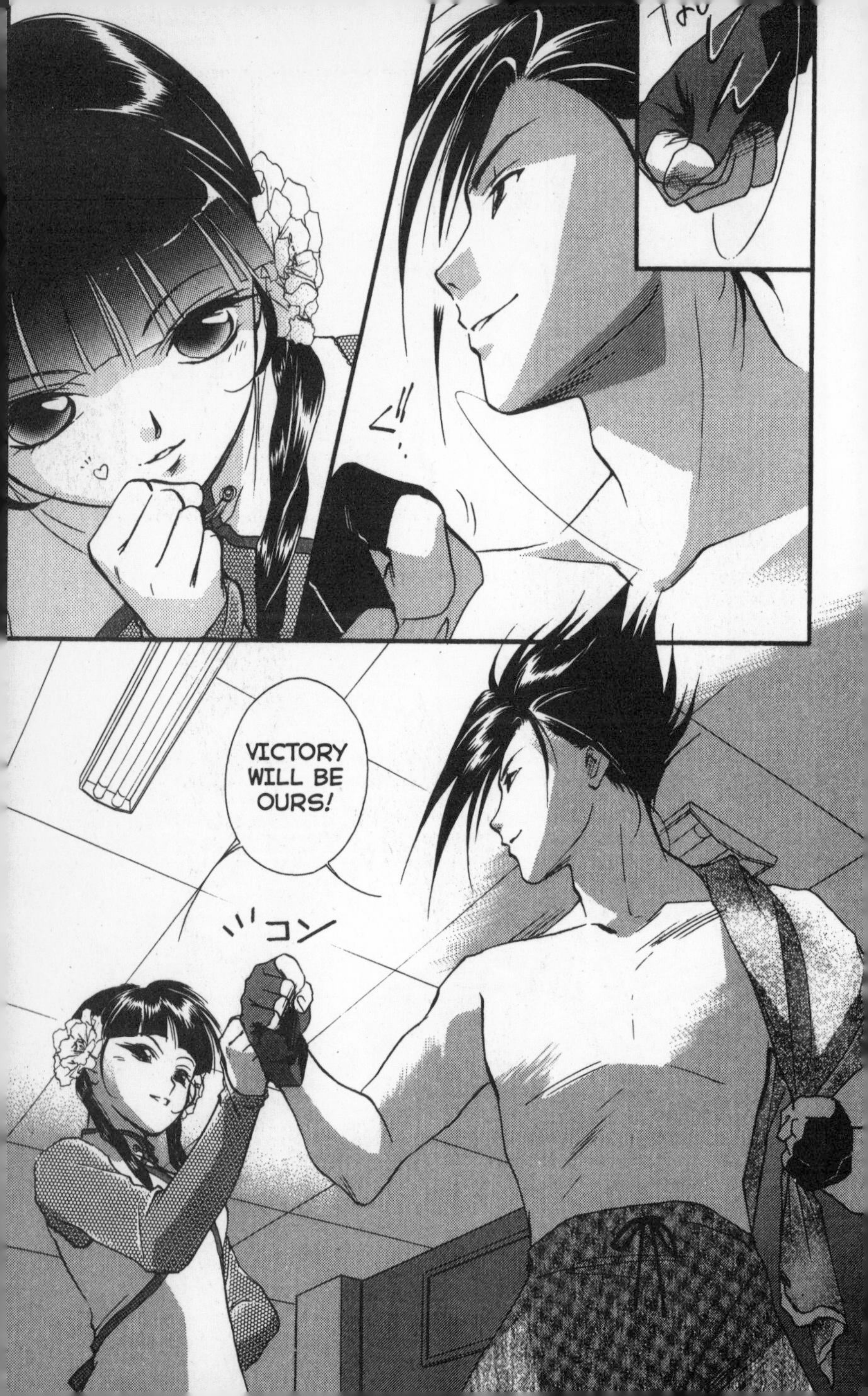
VICTORY WILL BE OURS!
コン

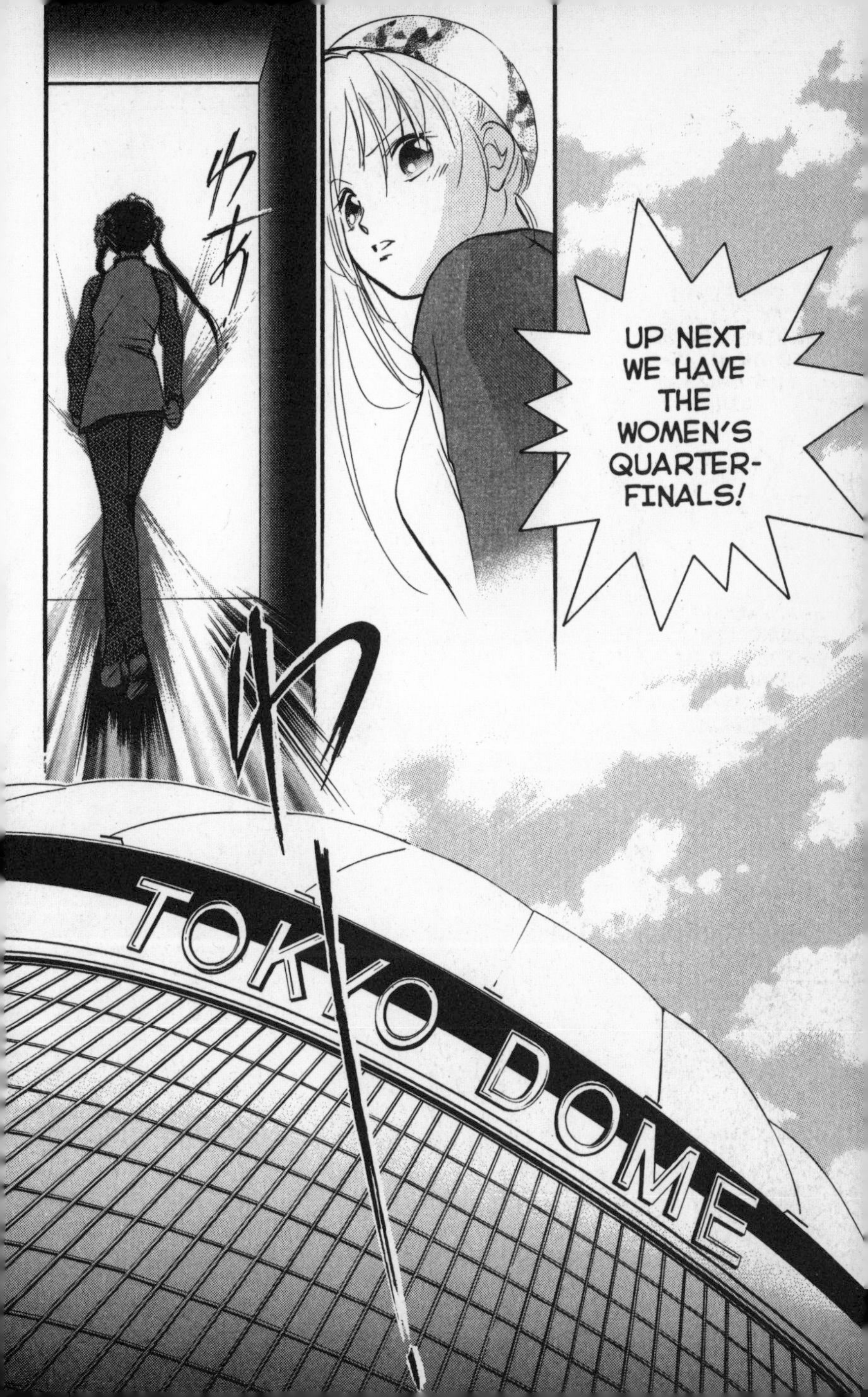
UP NEXT WE HAVE THE WOMEN'S QUARTER-FINALS!
TOKYO DOME

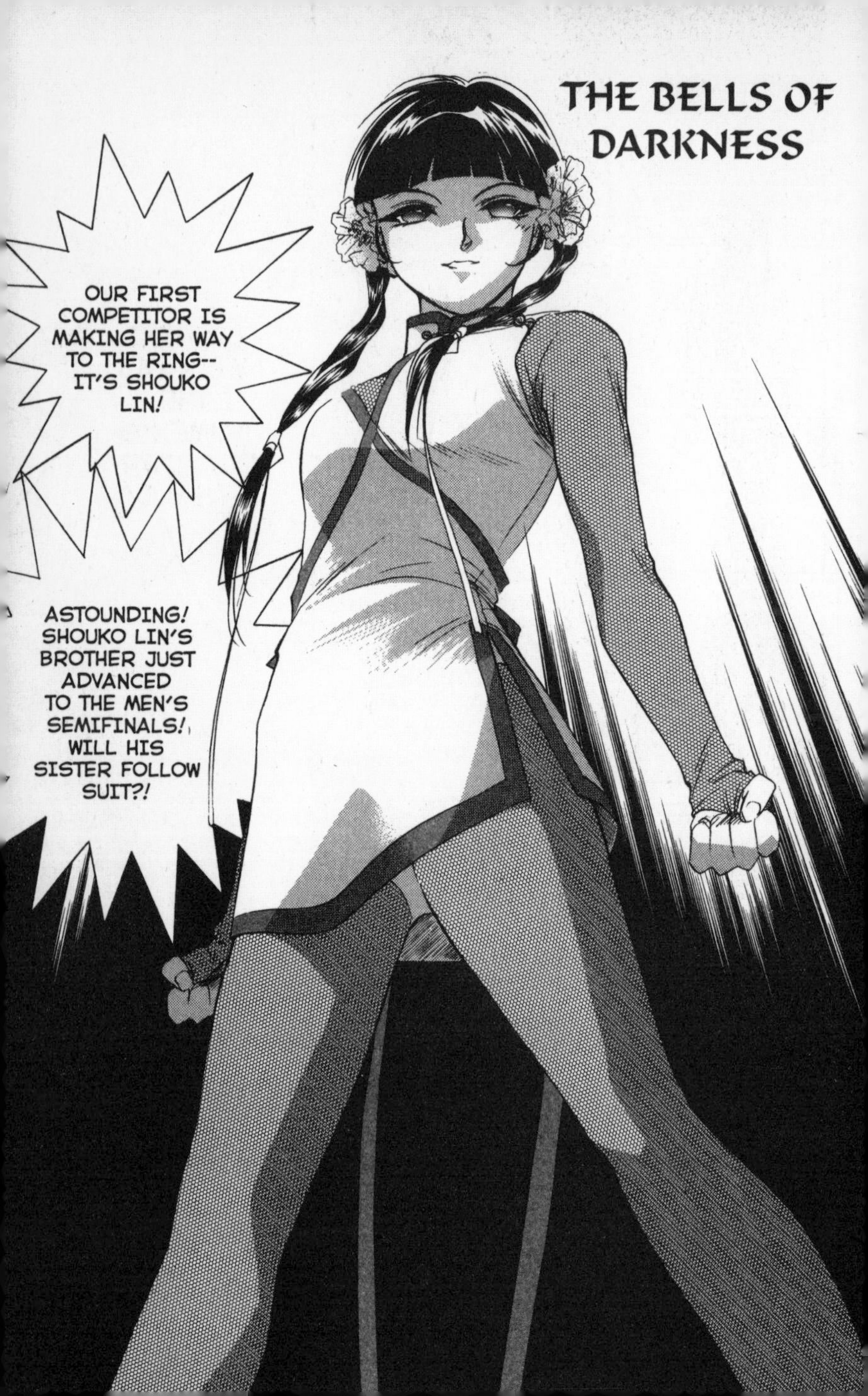
THE BELLS OF DARKNESS
OUR FIRST COMPETITOR IS MAKING HER WAY TO THE RING-- IT'S SHOUKO LIN!
ASTOUNDING! SHOUKO LIN'S BROTHER JUST ADVANCED TO THE MEN'S SEMIFINALS! WILL HIS SISTER FOLLOW SUIT?!

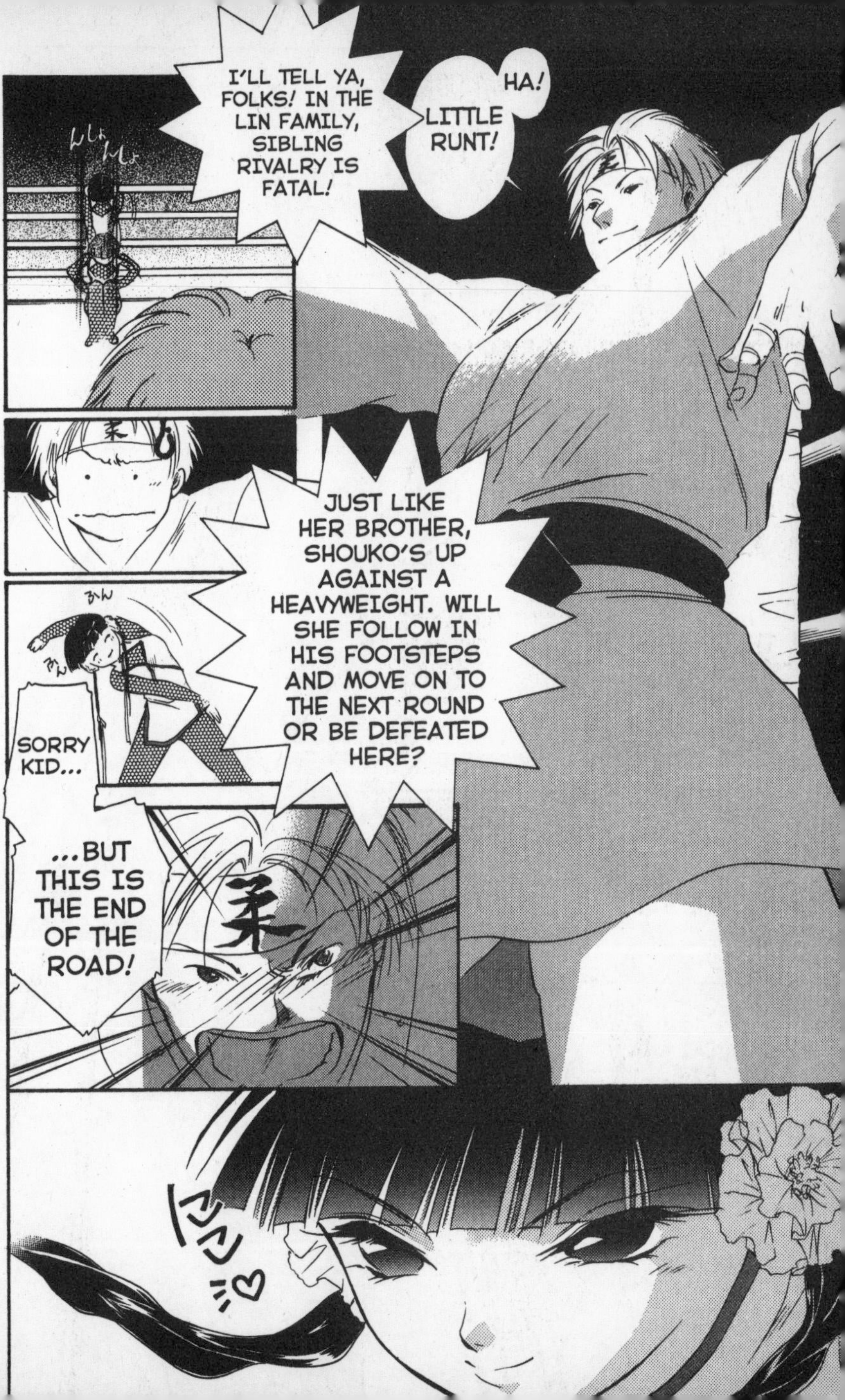
HA!
LITTLE RUNT!
I'LL TELL YA, FOLKS! IN THE LIN FAMILY, SIBLING RIVALRY IS FATAL!
JUST LIKE HER BROTHER, SHOUKO'S UP AGAINST A HEAVYWEIGHT. WILL SHE FOLLOW IN HIS FOOTSTEPS AND MOVE ON TO THE NEXT ROUND OR BE DEFEATED HERE?
SORRY KID...
...BUT THIS IS THE END OF THE ROAD!

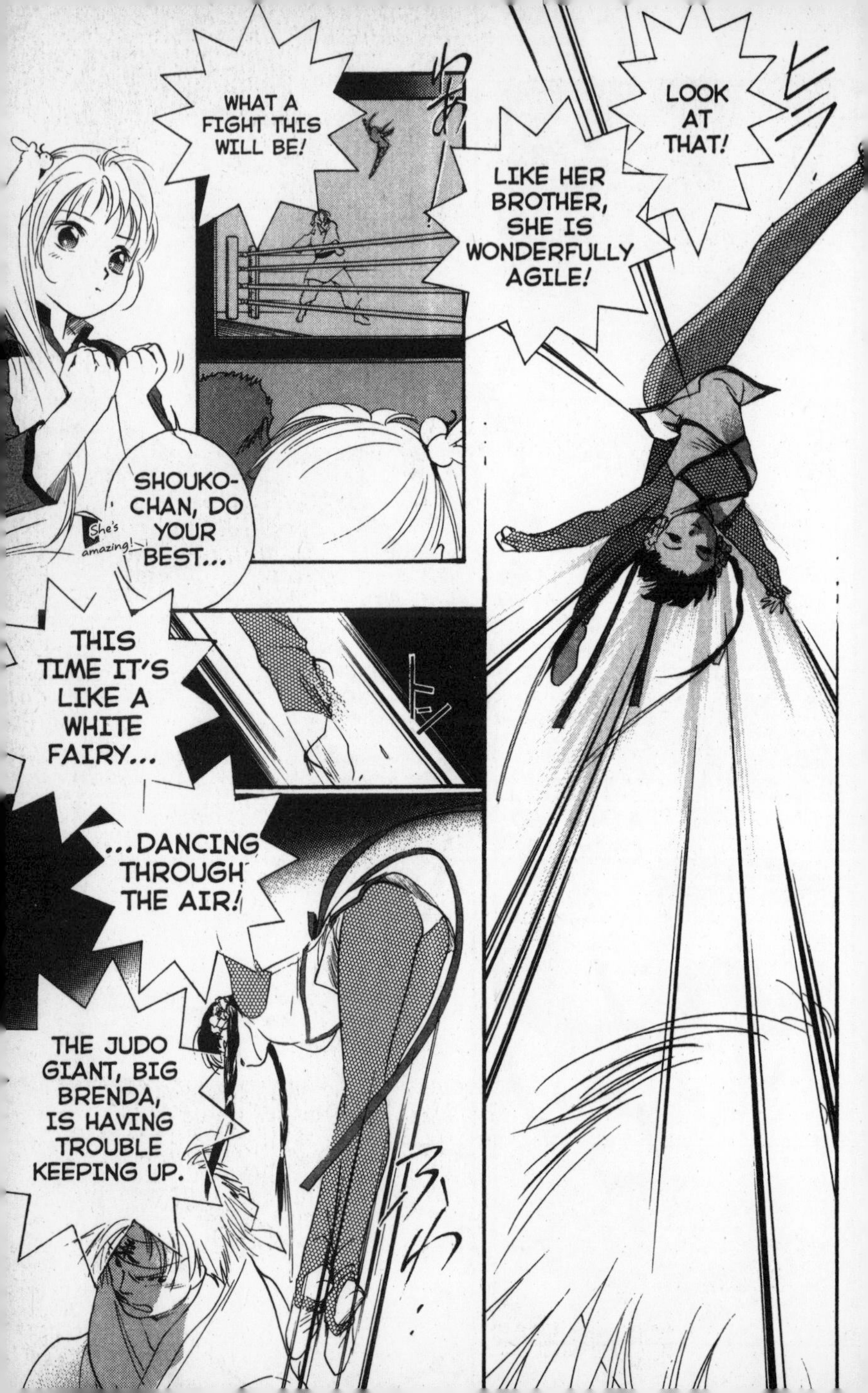
LOOK AT THAT!
LIKE HER BROTHER, SHE IS WONDERFULLY AGILE!
WHAT A FIGHT THIS WILL BE!
SHOUKO-CHAN, DO YOUR BEST...
She's amazing!
THIS TIME IT'S LIKE A WHITE FAIRY...
...DANCING THROUGH THE AIR!
THE JUDO GIANT, BIG BRENDA, IS HAVING TROUBLE KEEPING UP.

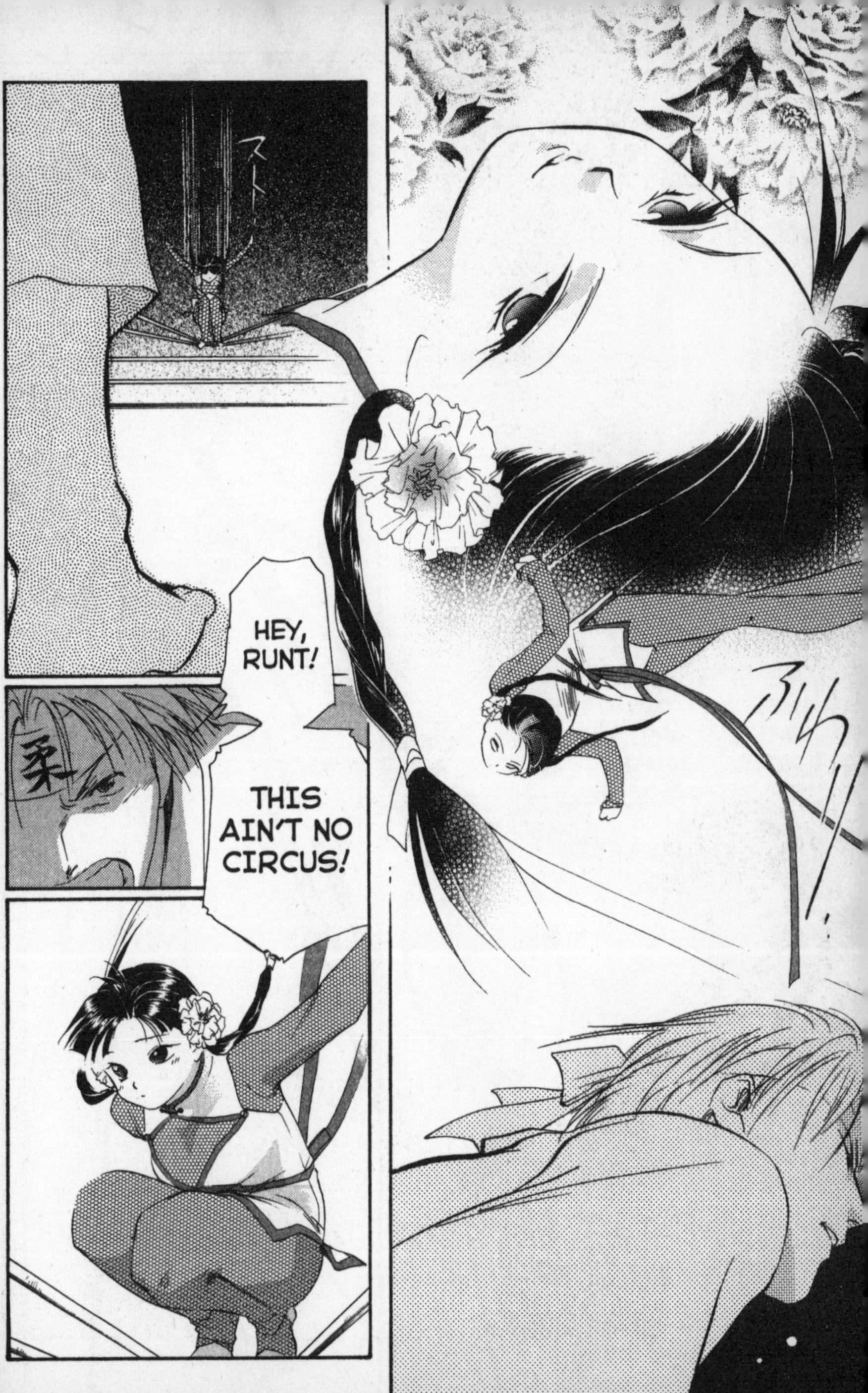
ふわ
ストー
HEY, RUNT!
THIS AIN'T NO CIRCUS!

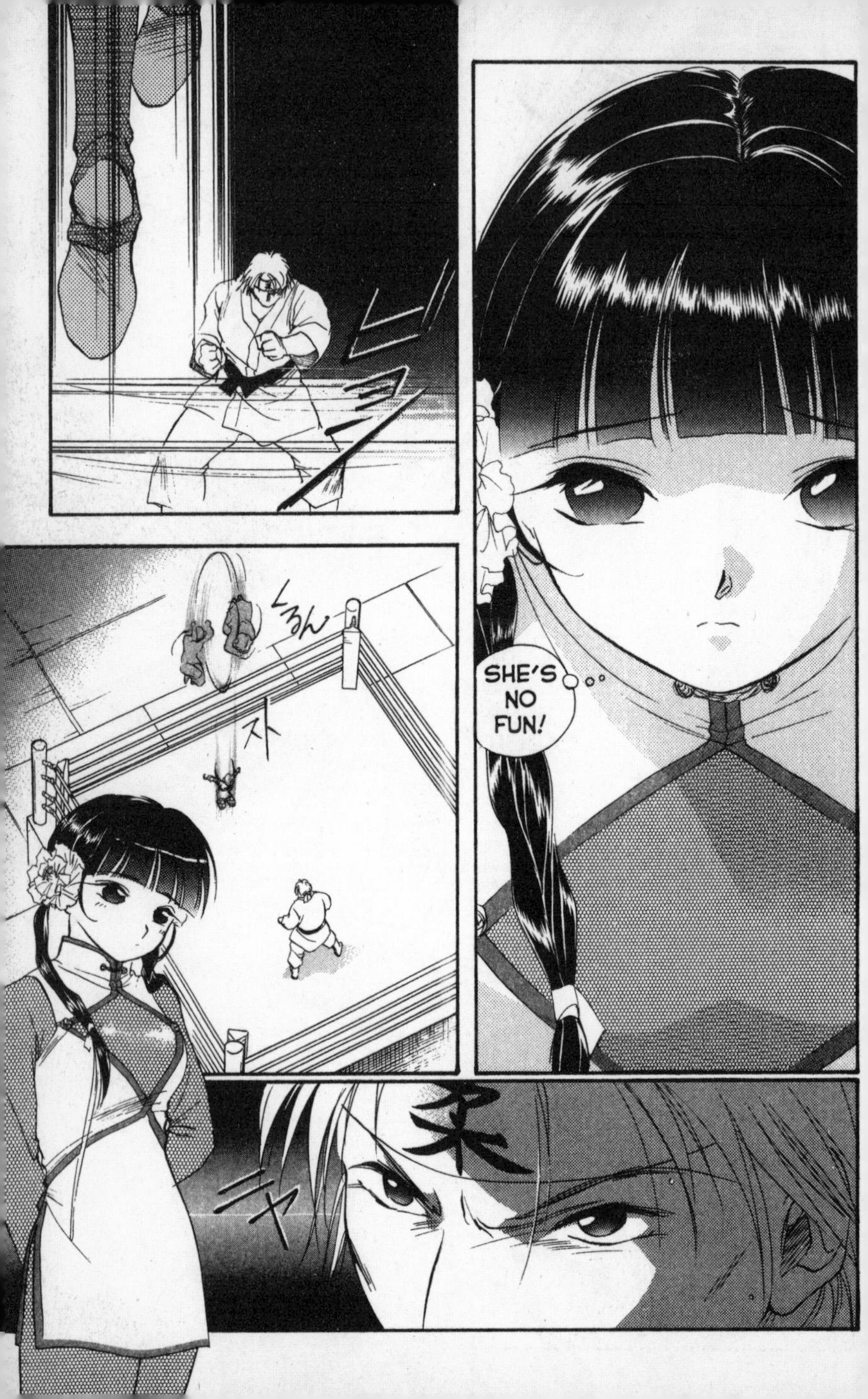

SHE'S NO FUN!
くるん
スト
ニヤ

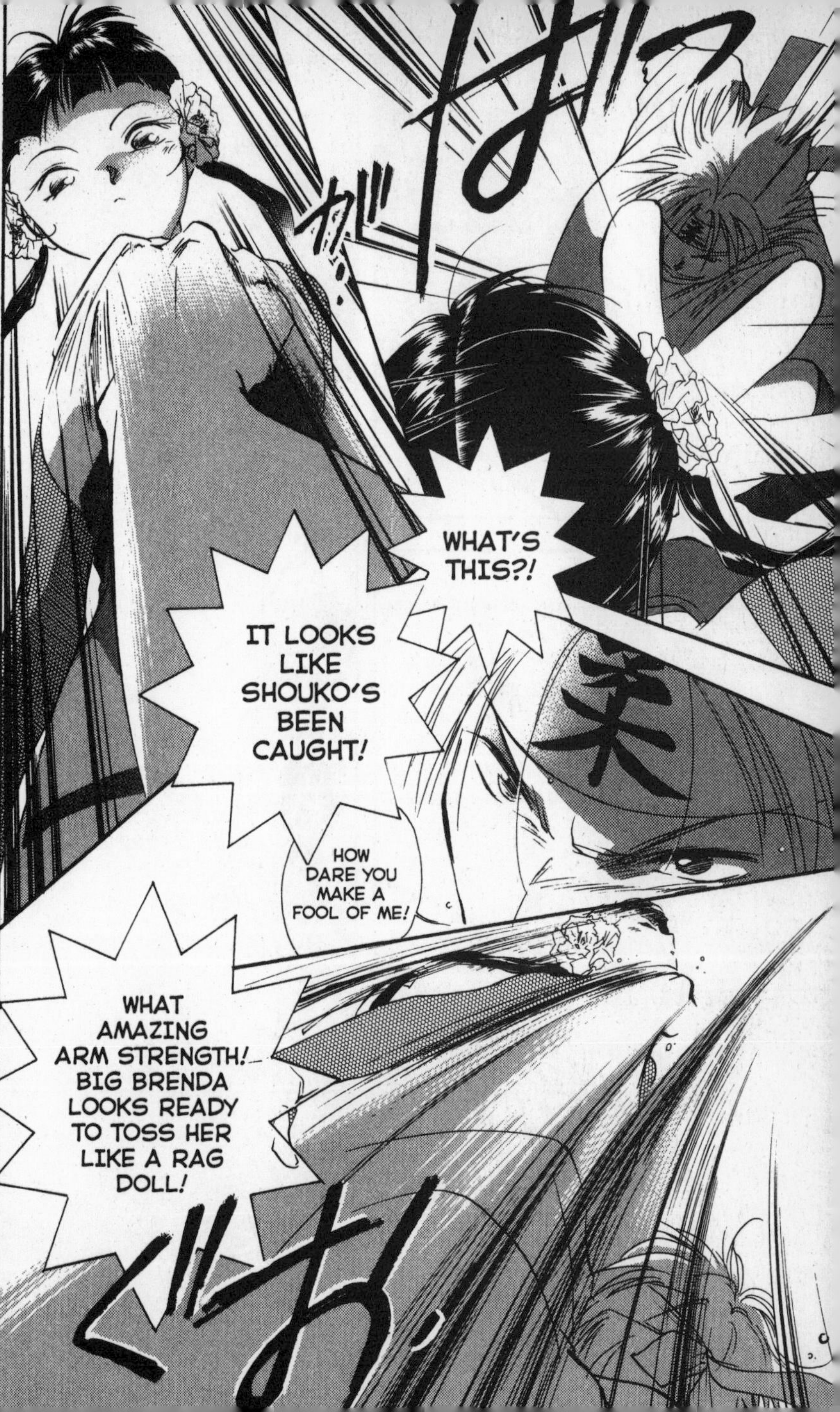
WHAT'S THIS?!
IT LOOKS LIKE SHOUKO'S BEEN CAUGHT!
HOW DARE YOU MAKE A FOOL OF ME!
WHAT AMAZING ARM STRENGTH! BIG BRENDA LOOKS READY TO TOSS HER LIKE A RAG DOLL!

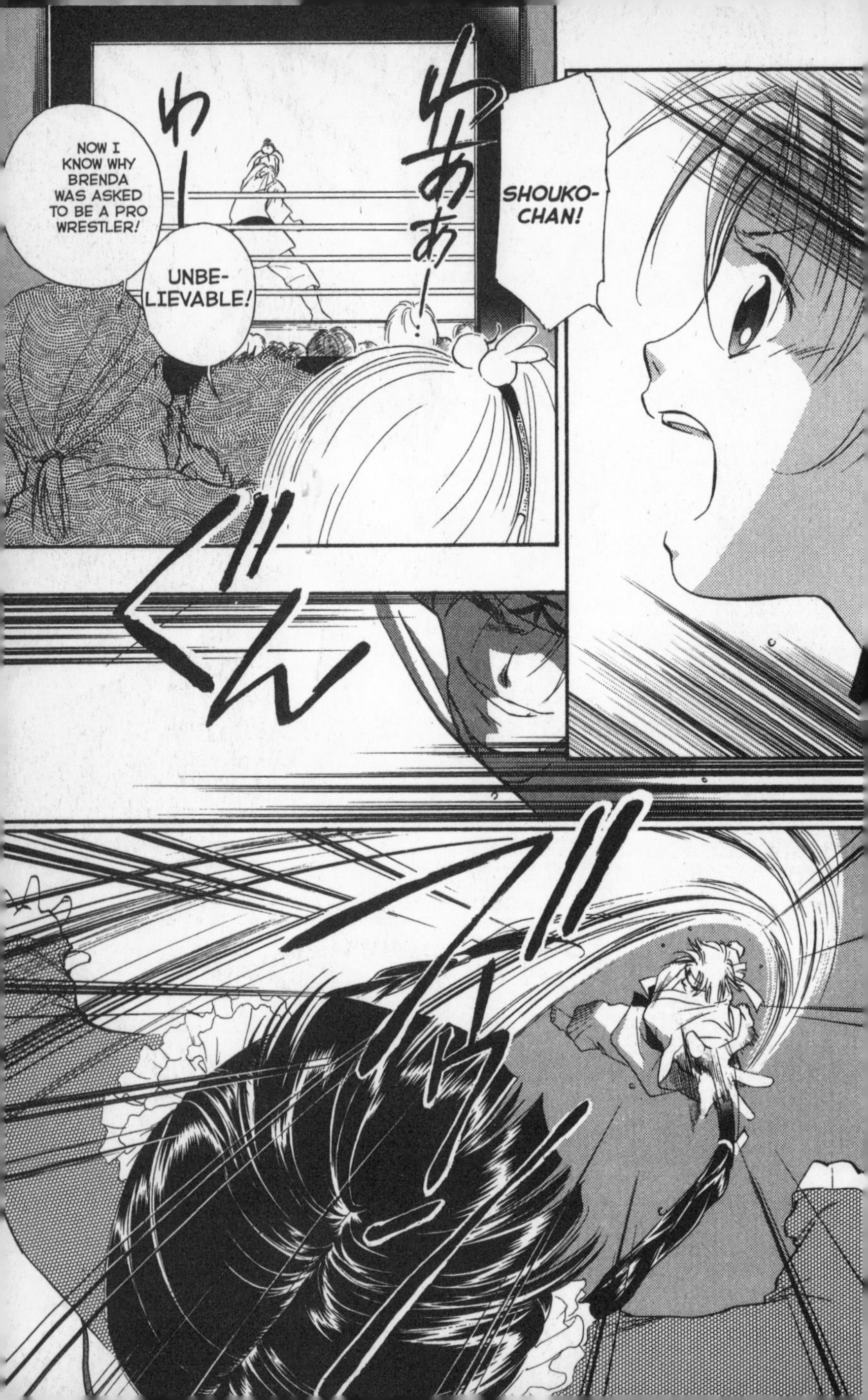
SHOUKO-CHAN!
NOW I KNOW WHY BRENDA WAS ASKED TO BE A PRO WRESTLER!
UNBE-LIEVABLE!

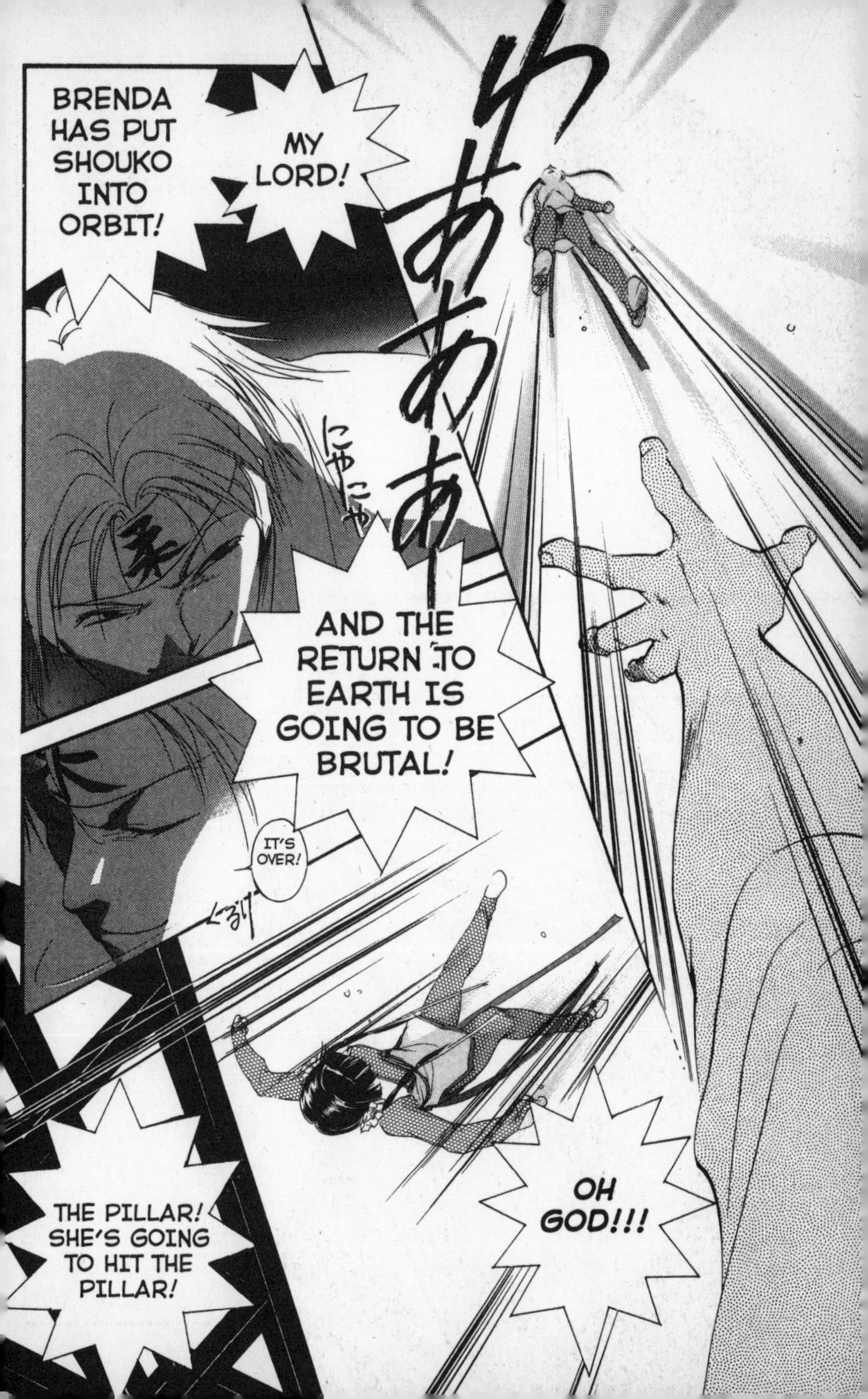
BRENDA HAS PUT SHOUKO INTO ORBIT!
MY LORD!
わあああ
にやにや
AND THE RETURN TO EARTH IS GOING TO BE BRUTAL!
IT'S OVER!
OH GOD!!!
THE PILLAR! SHE'S GOING TO HIT THE PILLAR!

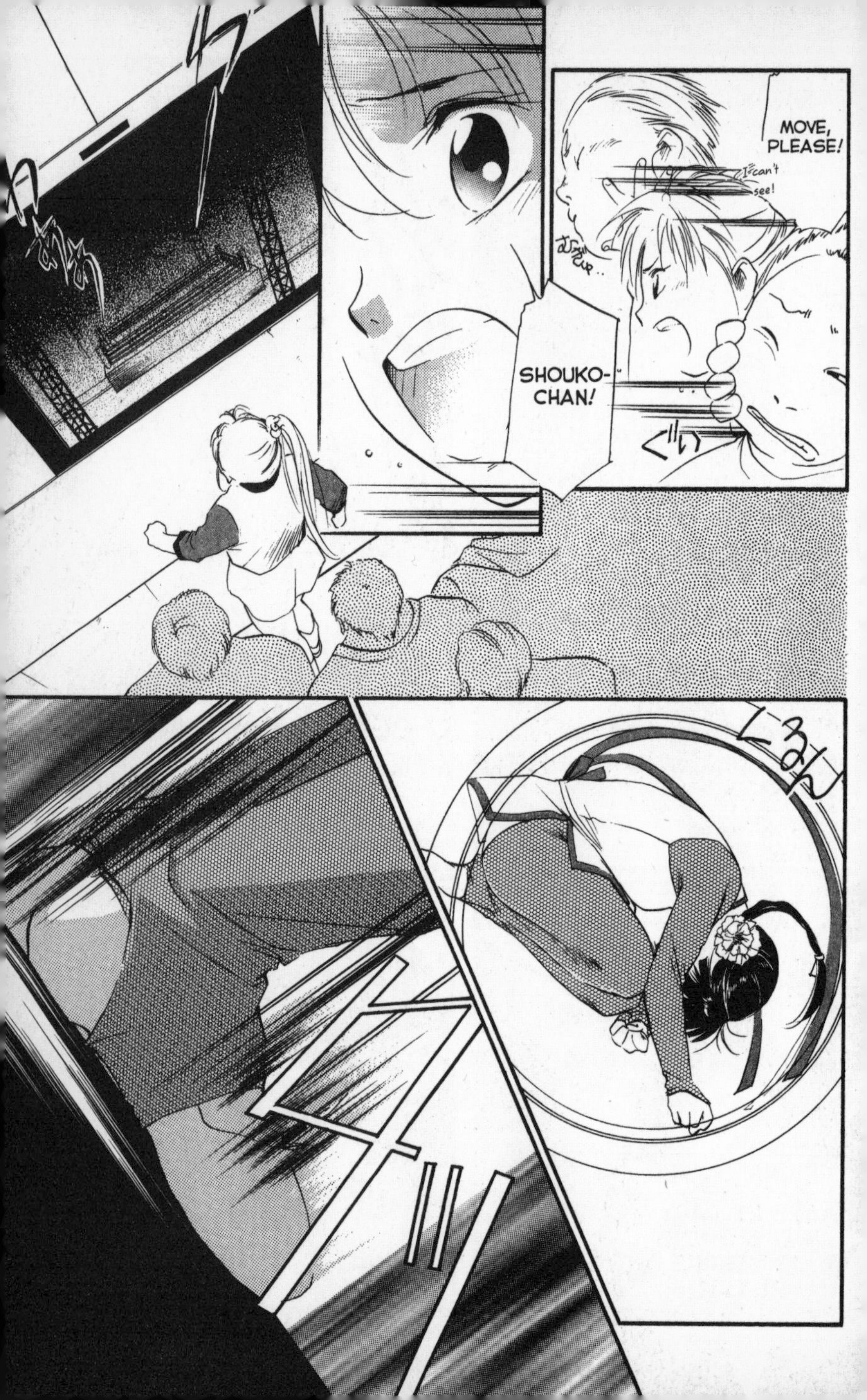
MOVE, PLEASE!
I can't see!
SHOUKO-CHAN!

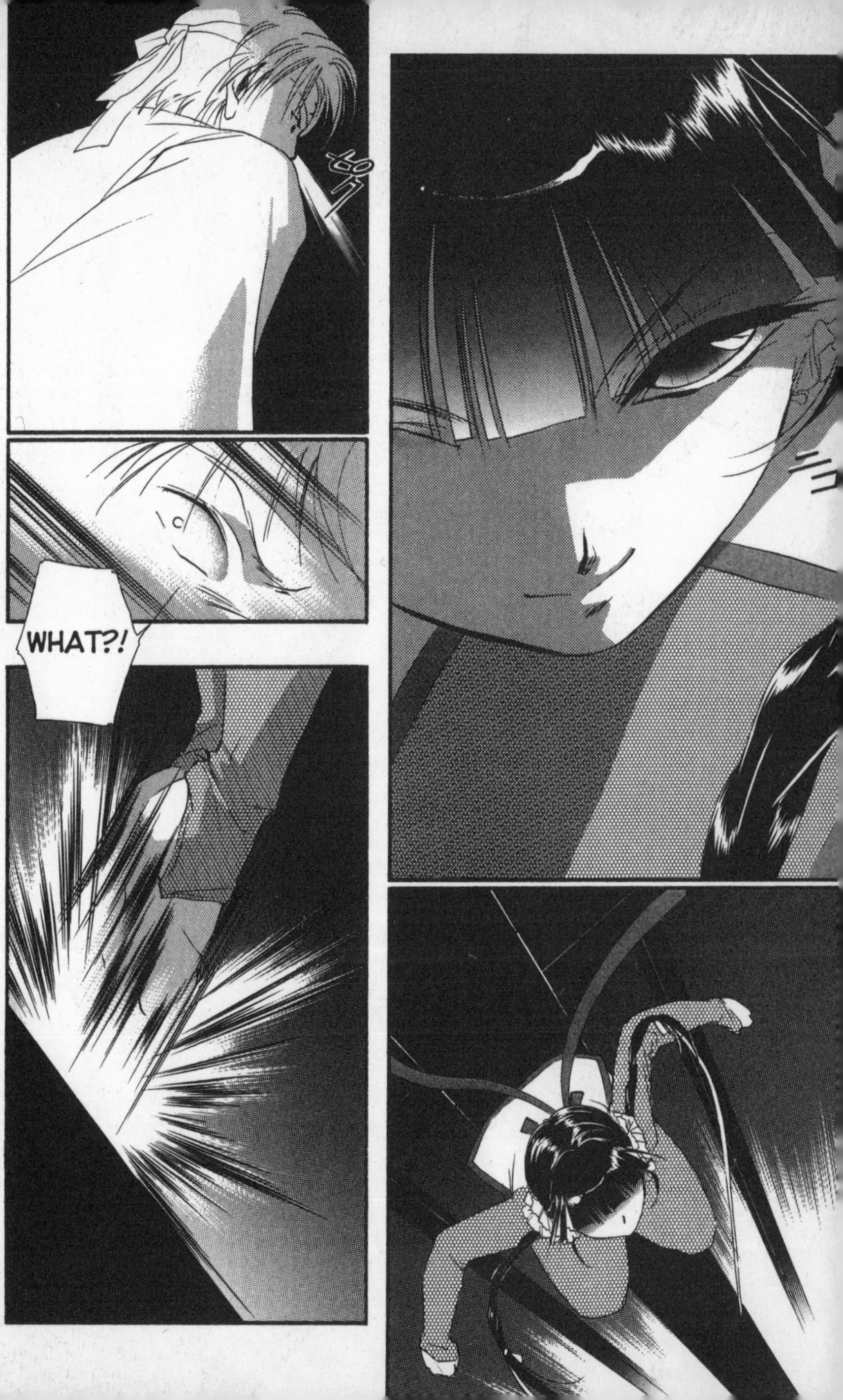
WHAT?!

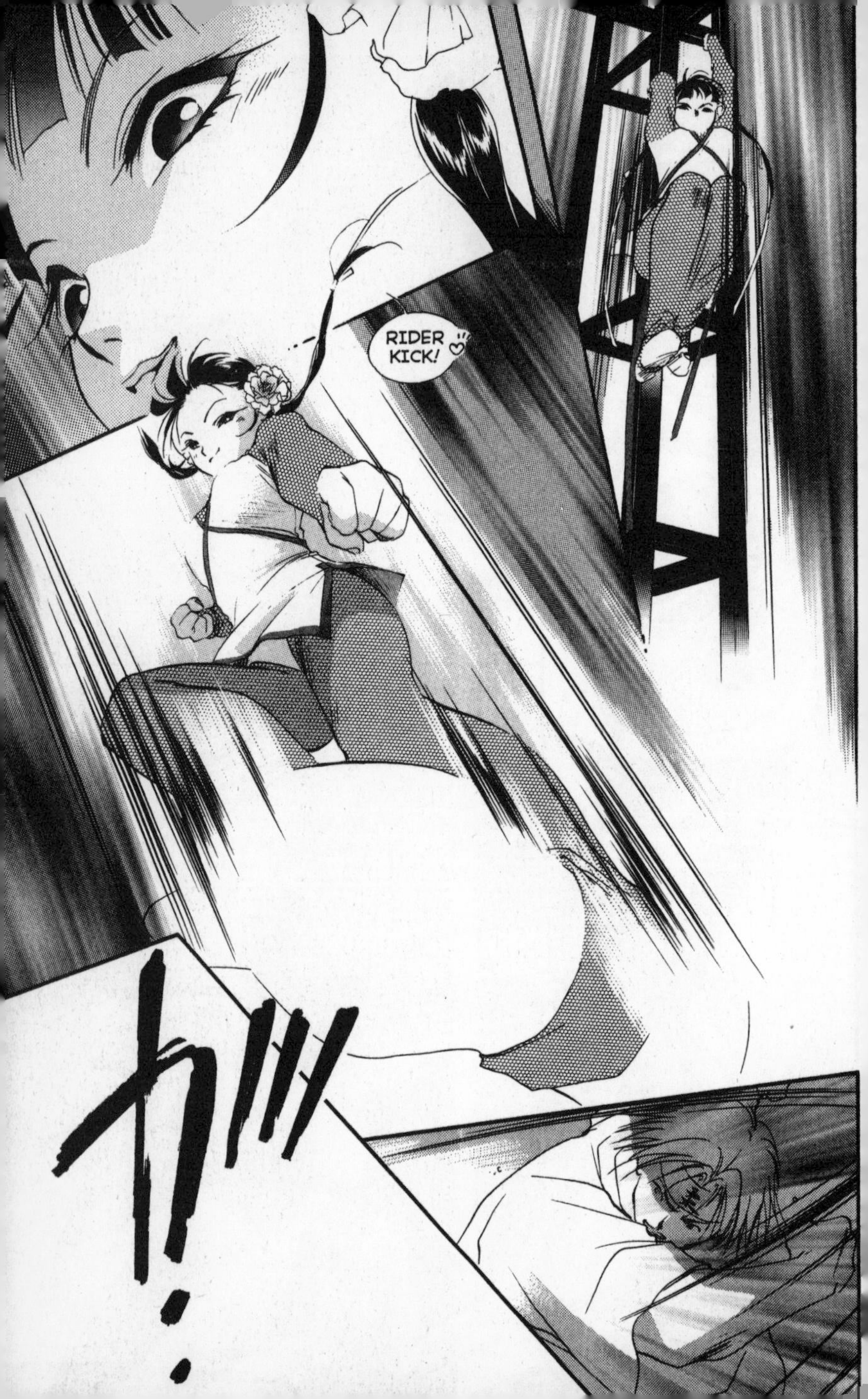
RIDER KICK!

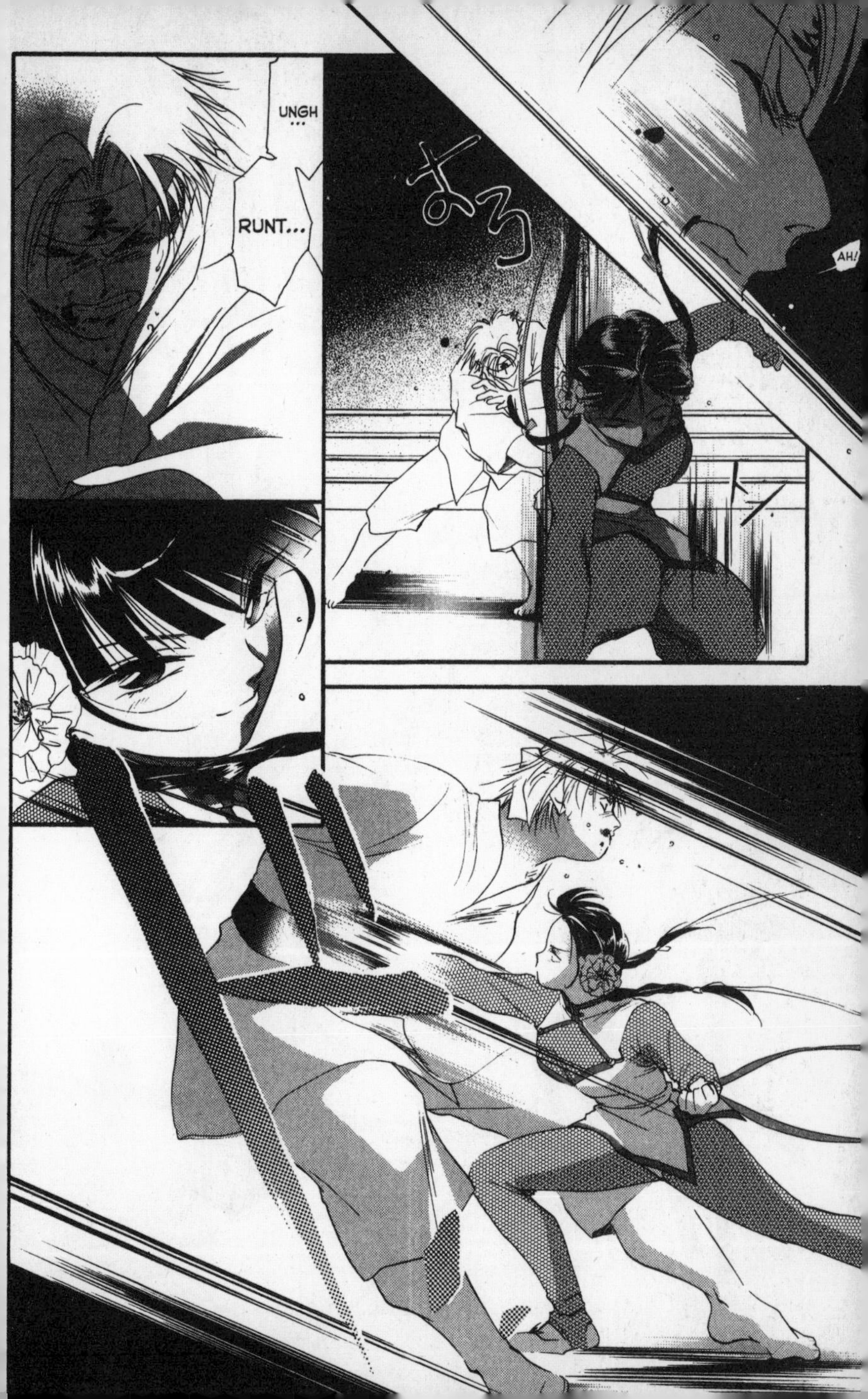
AH!
まろっ
トッ
UNGH...
RUNT...

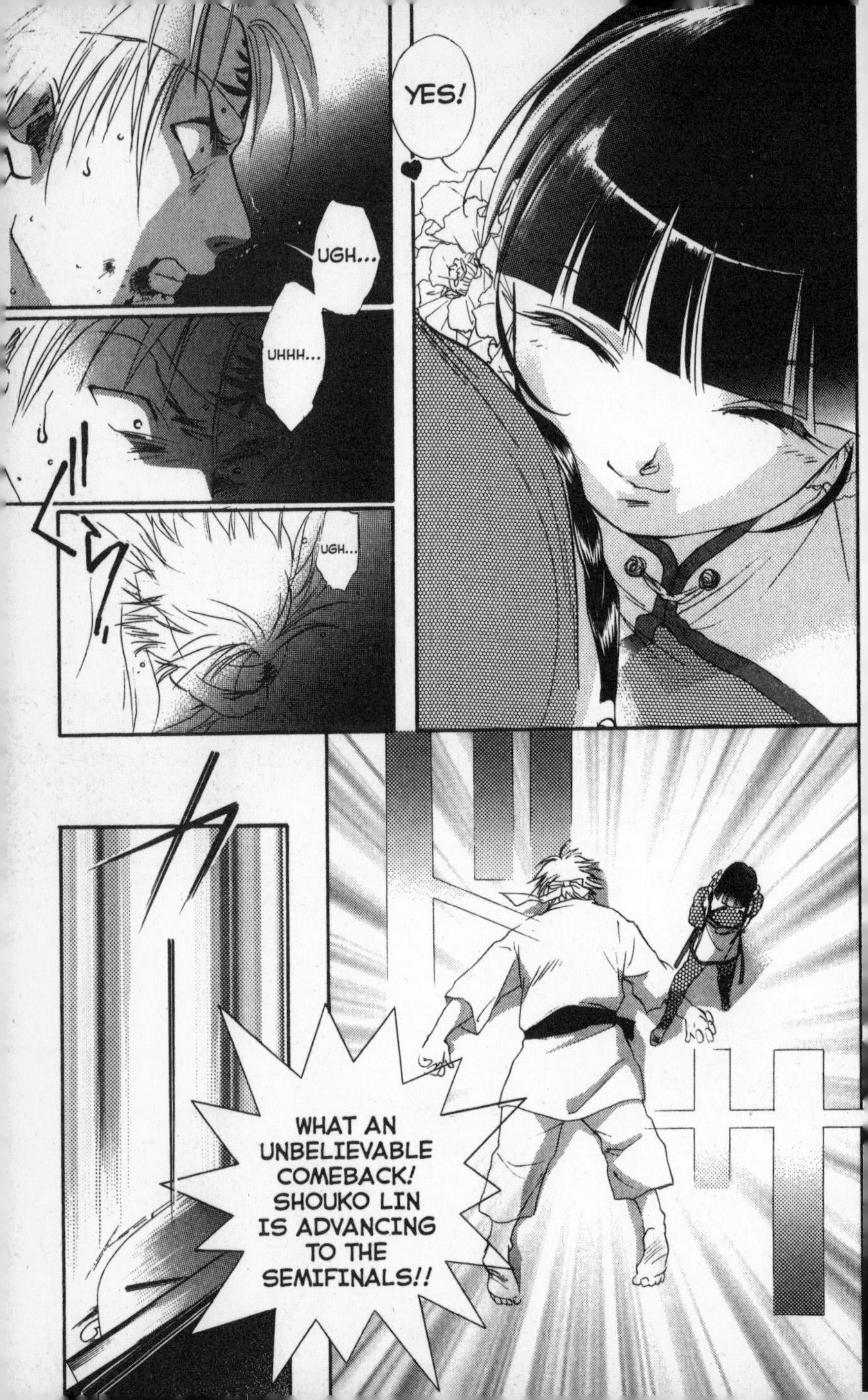
YES!
UGH...
UHHH...
UGH...
WHAT AN UNBELIEVABLE COMEBACK! SHOUKO LIN IS ADVANCING TO THE SEMIFINALS!!

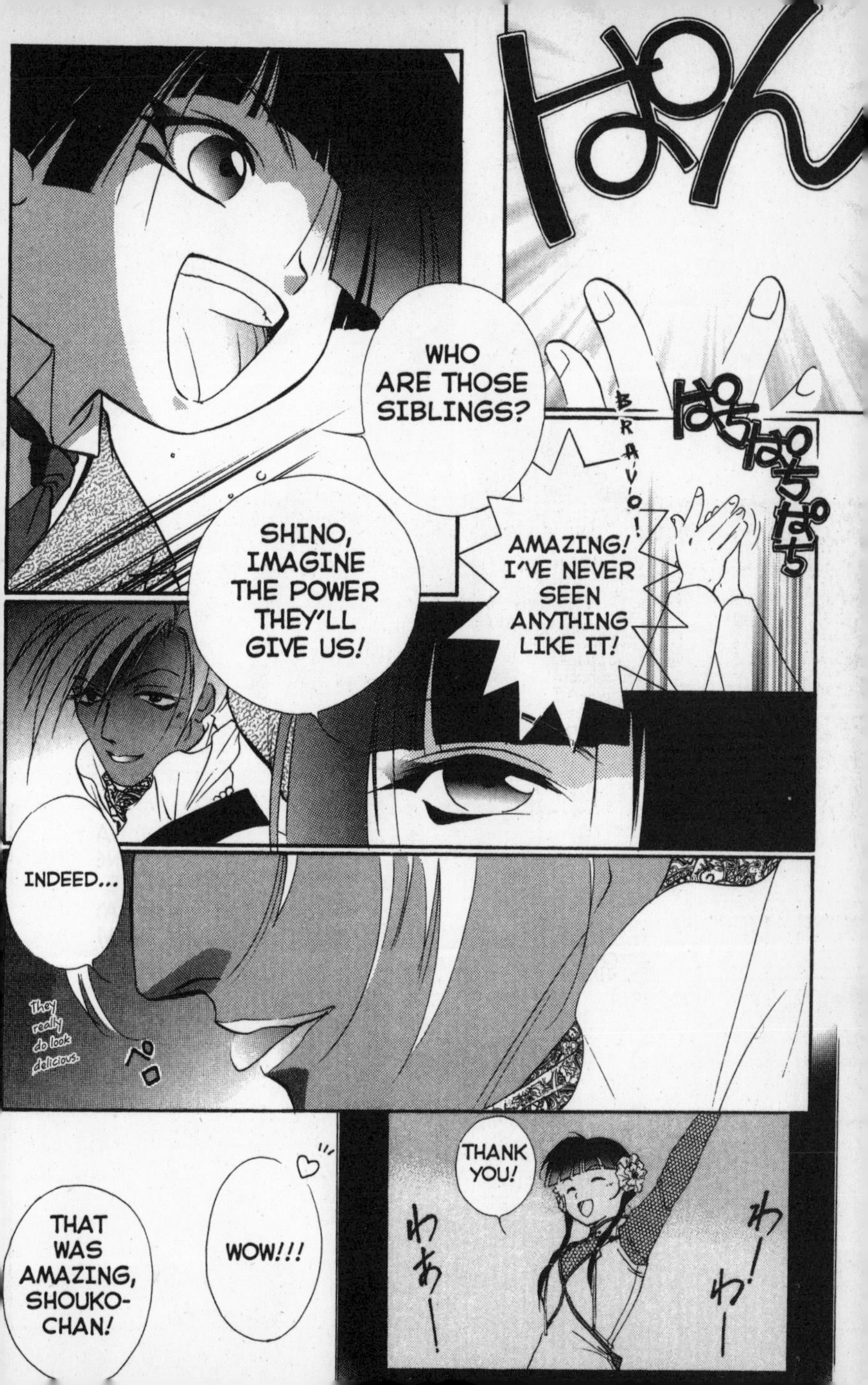
ぱん
ぱちぱちぱち
BRAVO!
AMAZING! I'VE NEVER SEEN ANYTHING LIKE IT!
WHO ARE THOSE SIBLINGS?
SHINO, IMAGINE THE POWER THEY'LL GIVE US!
INDEED...
They really do look delicious.
ぺろ
わーわー
THANK YOU!
わぁー
WOW!!!
THAT WAS AMAZING, SHOUKO-CHAN!

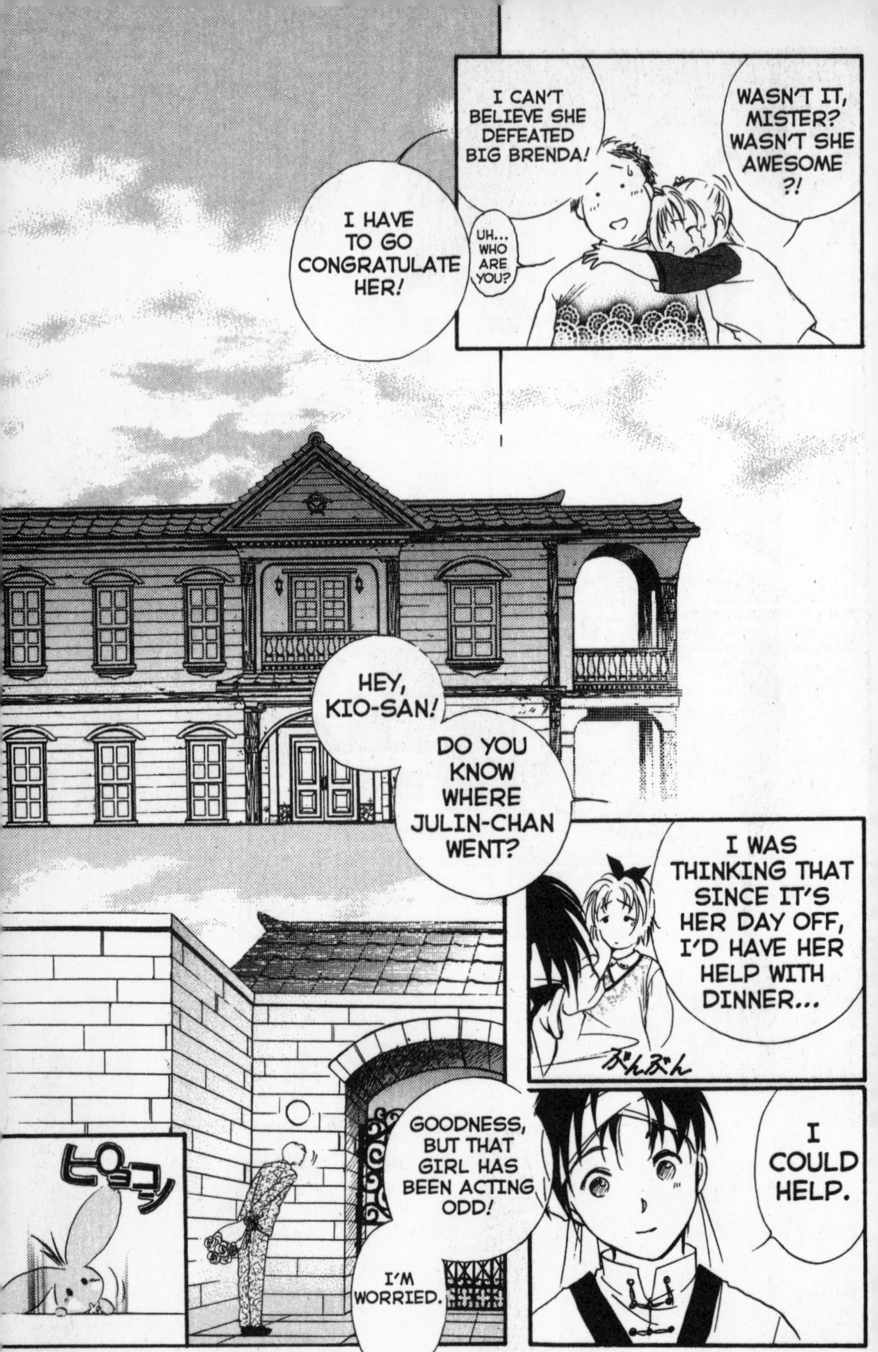
WASN'T IT, MISTER? WASN'T SHE AWESOME ?!
UH... WHO ARE YOU?
I CAN'T BELIEVE SHE DEFEATED BIG BRENDA!
I HAVE TO GO CONGRATULATE HER!
HEY, KIO-SAN!
DO YOU KNOW WHERE JULIN-CHAN WENT?
I WAS THINKING THAT SINCE IT'S HER DAY OFF, I'D HAVE HER HELP WITH DINNER...
ぶんぶん
I COULD HELP.
GOODNESS, BUT THAT GIRL HAS BEEN ACTING ODD!
I'M WORRIED.
ピョコン

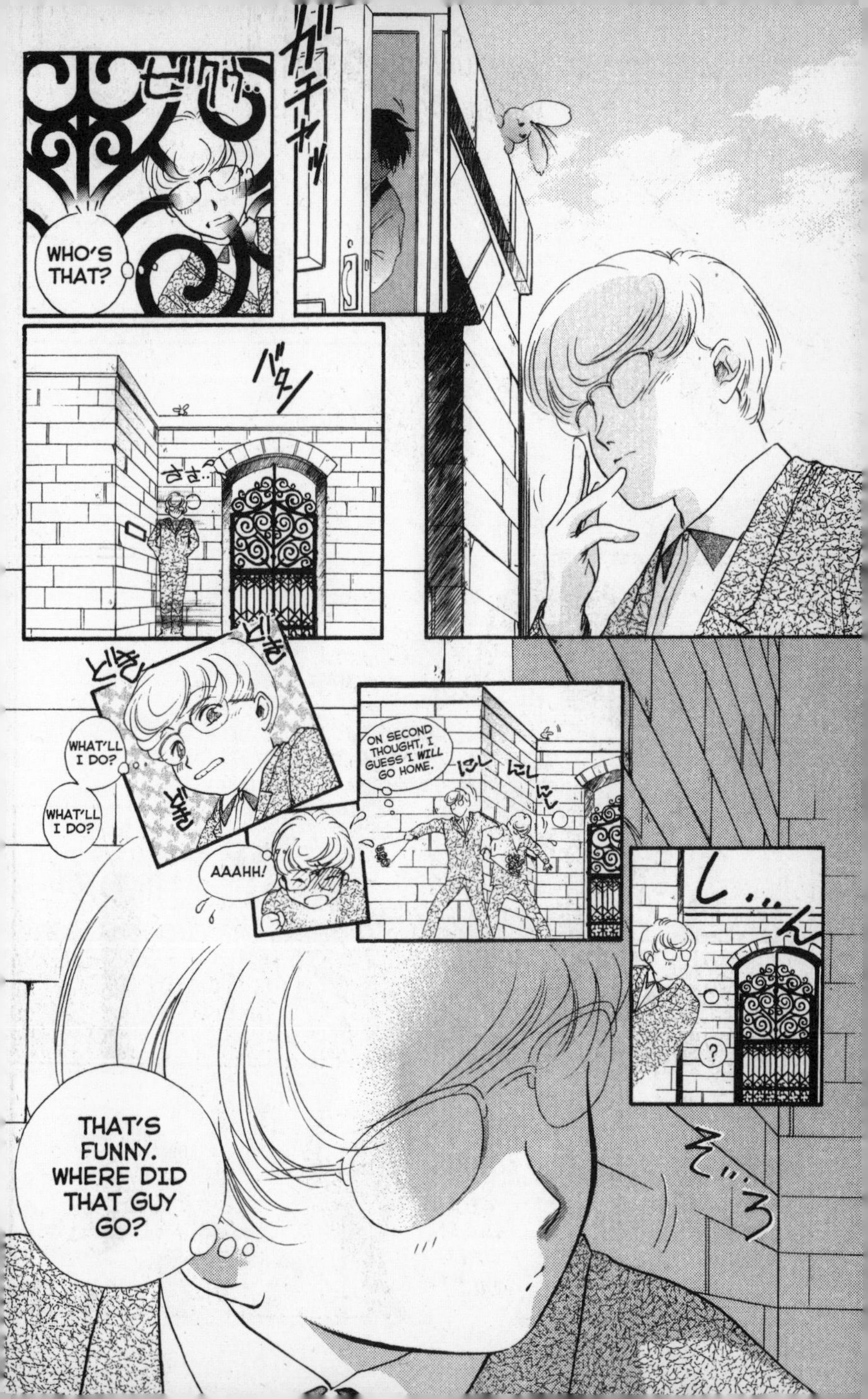

ガチャッ
ビクッ
WHO'S THAT?
バタン
ささ…
ON SECOND THOUGHT, I GUESS I *WILL* GO HOME.
AAAHH!
WHAT'LL I DO?
WHAT'LL I DO?
?
THAT'S FUNNY. WHERE DID THAT GUY GO?

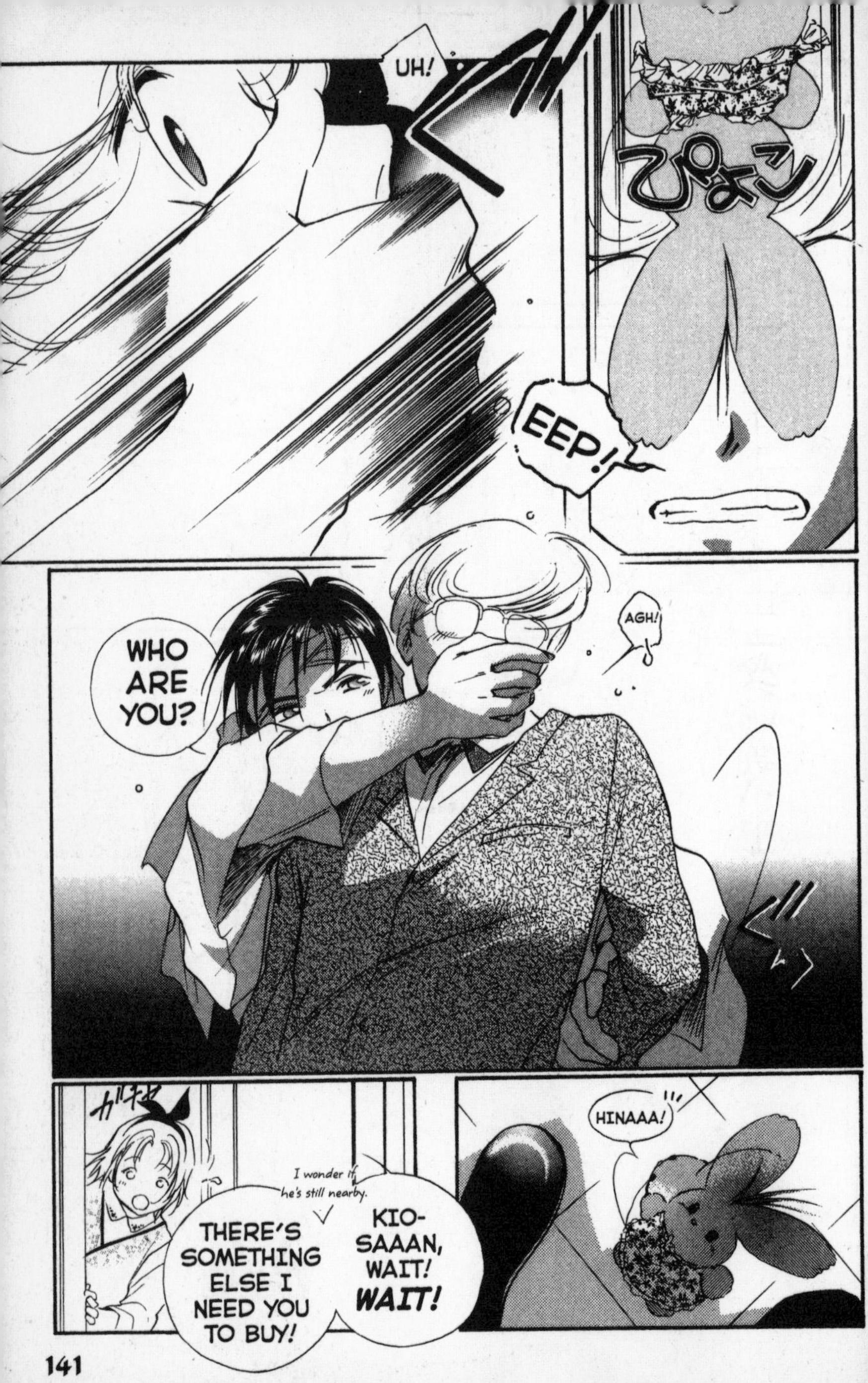
ぴょン
EEP!
UH!
AGH!
WHO ARE YOU?
HINAAA!
ガチャ
KIO-SAAAN, WAIT! WAIT!
I wonder if he's still nearby.
THERE'S SOMETHING ELSE I NEED YOU TO BUY!

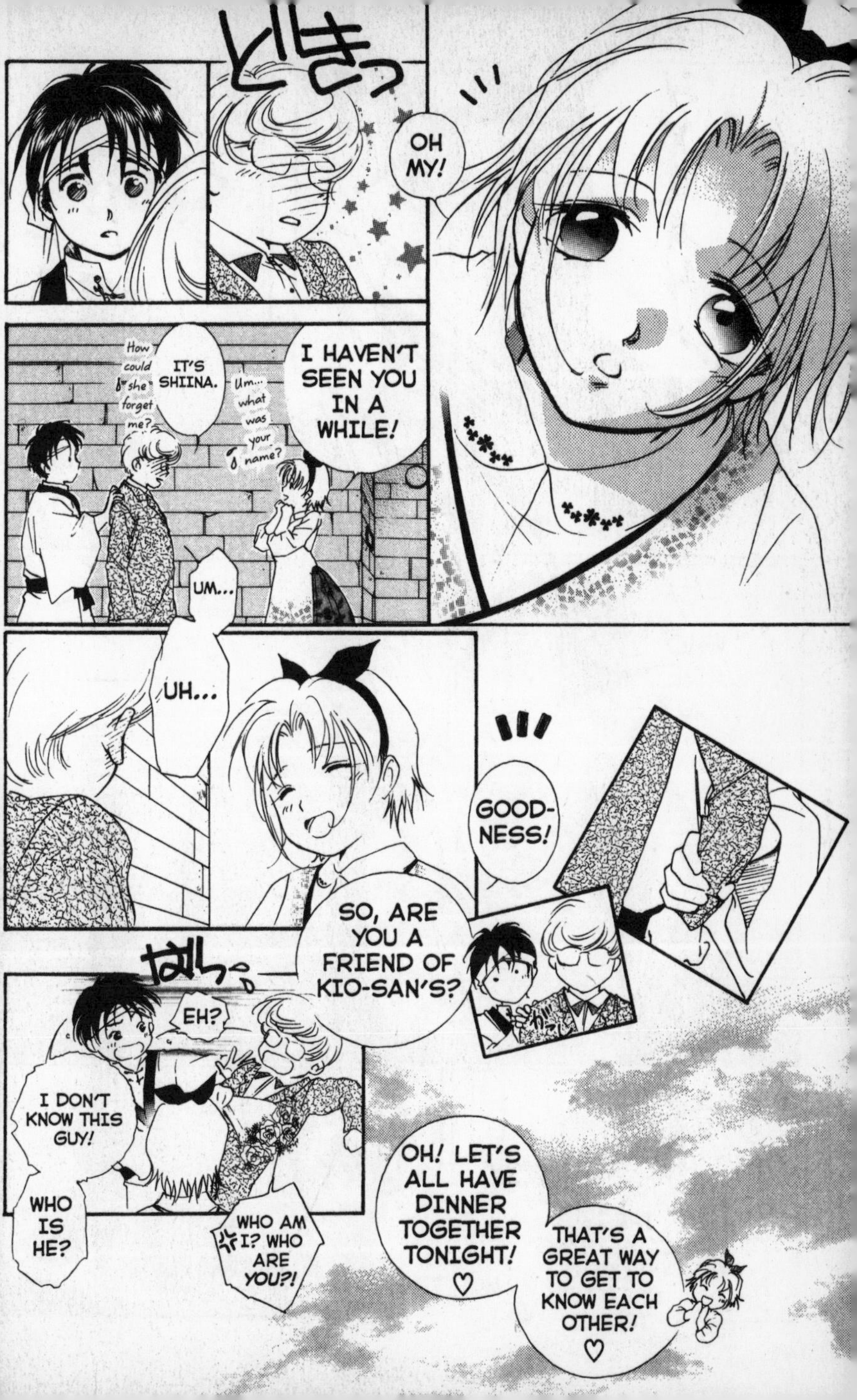
OH MY!
どきっ
I HAVEN'T SEEN YOU IN A WHILE!
Um... what was your name?
IT'S SHIINA.
How could she forget me?
UM...
GOODNESS!
UH...
SO, ARE YOU A FRIEND OF KIO-SAN'S?
OH! LET'S ALL HAVE DINNER TOGETHER TONIGHT! ♡
THAT'S A GREAT WAY TO GET TO KNOW EACH OTHER! ♡
EH?
I DON'T KNOW THIS GUY!
WHO AM I? WHO ARE YOU?!
WHO IS HE?

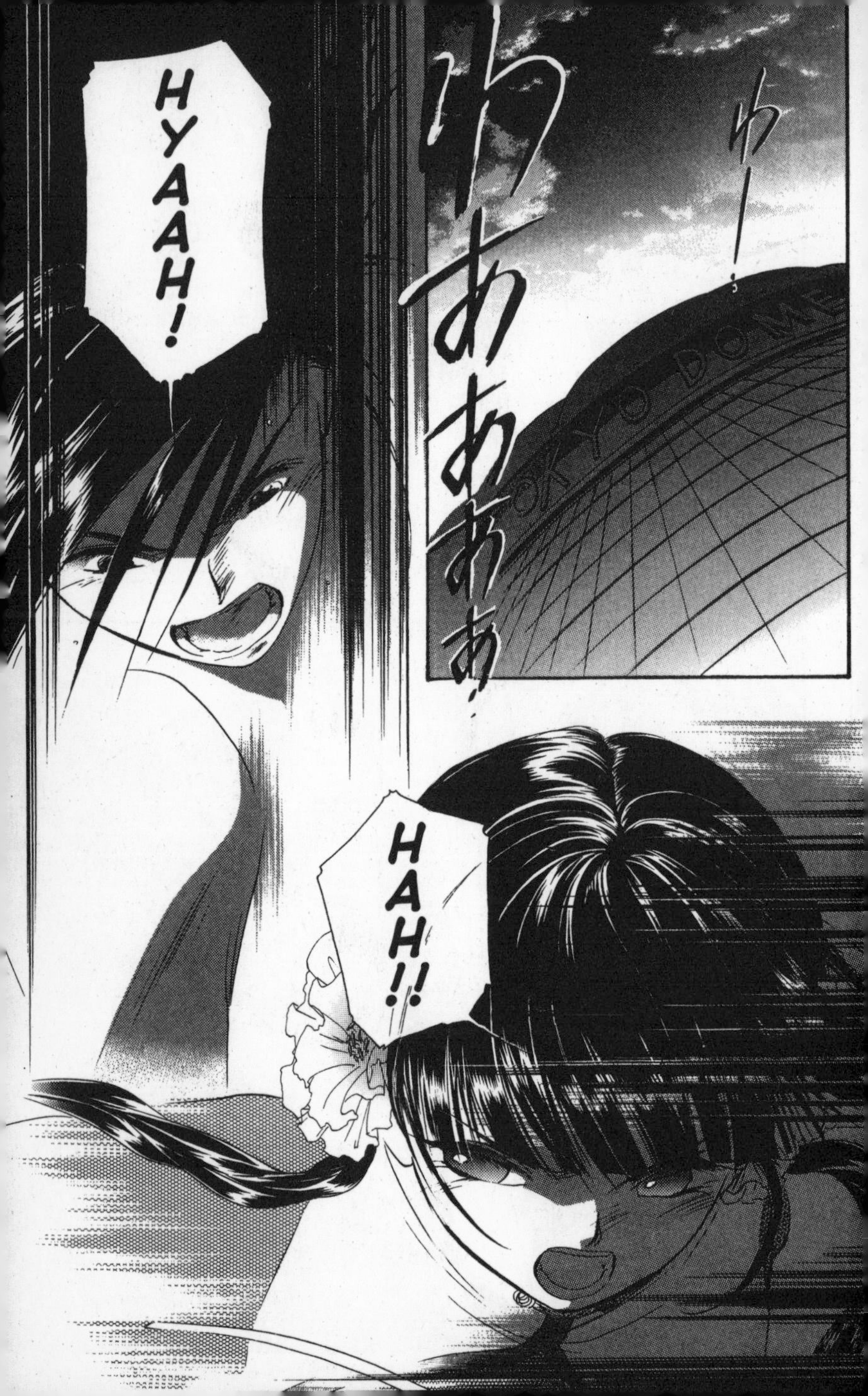
わー！
わああああ…
HAH!!
HYAAAH!

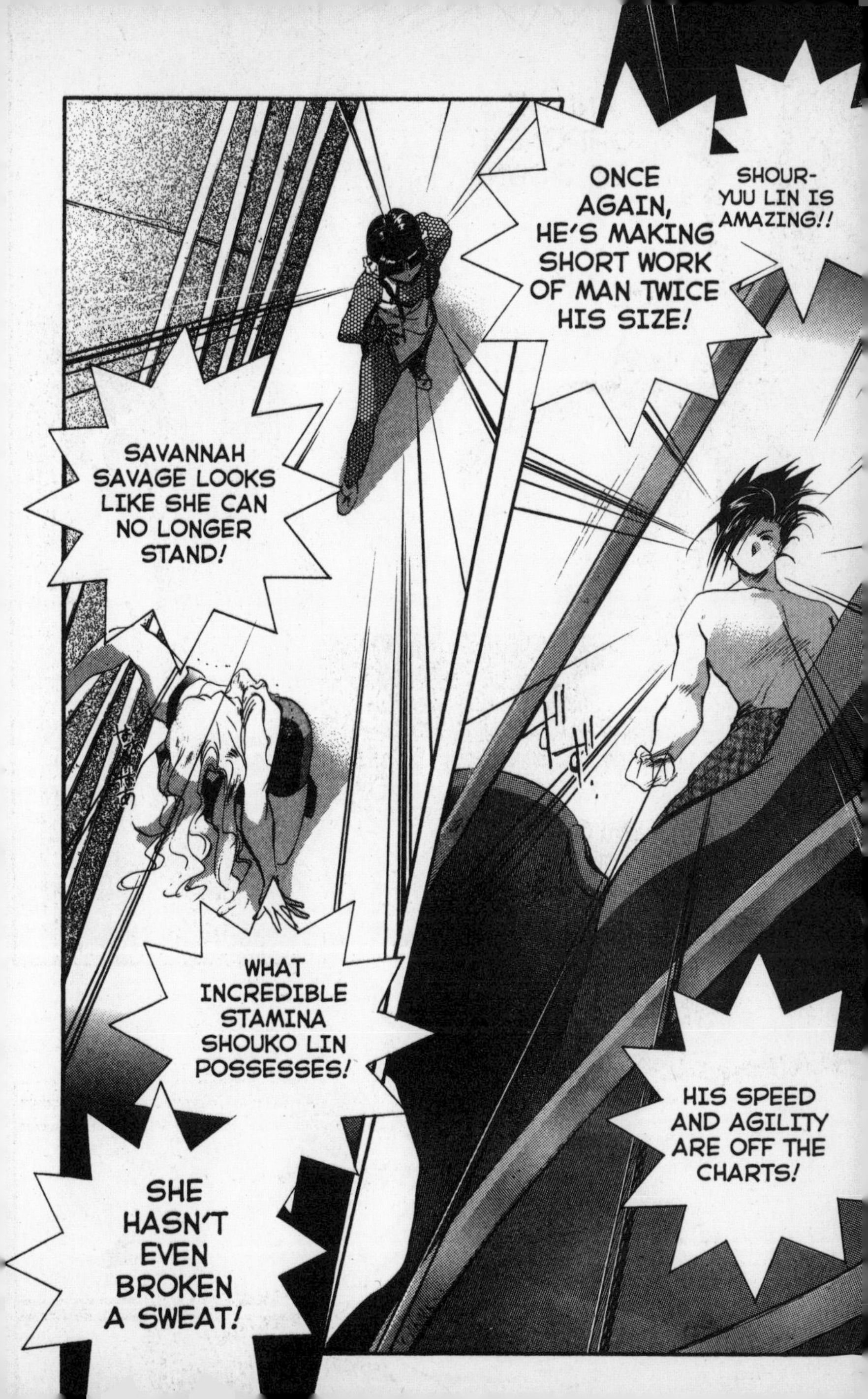
SHOUR-YUU LIN IS AMAZING!!
ONCE AGAIN, HE'S MAKING SHORT WORK OF MAN TWICE HIS SIZE!
SAVANNAH SAVAGE LOOKS LIKE SHE CAN NO LONGER STAND!
HIS SPEED AND AGILITY ARE OFF THE CHARTS!
WHAT INCREDIBLE STAMINA SHOUKO LIN POSSESSES!
SHE HASN'T EVEN BROKEN A SWEAT!

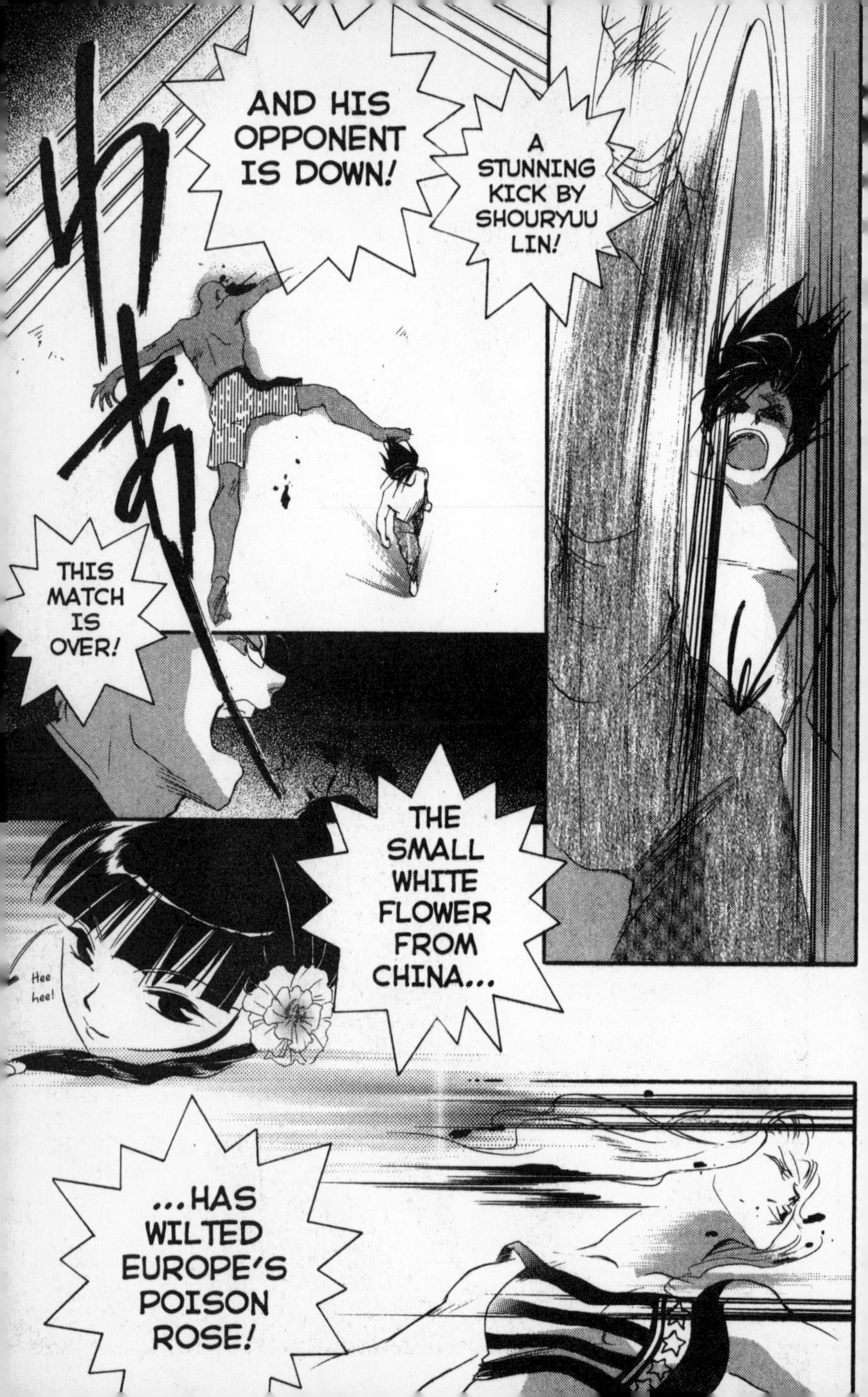
A STUNNING KICK BY SHOURYUU LIN!
AND HIS OPPONENT IS DOWN!
THIS MATCH IS OVER!
THE SMALL WHITE FLOWER FROM CHINA...
Hee hee!
...HAS WILTED EUROPE'S POISON ROSE!

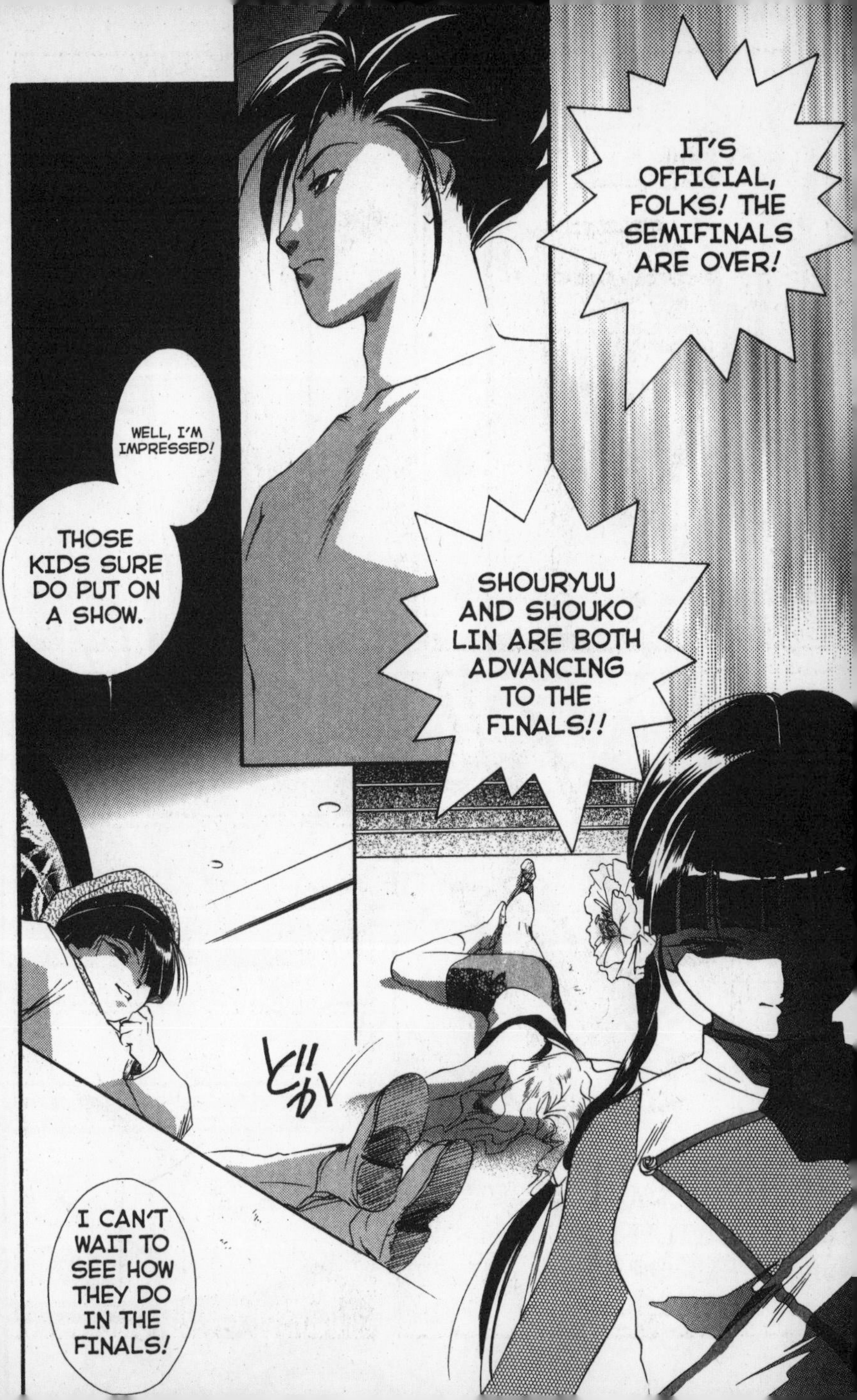
IT'S OFFICIAL, FOLKS! THE SEMIFINALS ARE OVER!
SHOURYUU AND SHOUKO LIN ARE BOTH ADVANCING TO THE FINALS!!
WELL, I'M IMPRESSED!
THOSE KIDS SURE DO PUT ON A SHOW.
I CAN'T WAIT TO SEE HOW THEY DO IN THE FINALS!

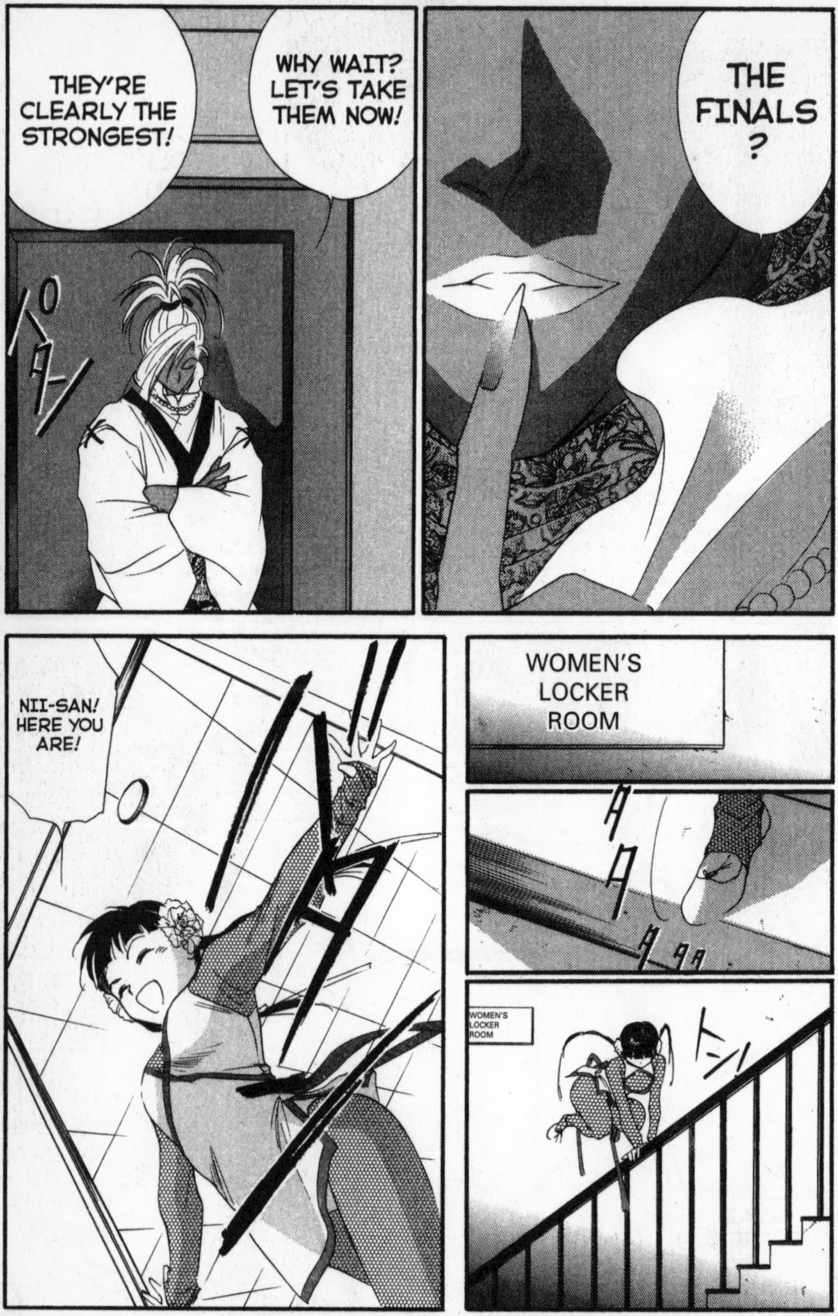
THE FINALS ?
WHY WAIT? LET'S TAKE THEM NOW!
THEY'RE CLEARLY THE STRONGEST!
パタン
WOMEN'S LOCKER ROOM
タタタタタタ
WOMEN'S LOCKER ROOM
トン!
NII-SAN! HERE YOU ARE!

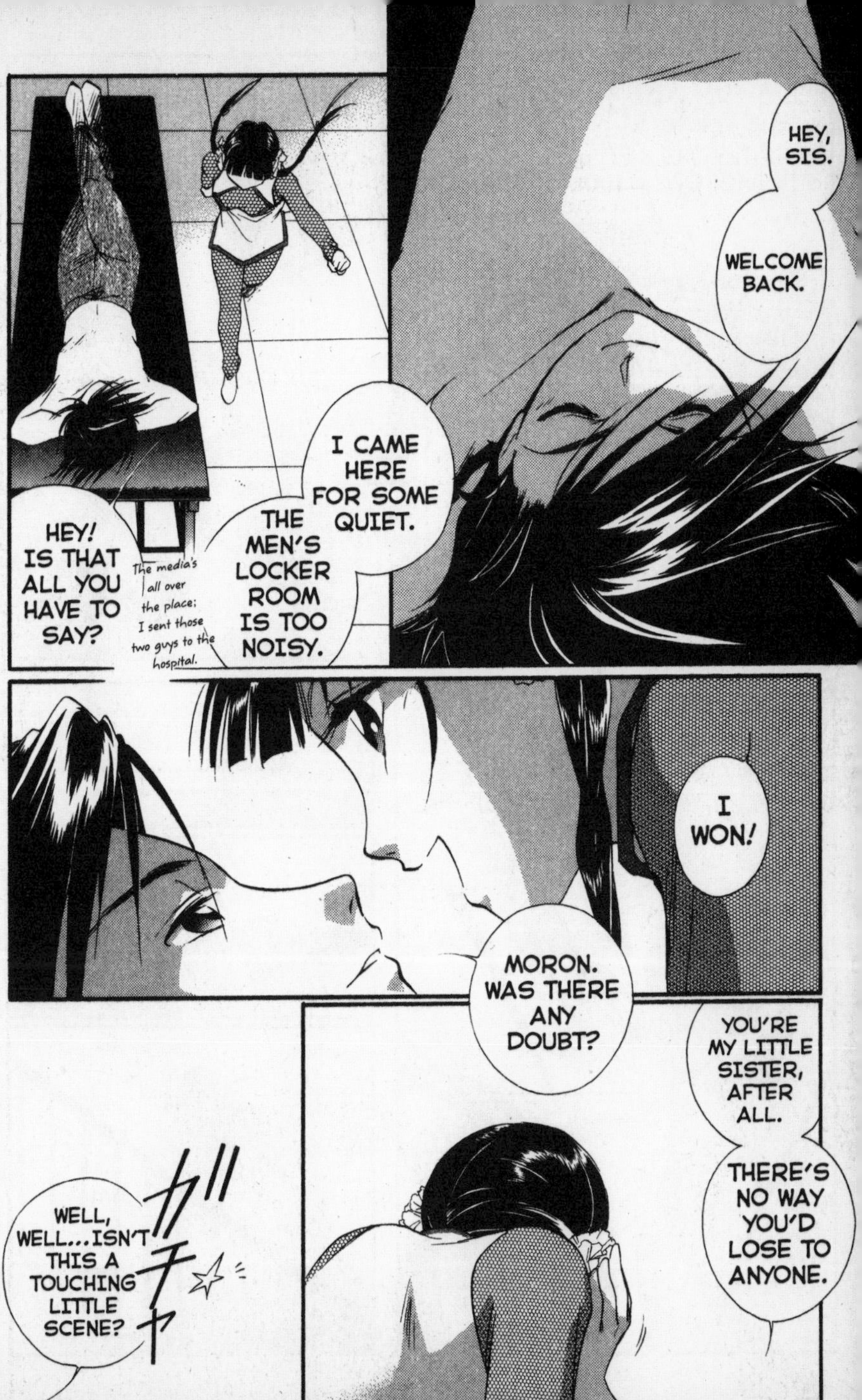
HEY, SIS.
WELCOME BACK.
I CAME HERE FOR SOME QUIET.
THE MEN'S LOCKER ROOM IS TOO NOISY.
The media's all over the place; I sent those two guys to the hospital.
HEY! IS THAT ALL YOU HAVE TO SAY?
I WON!
MORON. WAS THERE ANY DOUBT?
YOU'RE MY LITTLE SISTER, AFTER ALL.
THERE'S NO WAY YOU'D LOSE TO ANYONE.
ガチャ
WELL, WELL...ISN'T THIS A TOUCHING LITTLE SCENE?

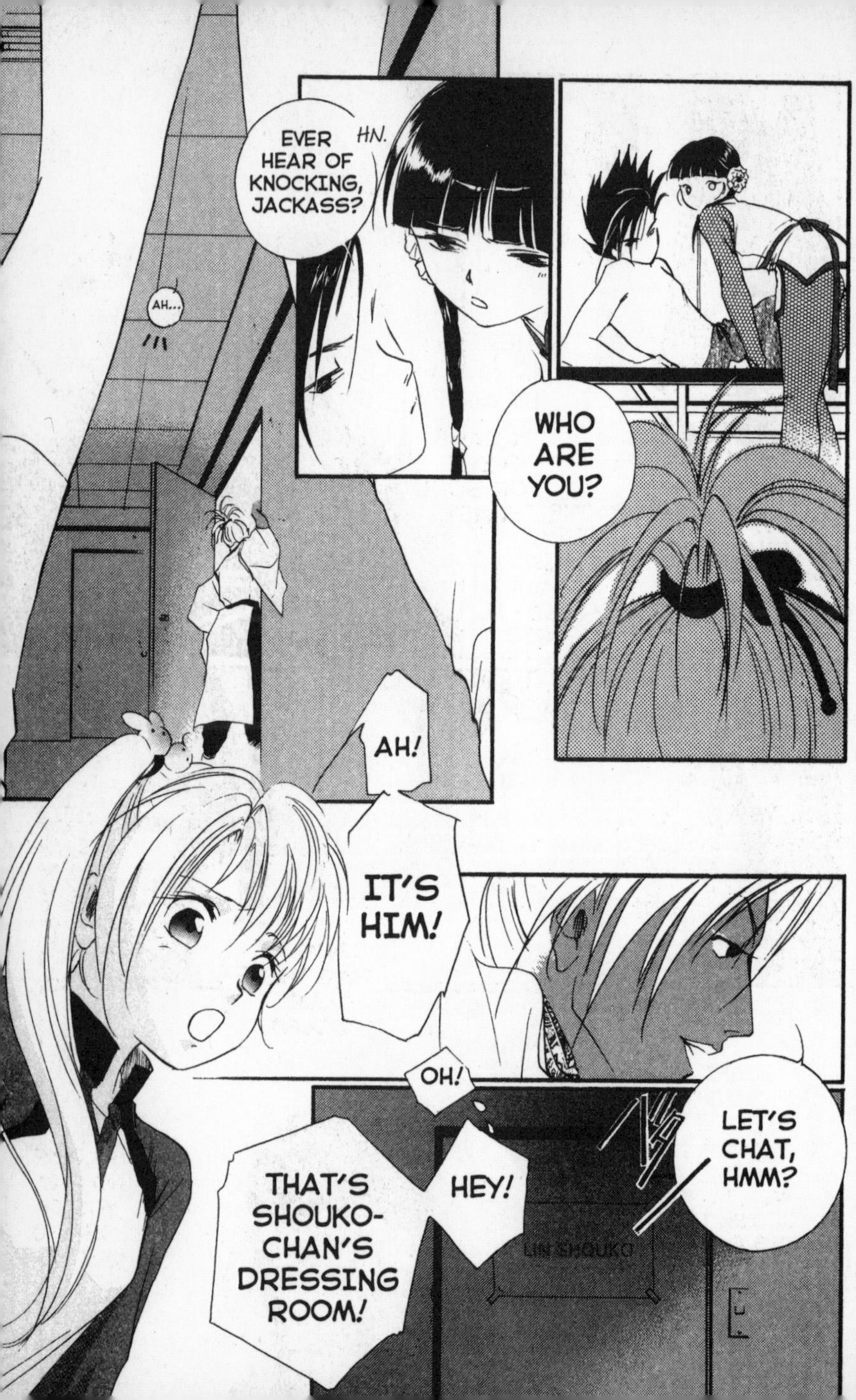
HN.
EVER HEAR OF KNOCKING, JACKASS?
WHO ARE YOU?
AH...
AH!
IT'S HIM!
LET'S CHAT, HMM?
OH!
HEY!
THAT'S SHOUKO-CHAN'S DRESSING ROOM!
LIN SHOUKO

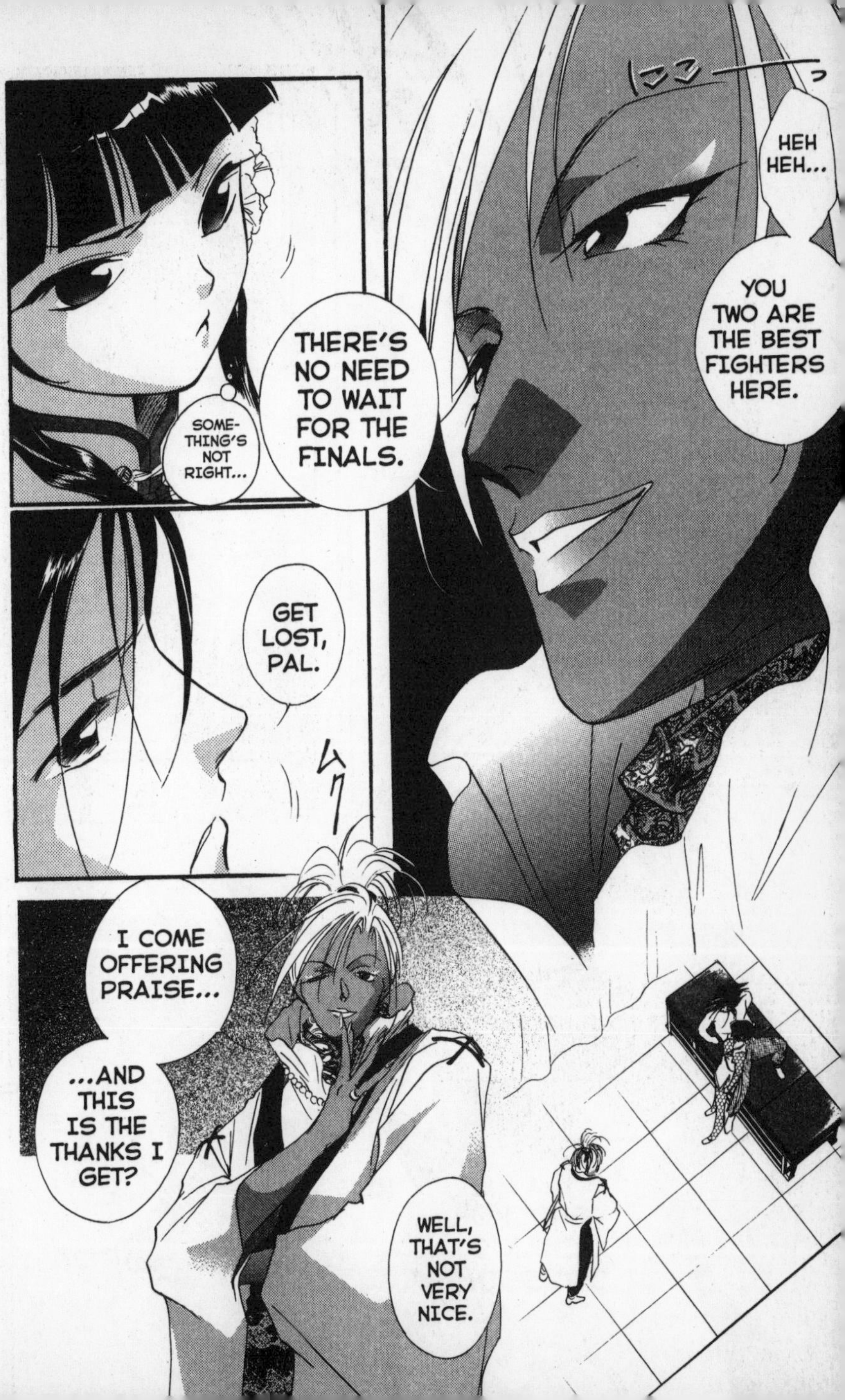
HEH HEH...
YOU TWO ARE THE BEST FIGHTERS HERE.
THERE'S NO NEED TO WAIT FOR THE FINALS.
SOME-THING'S NOT RIGHT...
GET LOST, PAL.
WELL, THAT'S NOT VERY NICE.
I COME OFFERING PRAISE...
...AND THIS IS THE THANKS I GET?

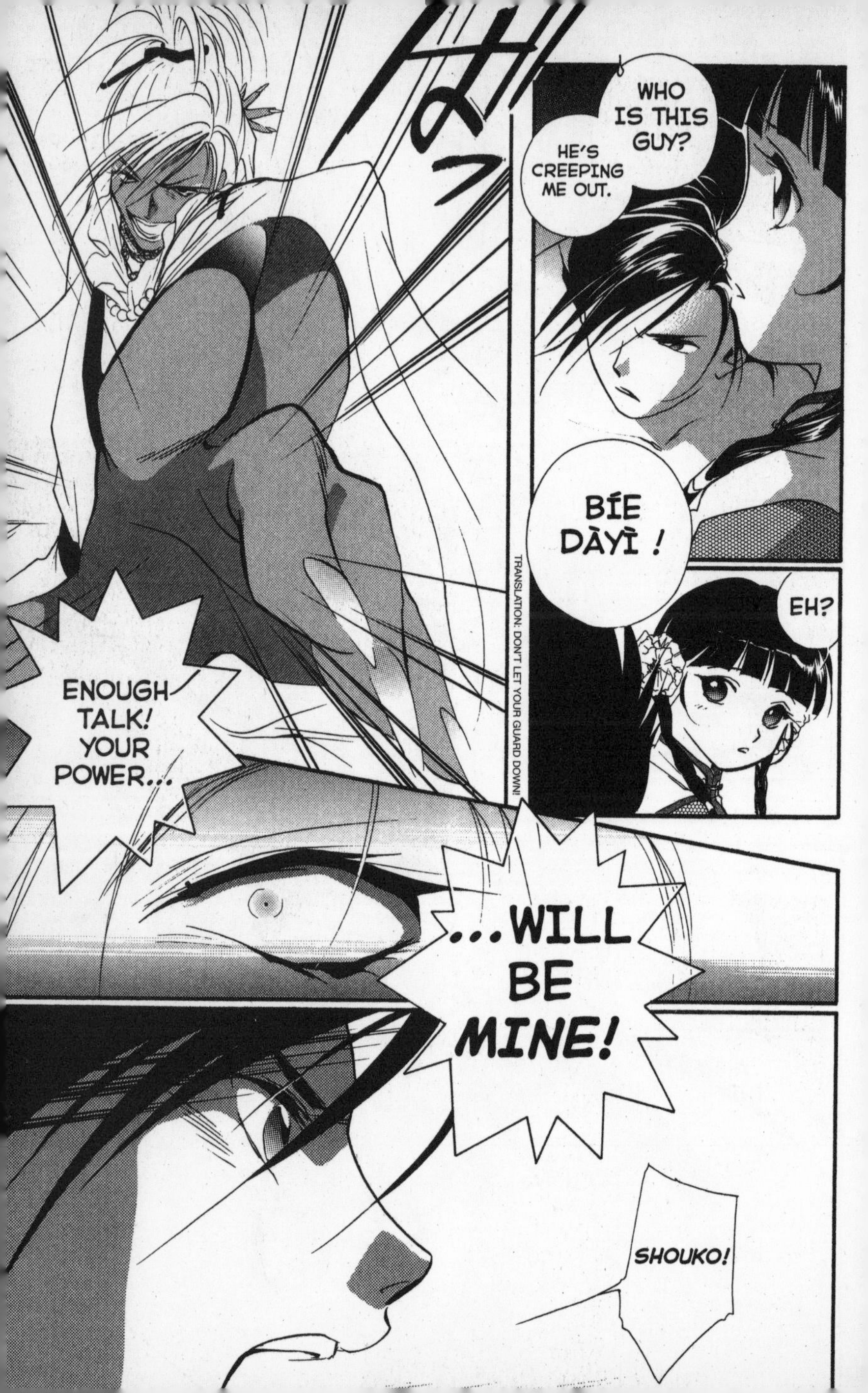
WHO IS THIS GUY?
HE'S CREEPING ME OUT.
BÍE DÀYÌ !
EH?
TRANSLATION: DON'T LET YOUR GUARD DOWN!
はっ
ENOUGH TALK! YOUR POWER...
...WILL BE MINE!
SHOUKO!

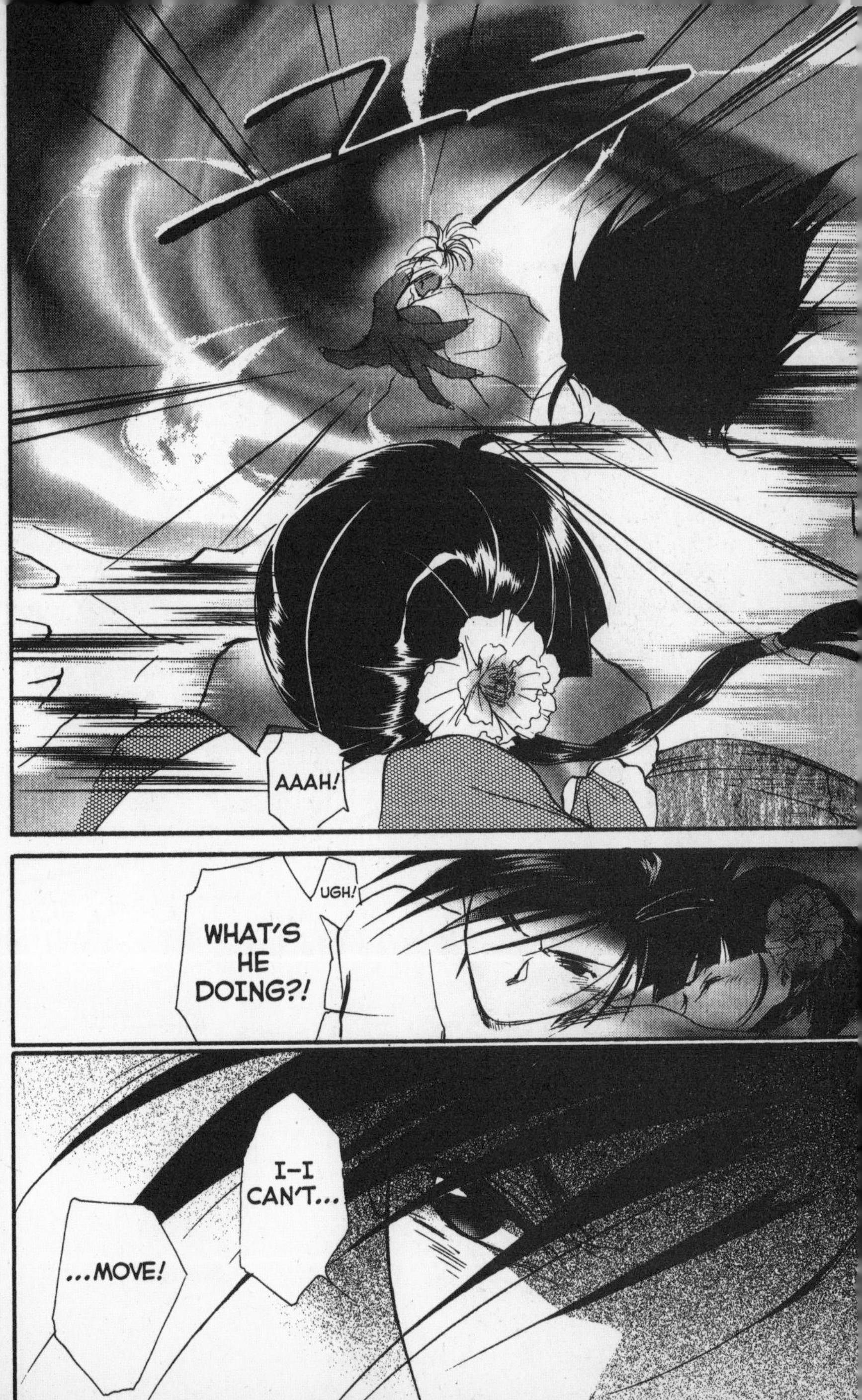
AAAH!
UGH!
WHAT'S HE DOING?!
I-I CAN'T...
...MOVE!

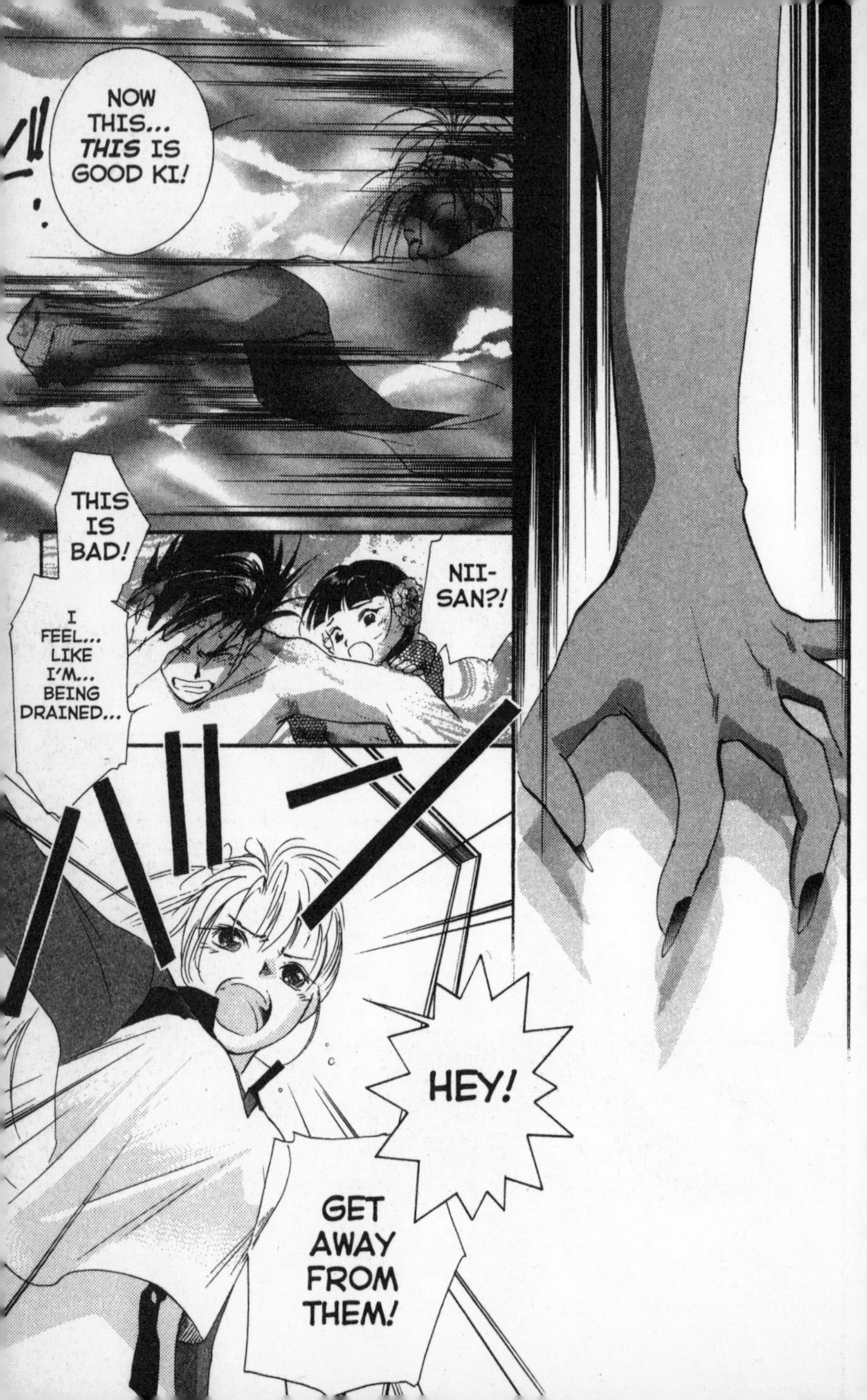
NOW THIS... THIS IS GOOD KI!
NII-SAN?!
THIS IS BAD!
I FEEL... LIKE I'M... BEING DRAINED...
HEY!
GET AWAY FROM THEM!

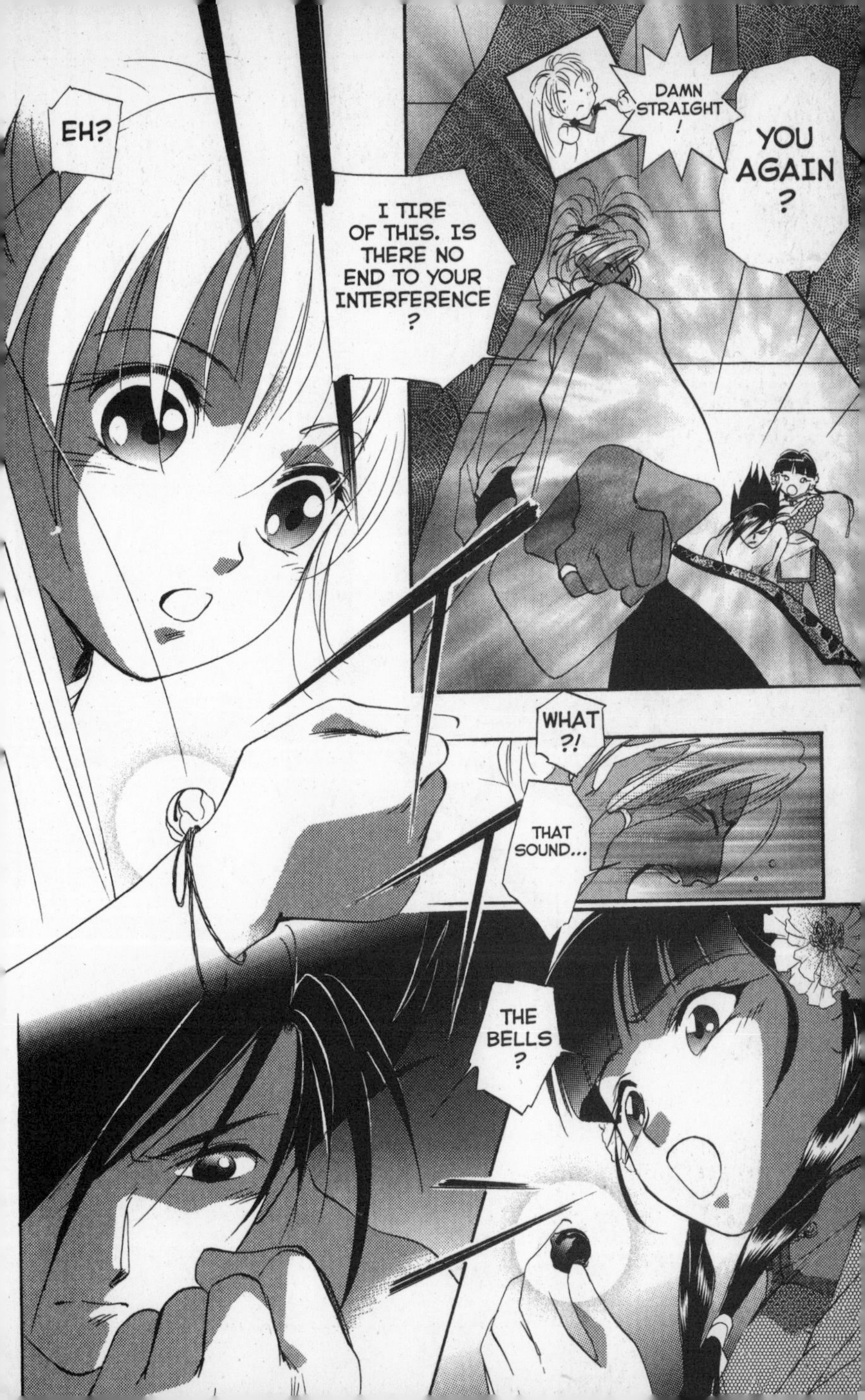
YOU AGAIN?
DAMN STRAIGHT!
I TIRE OF THIS. IS THERE NO END TO YOUR INTERFERENCE?
WHAT?!
THAT SOUND...
EH?
THE BELLS?

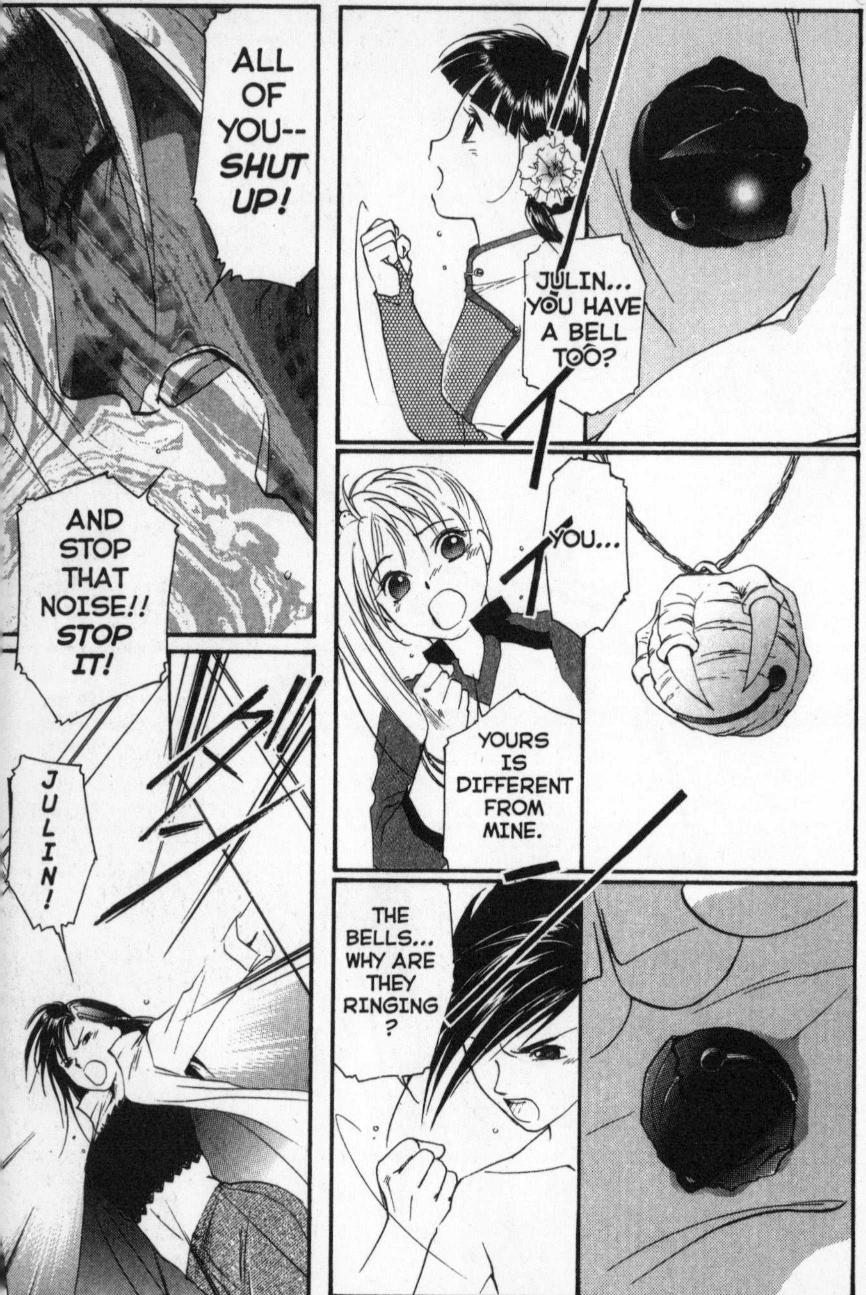
JULIN... YOU HAVE A BELL TOO?
YOU...
YOURS IS DIFFERENT FROM MINE.
THE BELLS... WHY ARE THEY RINGING?
ALL OF YOU-- SHUT UP!
AND STOP THAT NOISE!! STOP IT!
JULIN!

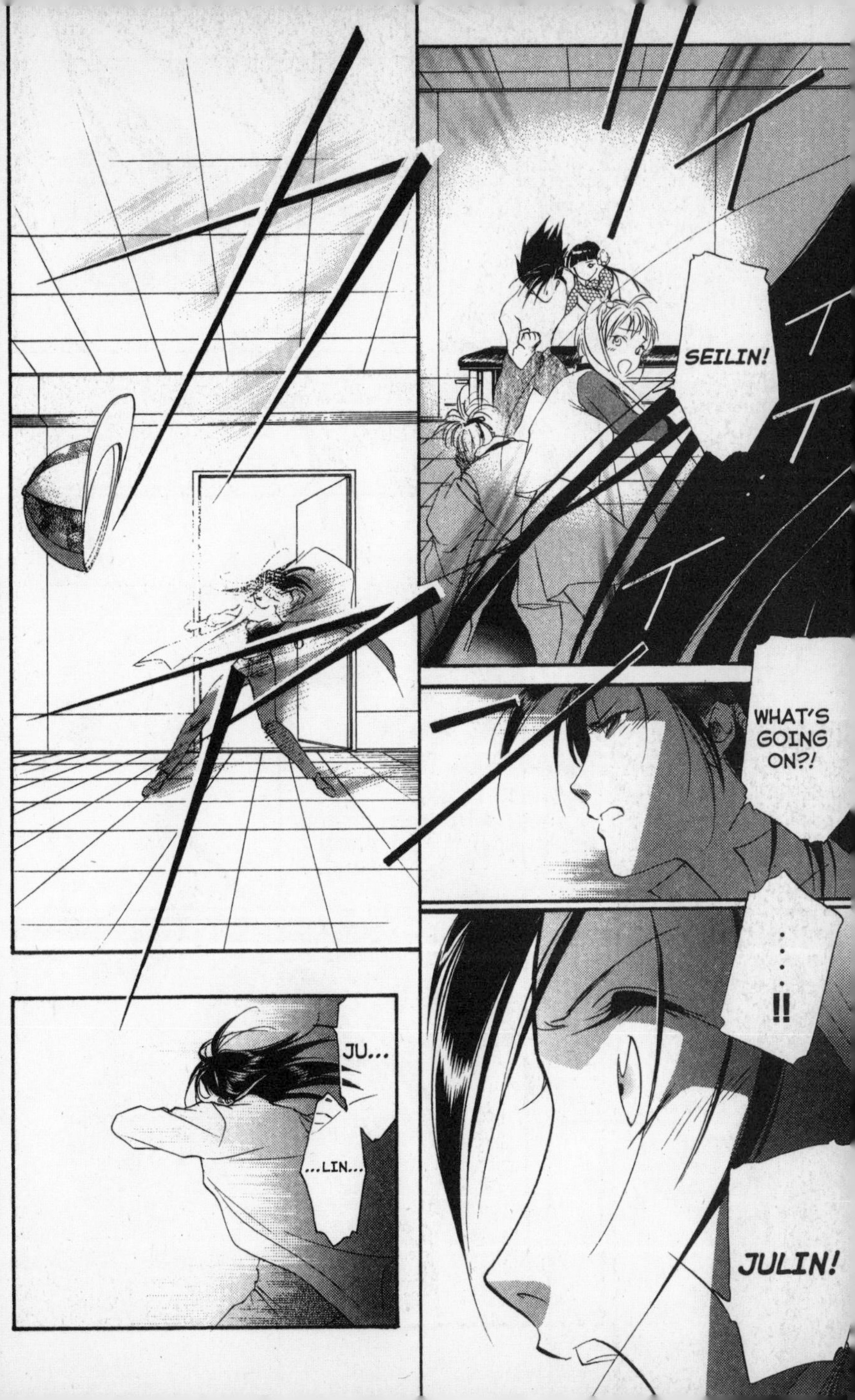
SEILIN!
WHAT'S GOING ON?!
. . . . !!
JULIN!
JU...
...LIN...

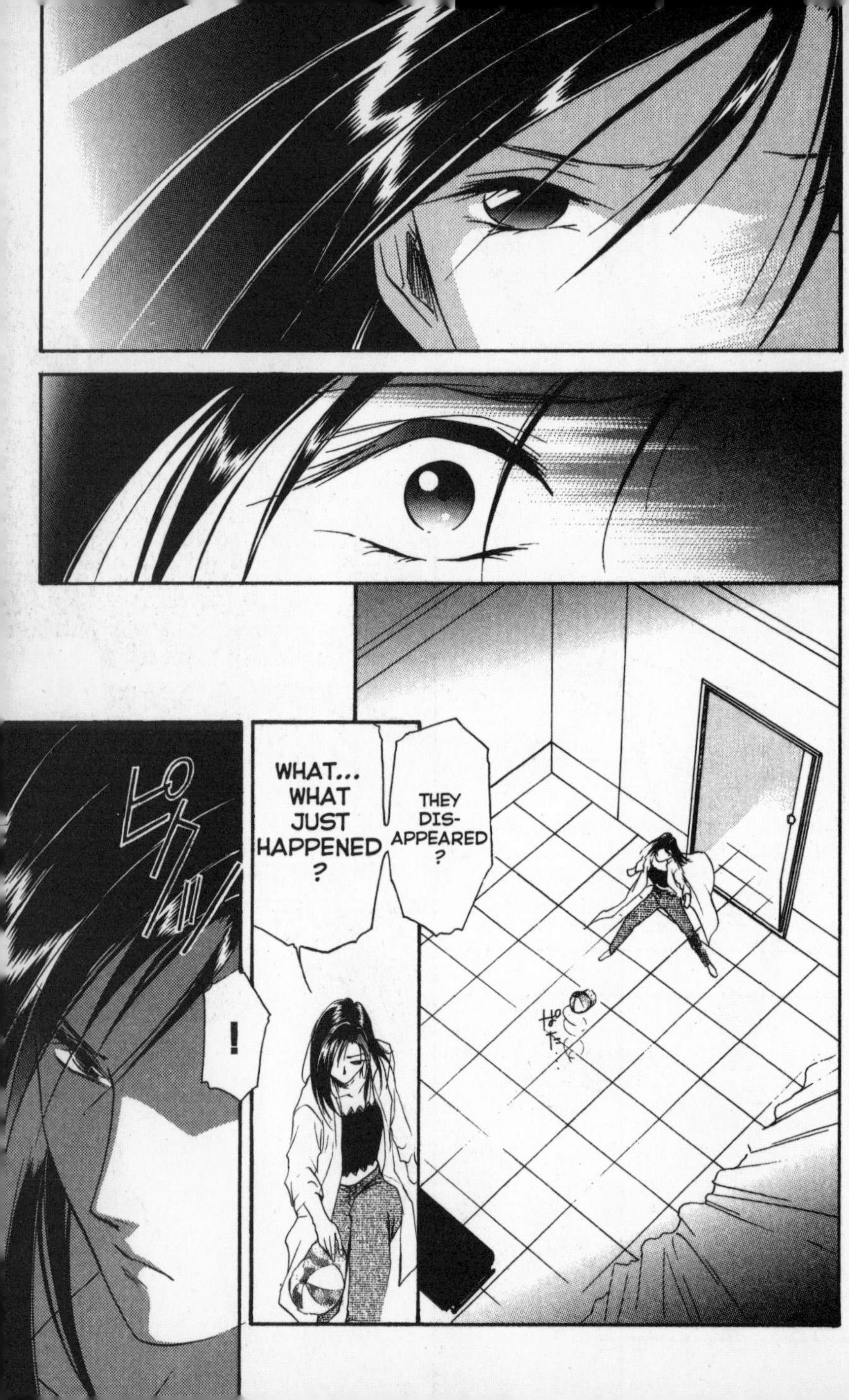
THEY DIS-APPEARED?
WHAT... WHAT JUST HAPPENED?
!

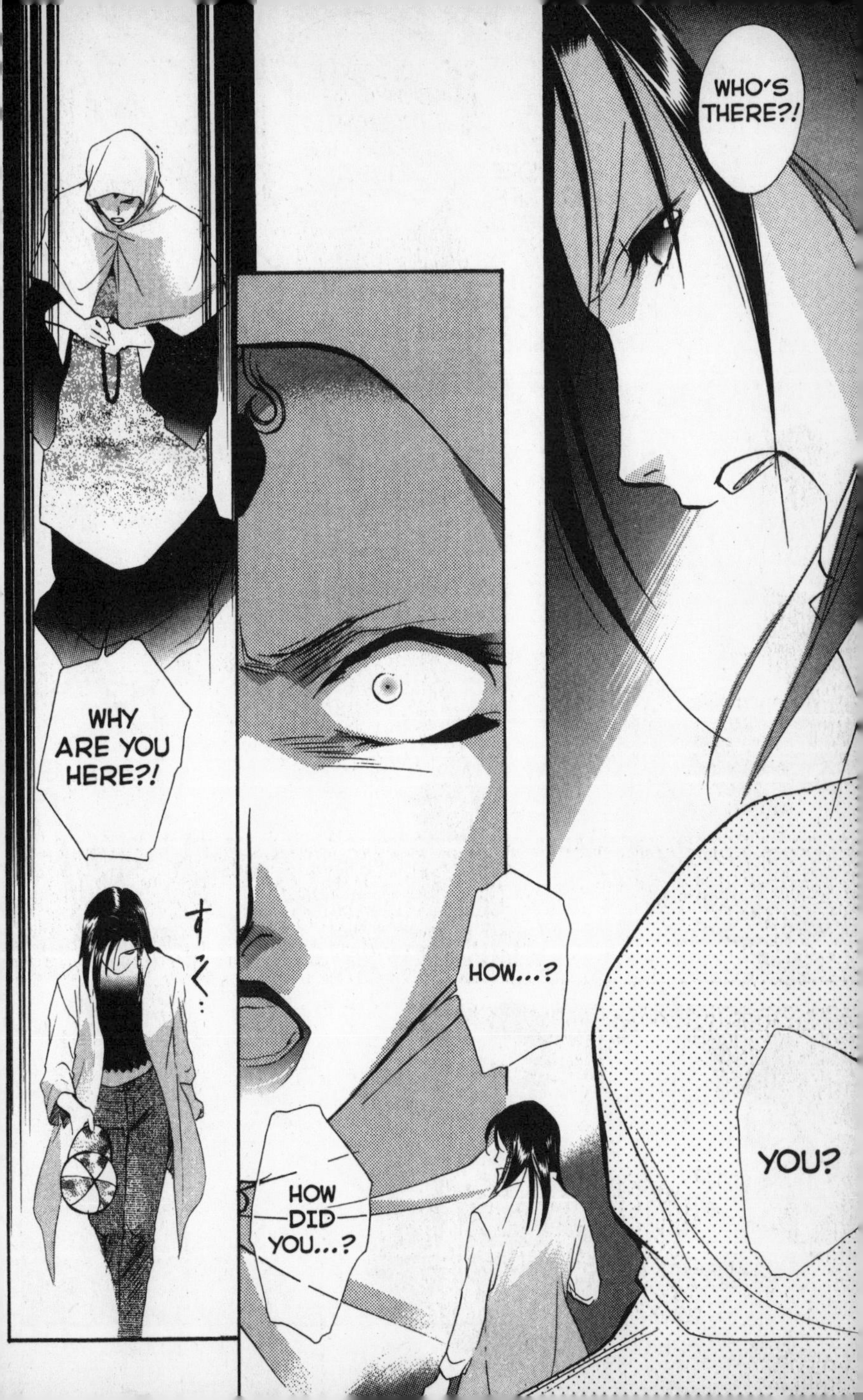
WHO'S THERE?!
YOU?
HOW...?
HOW DID YOU...?
WHY ARE YOU HERE?!
すく…

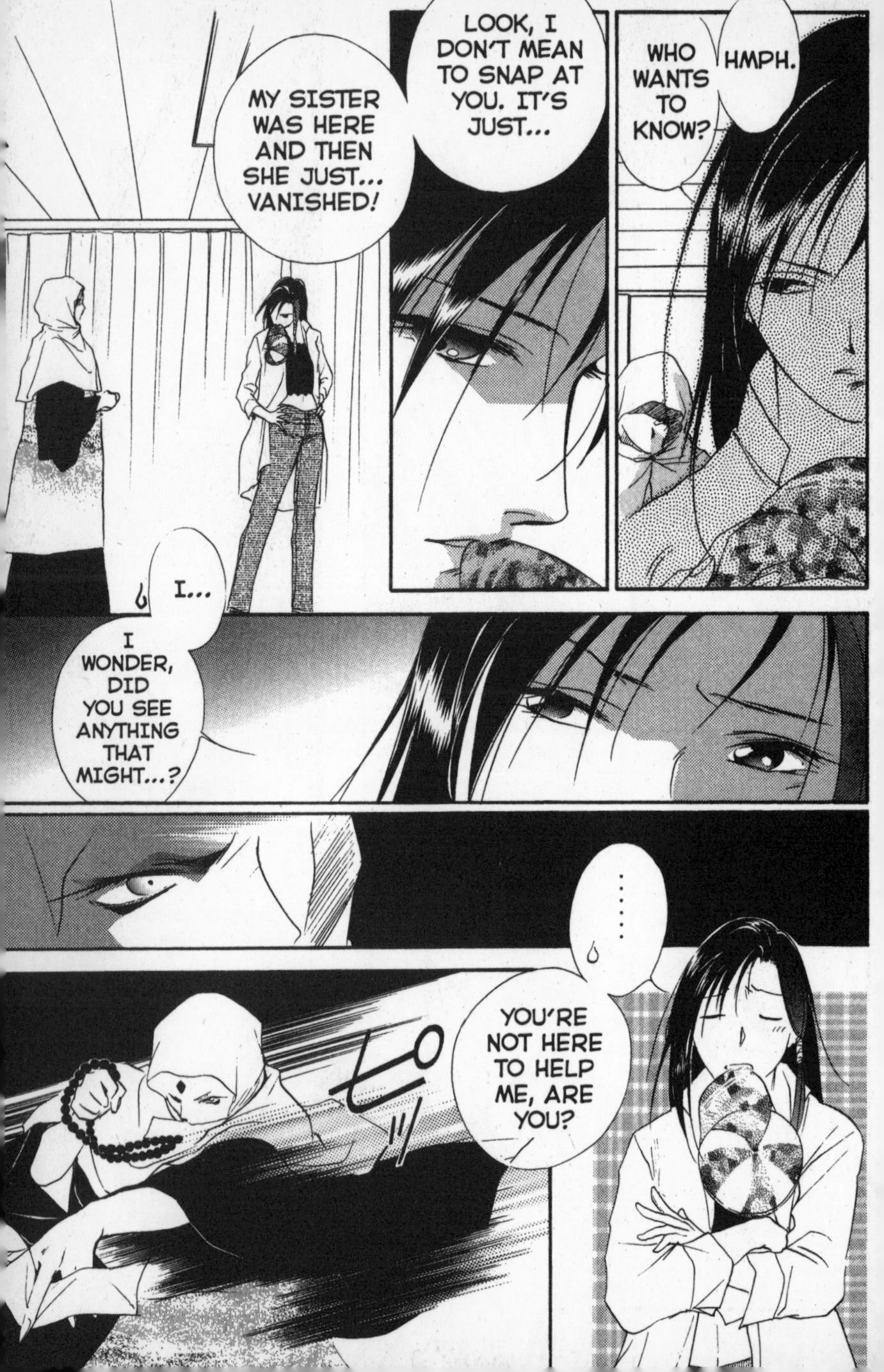
HMPH.
WHO WANTS TO KNOW?
LOOK, I DON'T MEAN TO SNAP AT YOU. IT'S JUST...
MY SISTER WAS HERE AND THEN SHE JUST... VANISHED!
I...
I WONDER, DID YOU SEE ANYTHING THAT MIGHT...?
......
YOU'RE NOT HERE TO HELP ME, ARE YOU?

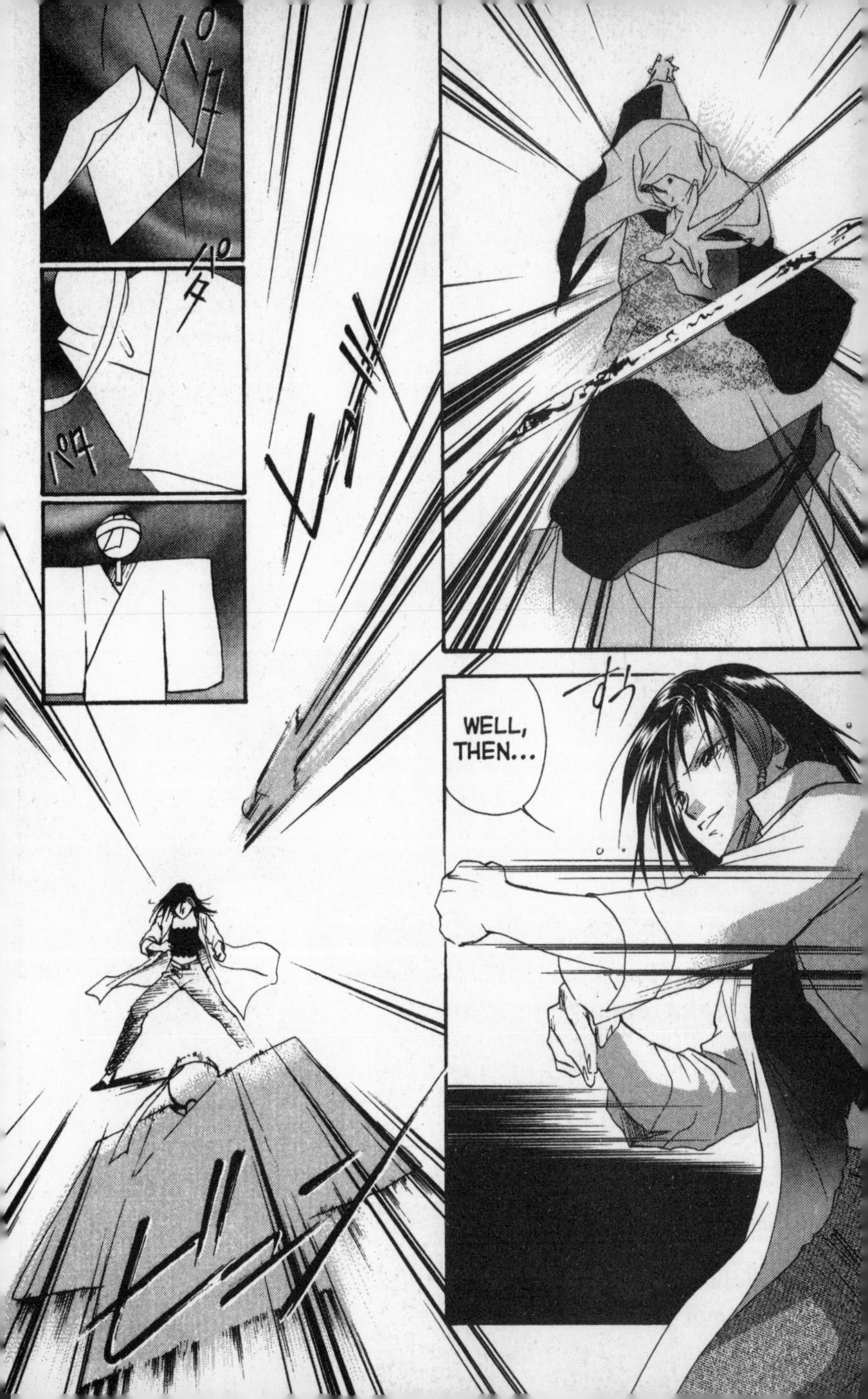
WELL, THEN...

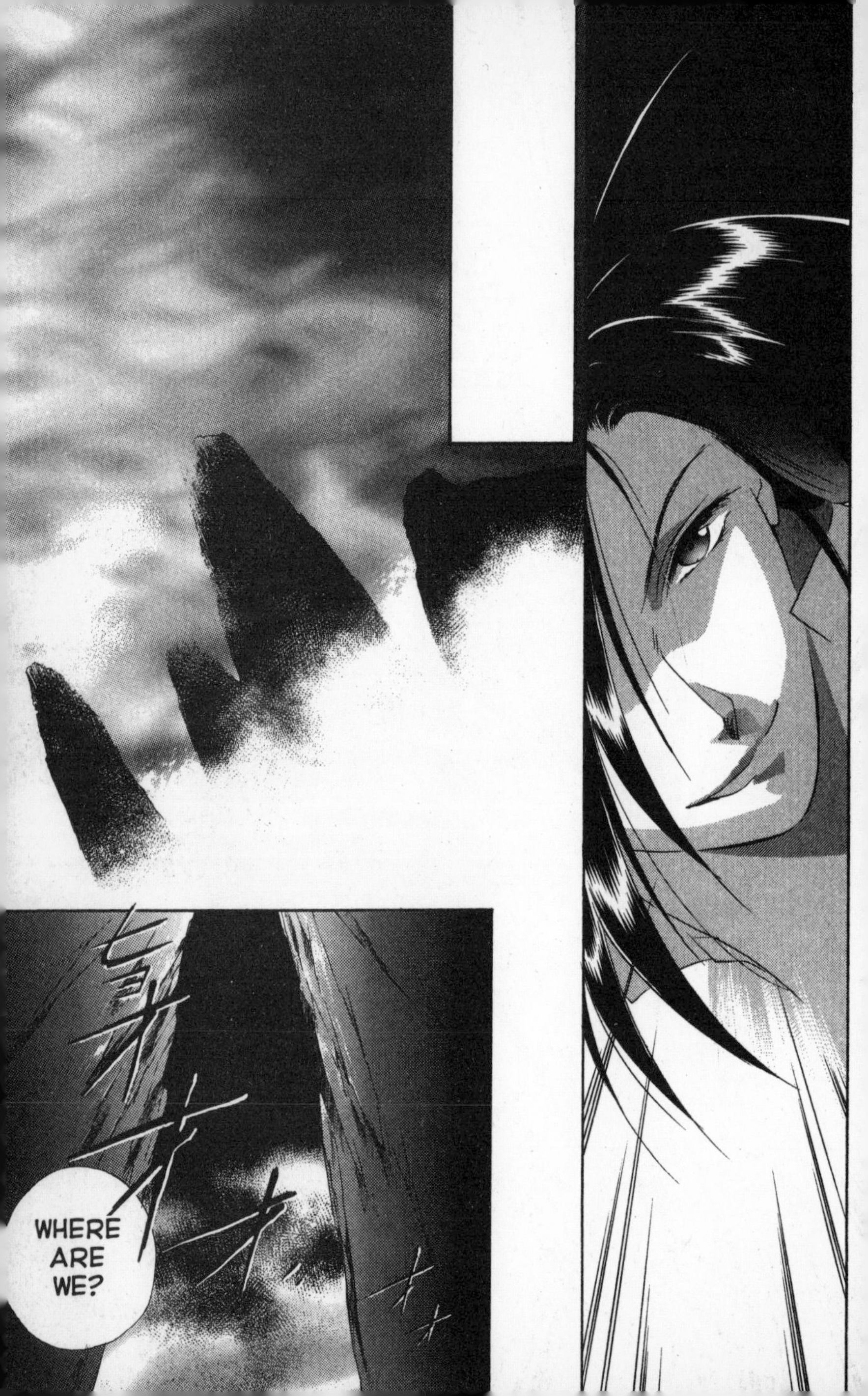
WHERE ARE WE?

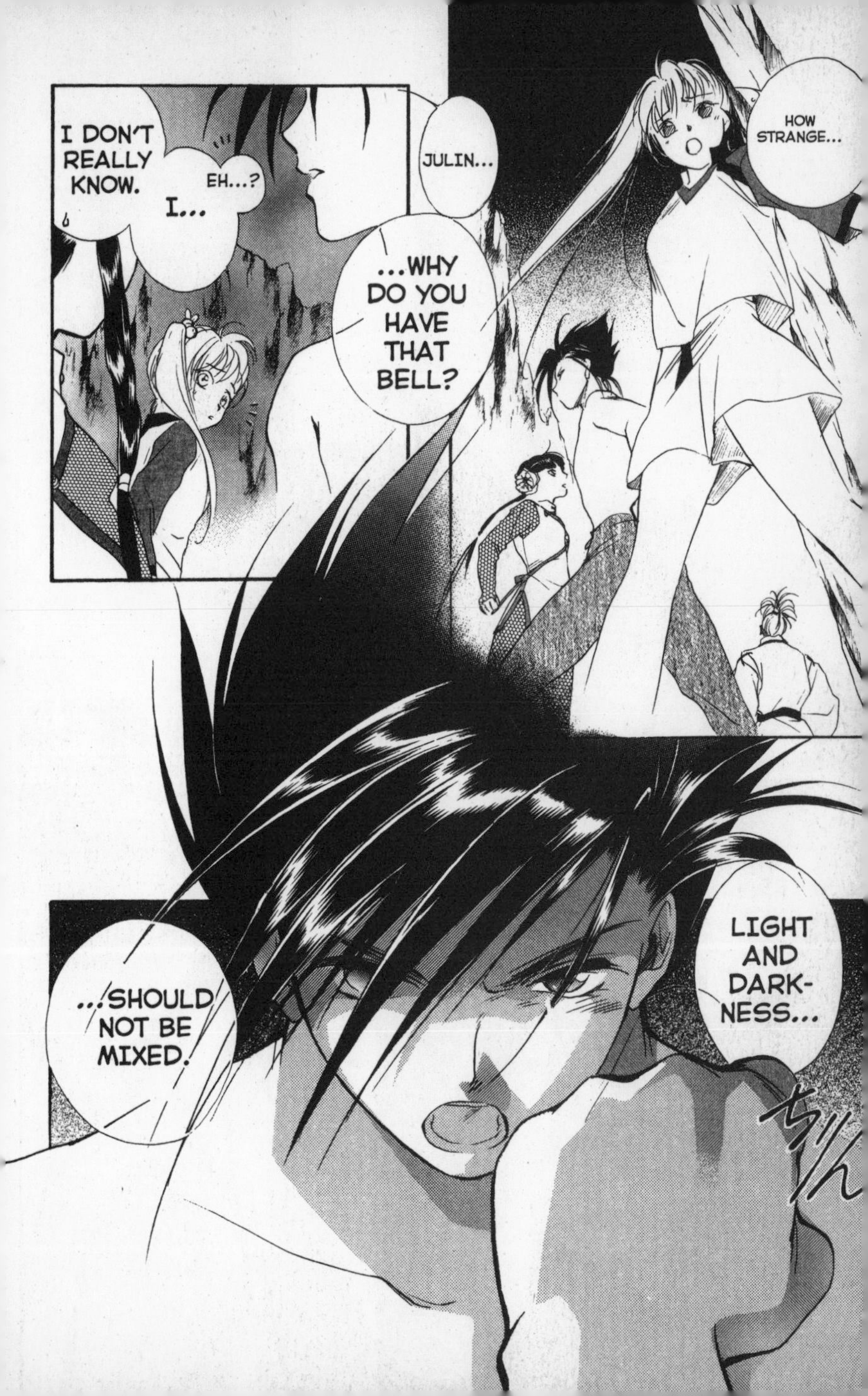
HOW STRANGE...
JULIN...
...WHY DO YOU HAVE THAT BELL?
EH...?
I...
I DON'T REALLY KNOW.
LIGHT AND DARK-NESS...
...SHOULD NOT BE MIXED.
ちりん

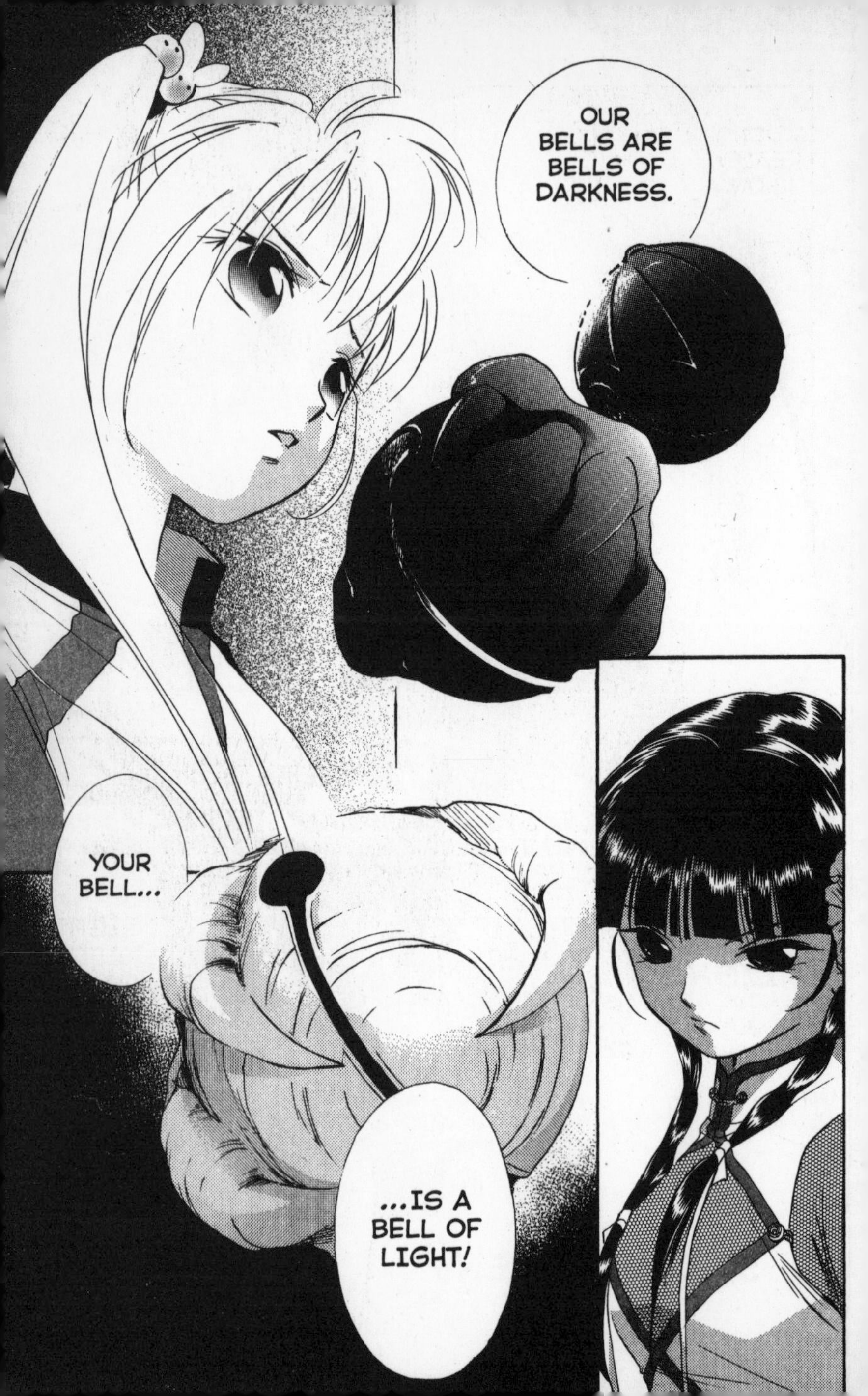

OUR BELLS ARE BELLS OF DARKNESS.
YOUR BELL...
...IS A BELL OF LIGHT!

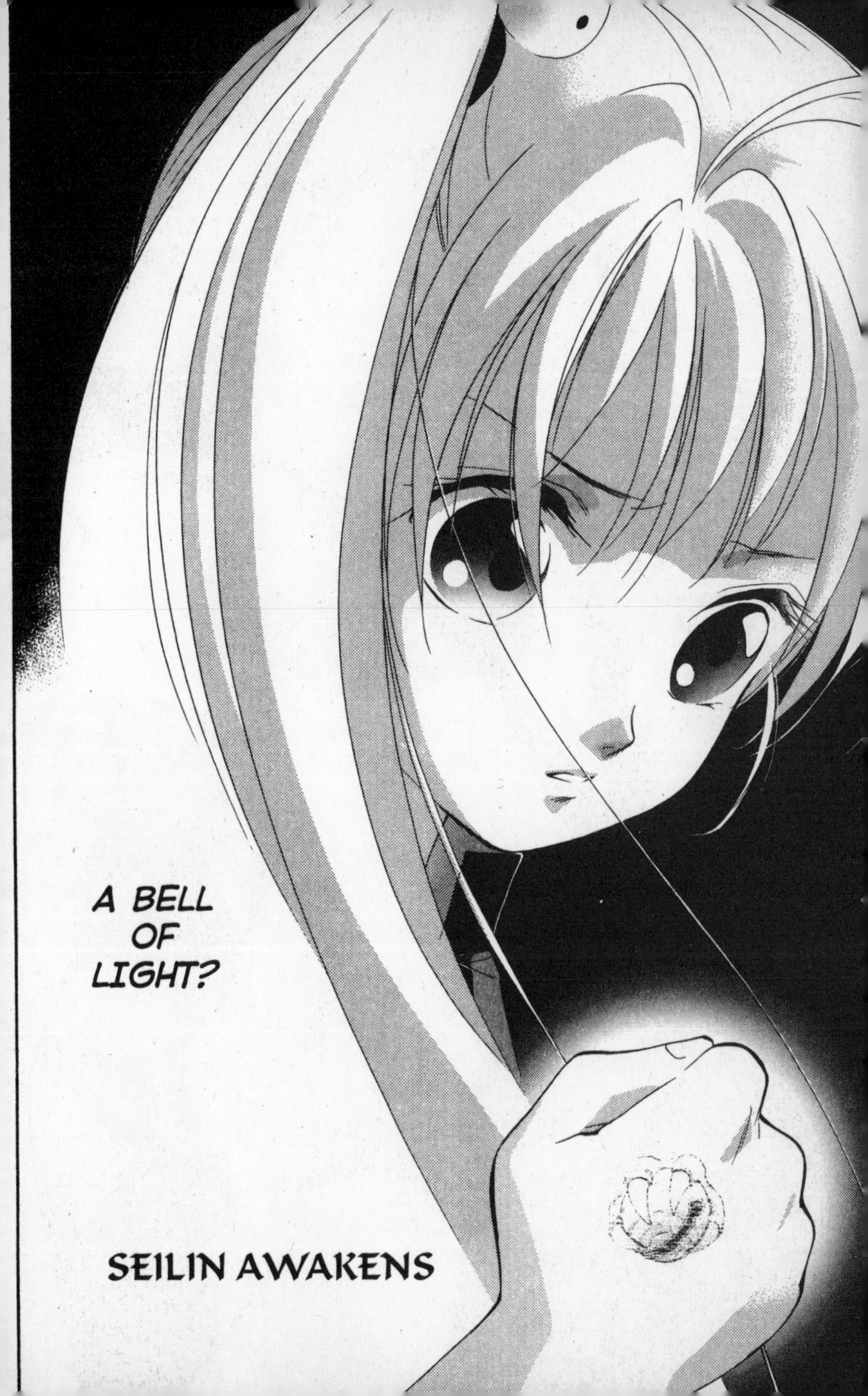
A BELL OF LIGHT?
SEILIN AWAKENS

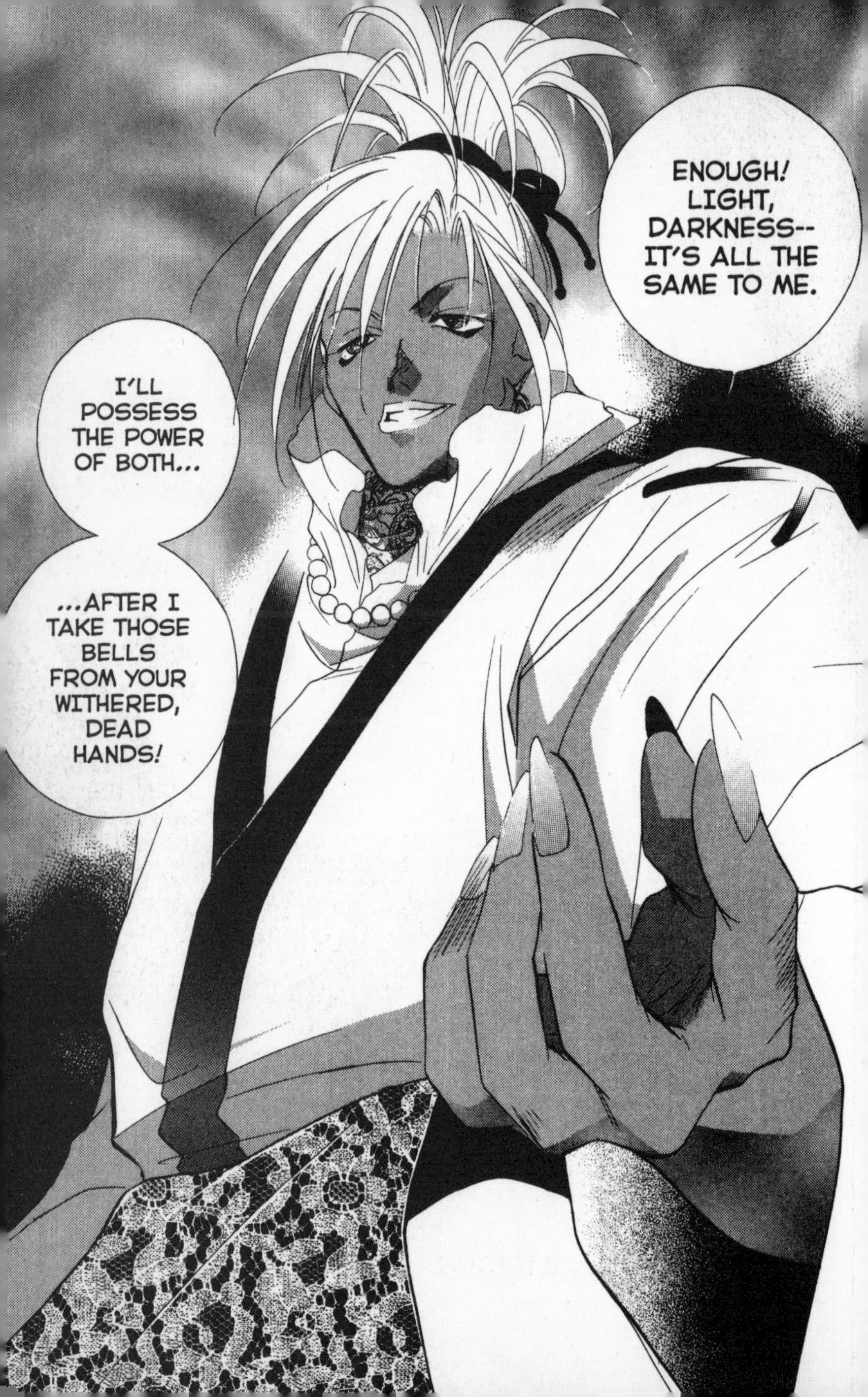
ENOUGH! LIGHT, DARKNESS-- IT'S ALL THE SAME TO ME.
I'LL POSSESS THE POWER OF BOTH...
...AFTER I TAKE THOSE BELLS FROM YOUR WITHERED, DEAD HANDS!

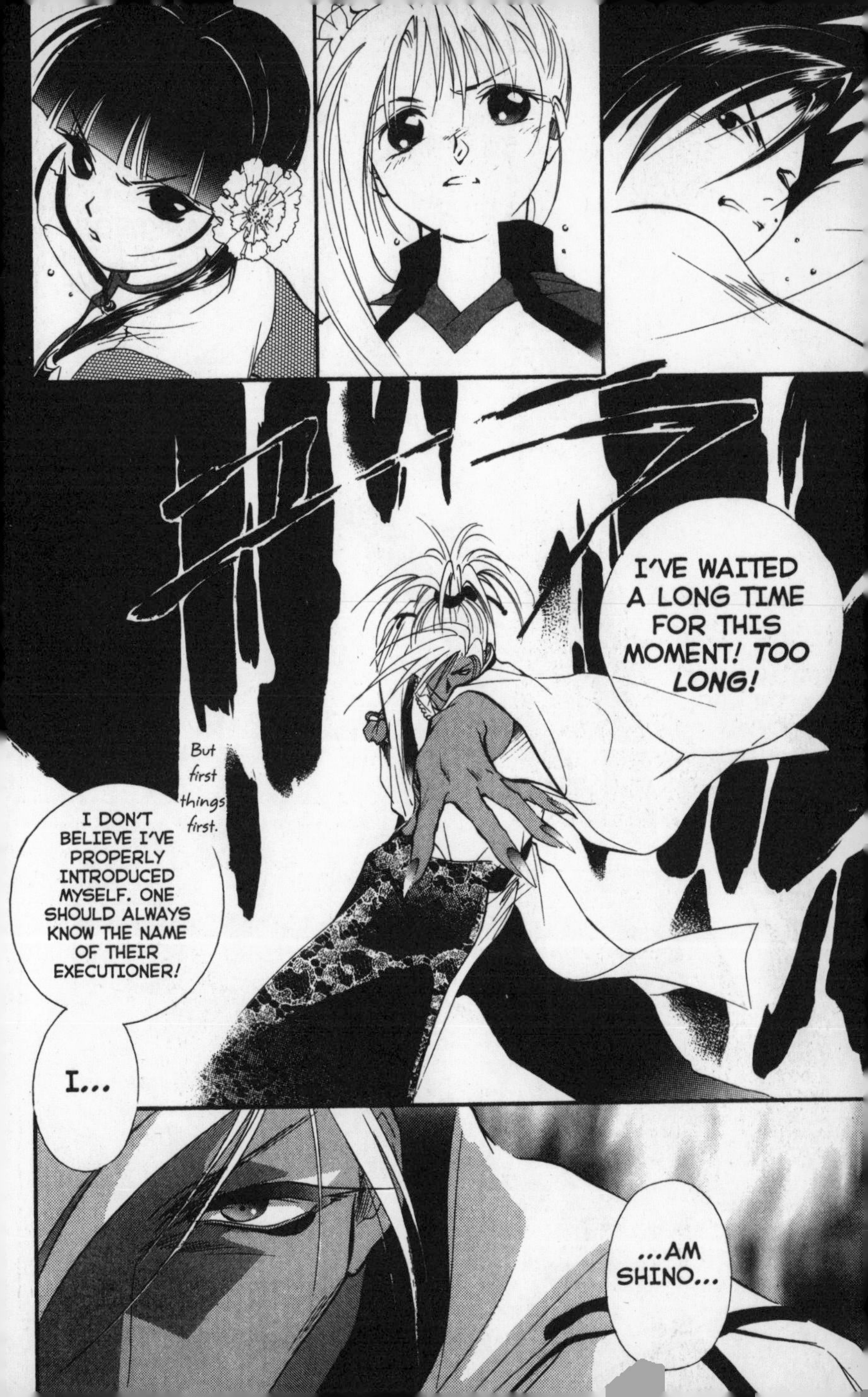
I'VE WAITED A LONG TIME FOR THIS MOMENT! TOO LONG!
But first things first.
I DON'T BELIEVE I'VE PROPERLY INTRODUCED MYSELF. ONE SHOULD ALWAYS KNOW THE NAME OF THEIR EXECUTIONER!
I...
...AM SHINO...

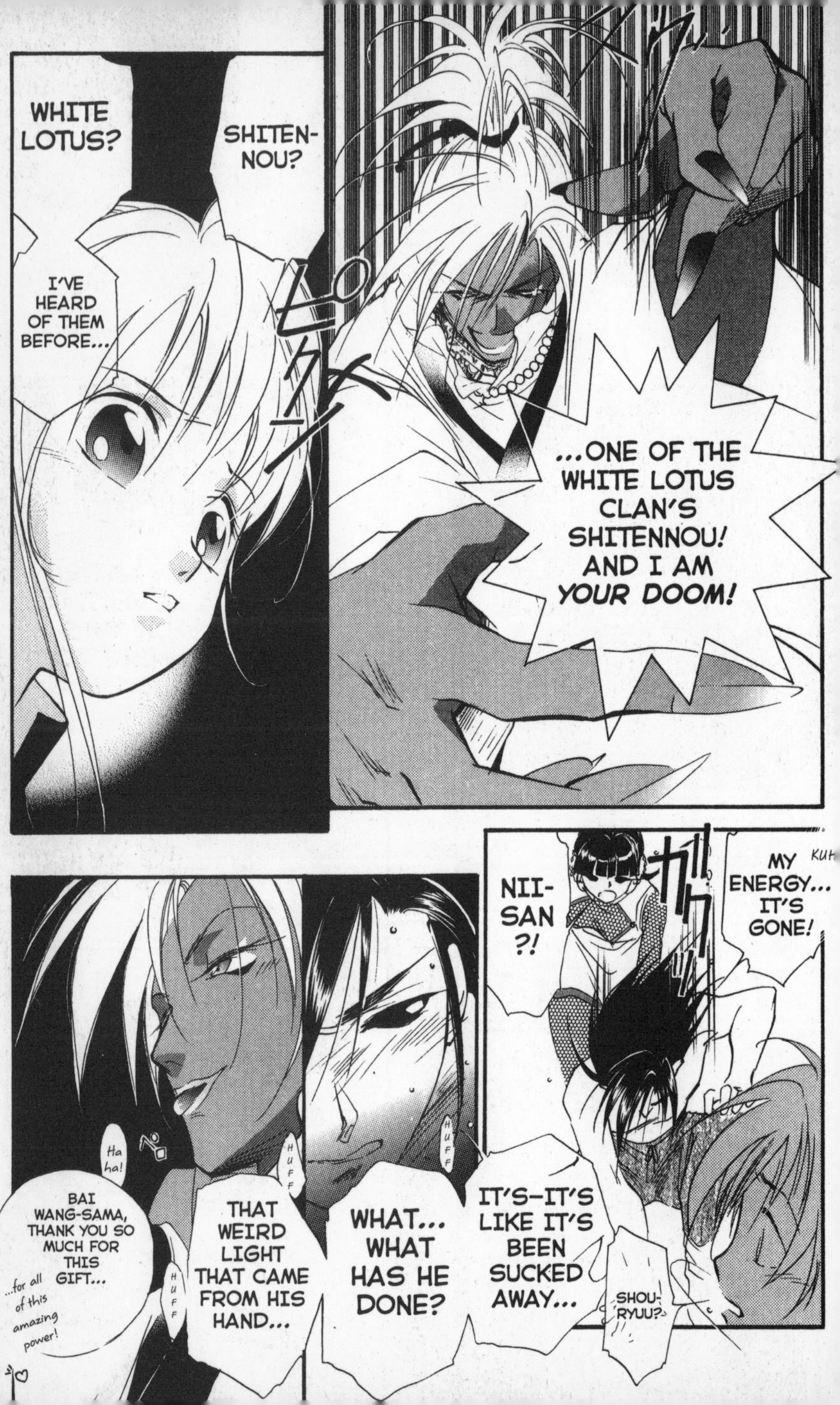
...ONE OF THE WHITE LOTUS CLAN'S SHITENNOU! AND I AM *YOUR DOOM!*
SHITEN-NOU?
WHITE LOTUS?
I'VE HEARD OF THEM BEFORE...
MY ENERGY... IT'S GONE!
KUH
NII-SAN?!
IT'S–IT'S LIKE IT'S BEEN SUCKED AWAY...
SHOU-RYUU?
HUFF
WHAT... WHAT HAS HE DONE?
THAT WEIRD LIGHT THAT CAME FROM HIS HAND...
HUFF
HUFF
Ha ha!
BAI WANG-SAMA, THANK YOU SO MUCH FOR THIS GIFT...
...for all of this amazing power!

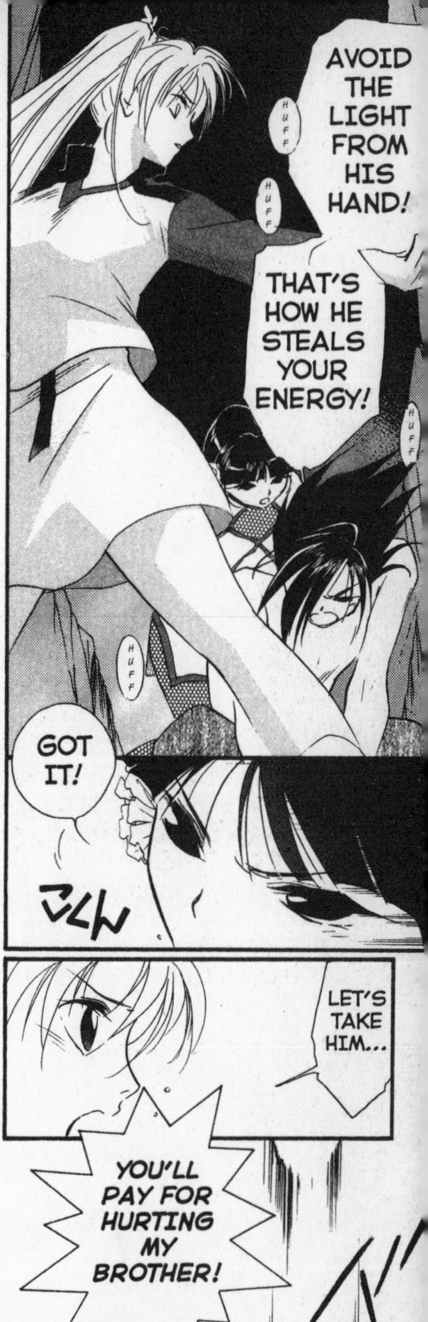
AVOID THE LIGHT FROM HIS HAND!
HUFF
HUFF
THAT'S HOW HE STEALS YOUR ENERGY!
HUFF
HUFF
GOT IT!
LET'S TAKE HIM...
YOU'LL PAY FOR HURTING MY BROTHER!
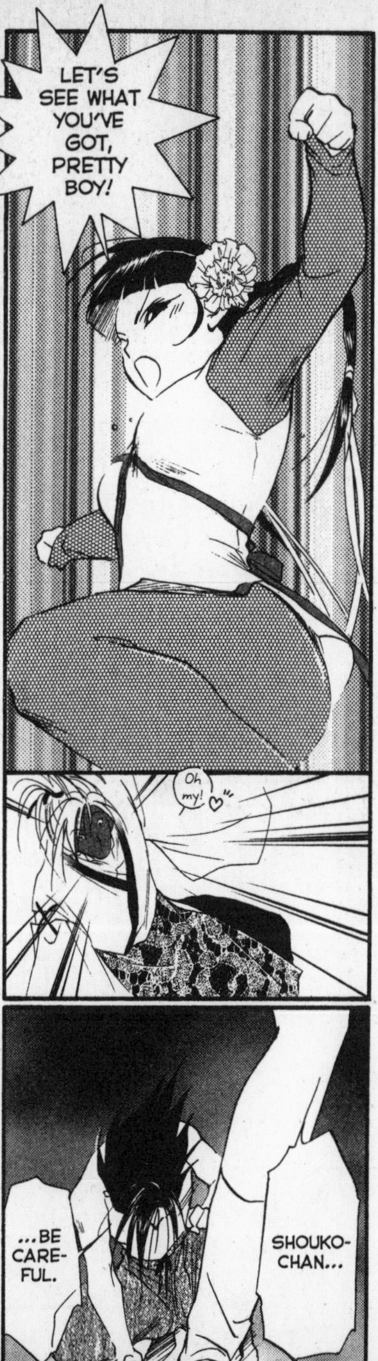
LET'S SEE WHAT YOU'VE GOT, PRETTY BOY!
Oh my!
SHOUKO-CHAN...
...BE CARE-FUL.

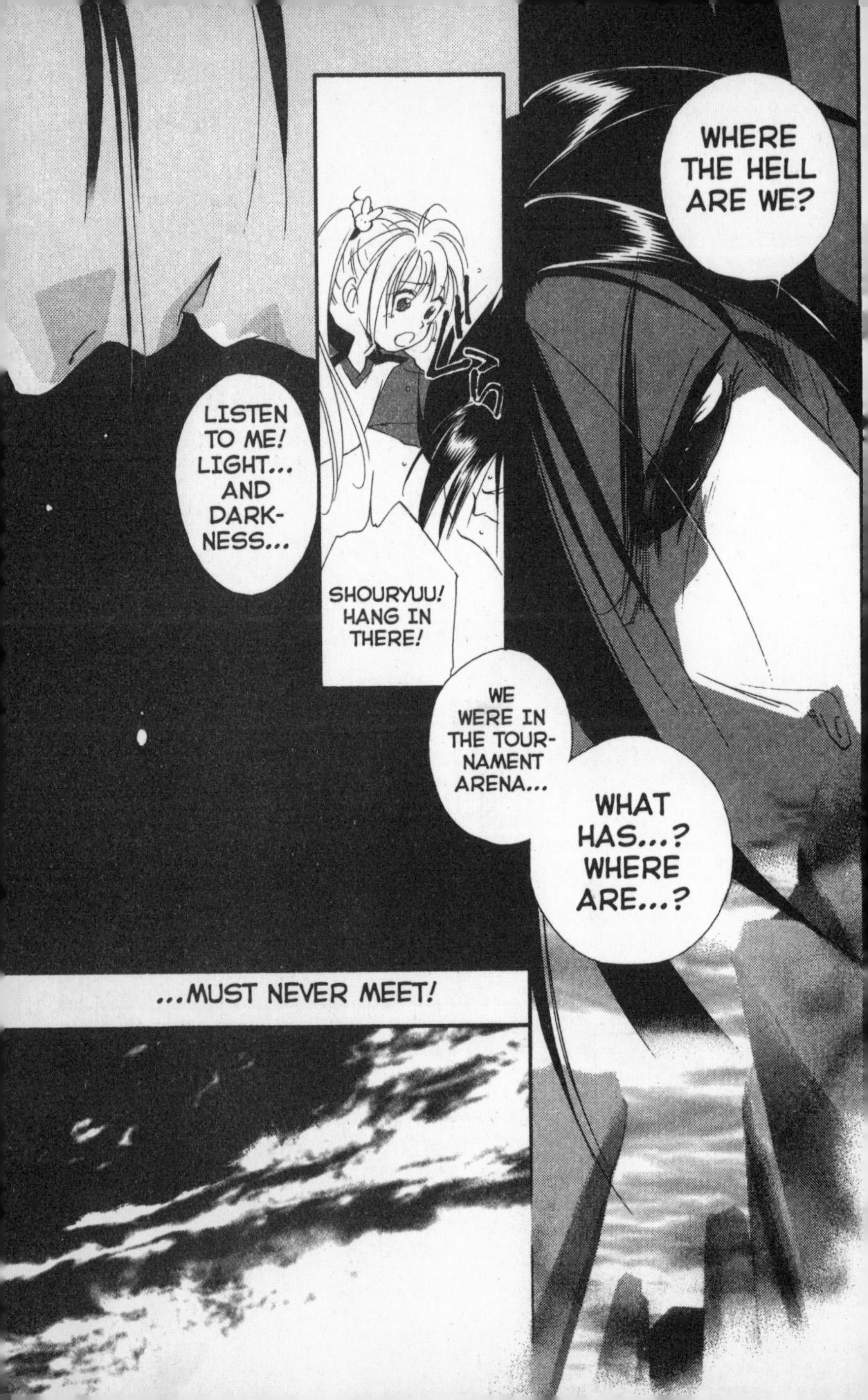
WHERE THE HELL ARE WE?
SHOURYUU! HANG IN THERE!
WE WERE IN THE TOURNAMENT ARENA...
WHAT HAS...? WHERE ARE...?
LISTEN TO ME! LIGHT... AND DARKNESS...
...MUST NEVER MEET!

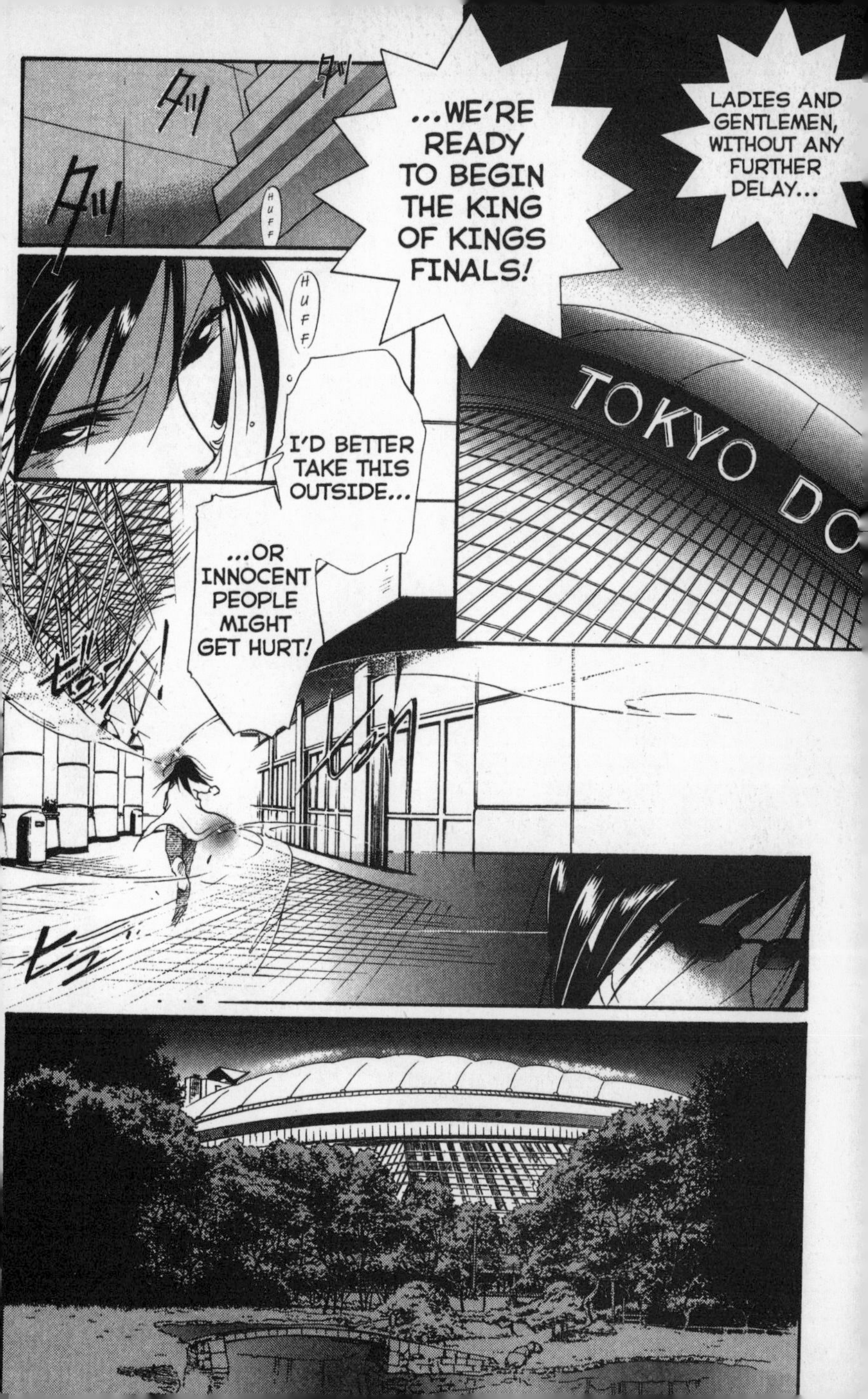
LADIES AND GENTLEMEN, WITHOUT ANY FURTHER DELAY...
...WE'RE READY TO BEGIN THE KING OF KINGS FINALS!
TOKYO DO
HUFF
HUFF
I'D BETTER TAKE THIS OUTSIDE...
...OR INNOCENT PEOPLE MIGHT GET HURT!

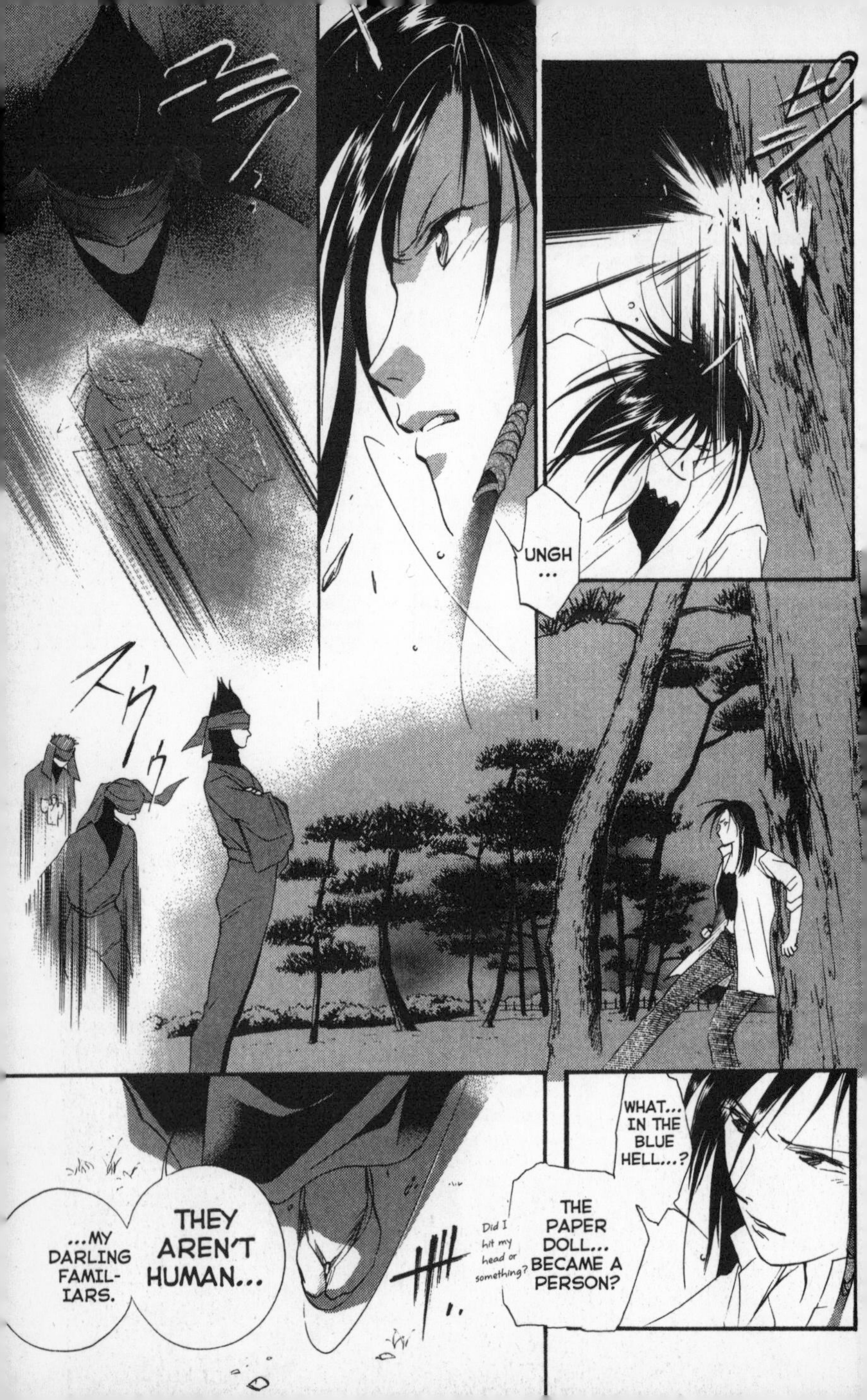
UNGH...
WHAT... IN THE BLUE HELL...?
THE PAPER DOLL... BECAME A PERSON?
Did I hit my head or something?
THEY AREN'T HUMAN...
...MY DARLING FAMILIARS.

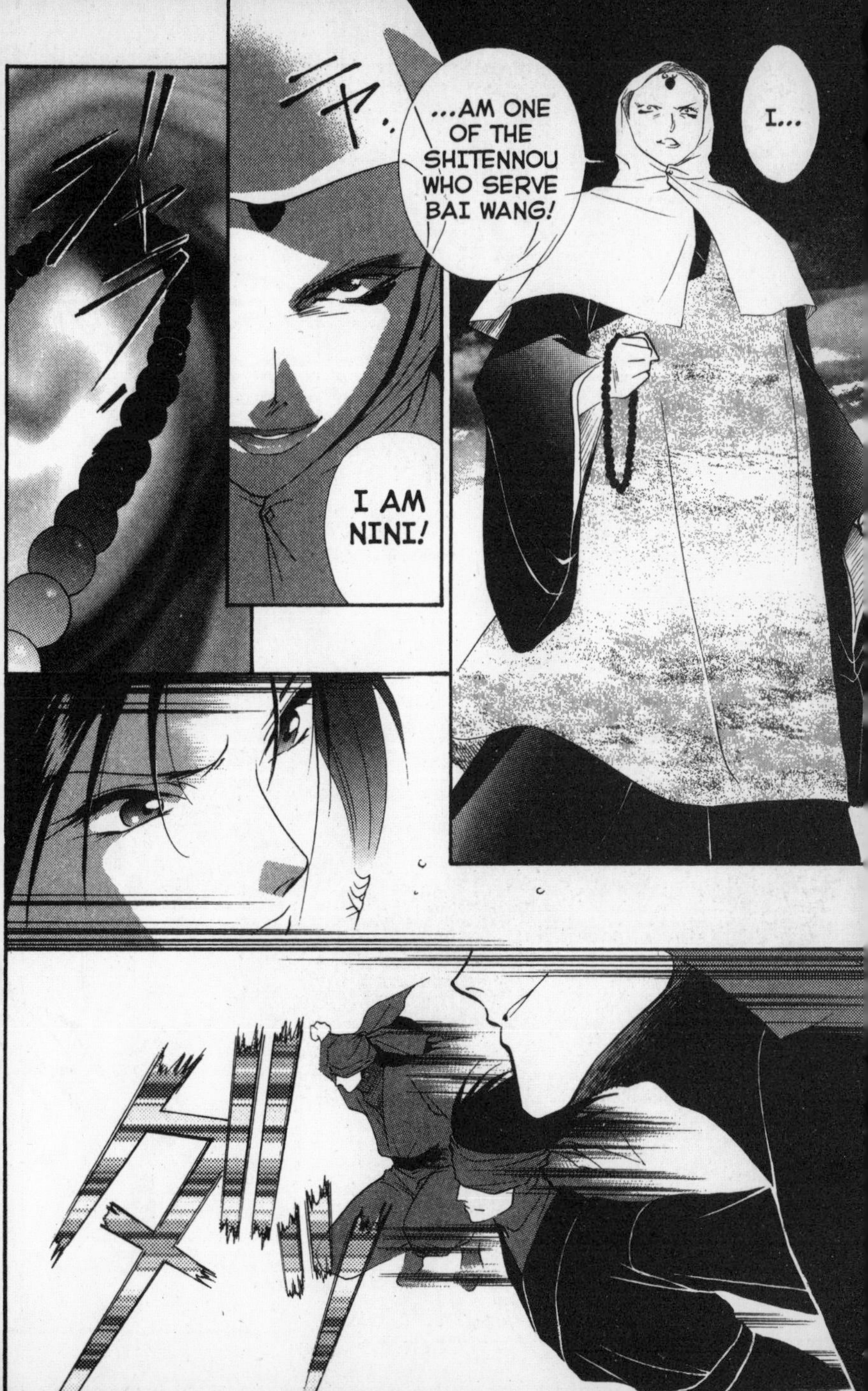
I...
...AM ONE OF THE SHITENNOU WHO SERVE BAI WANG!
ニヤ..
I AM NINI!

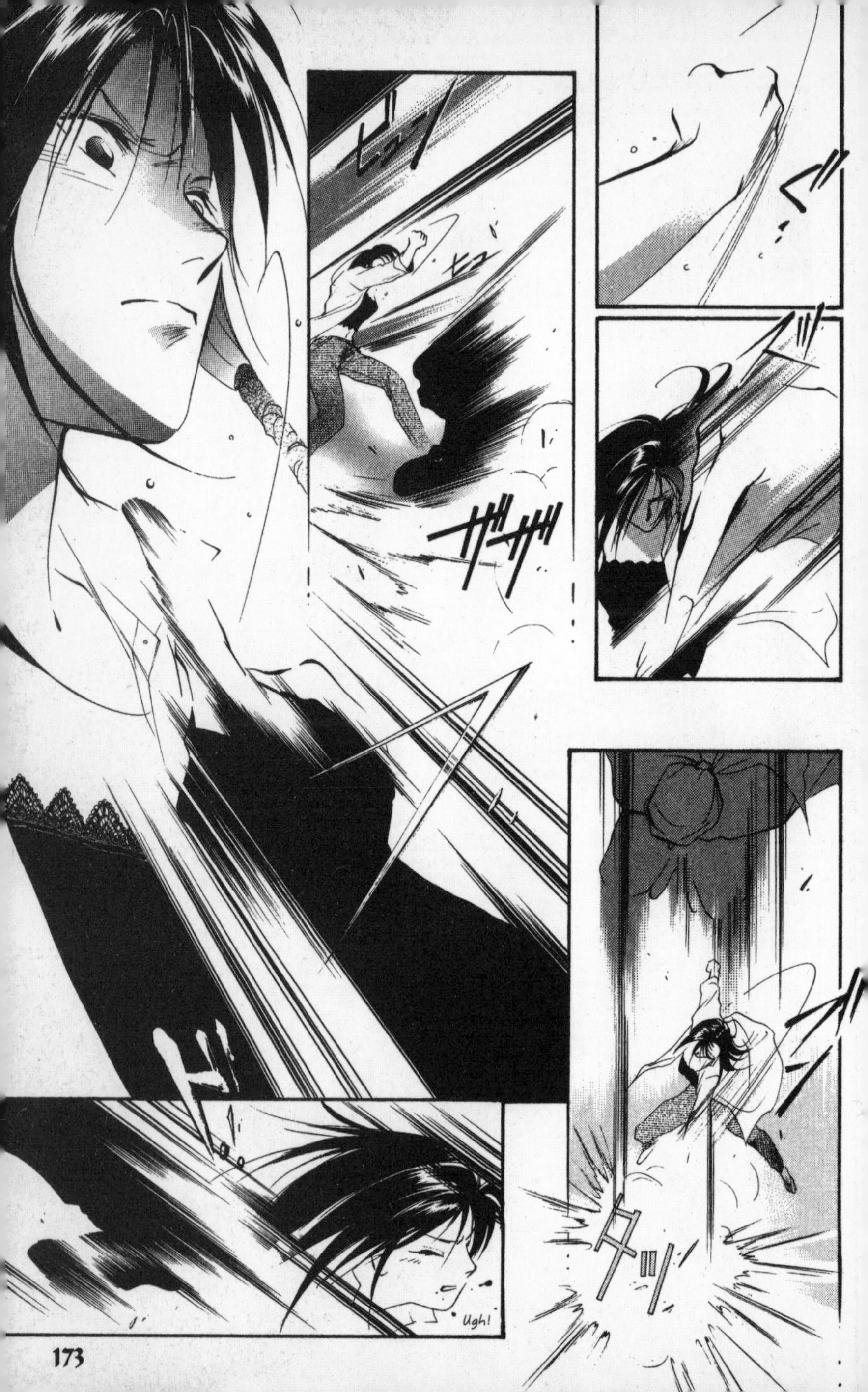
Ugh!

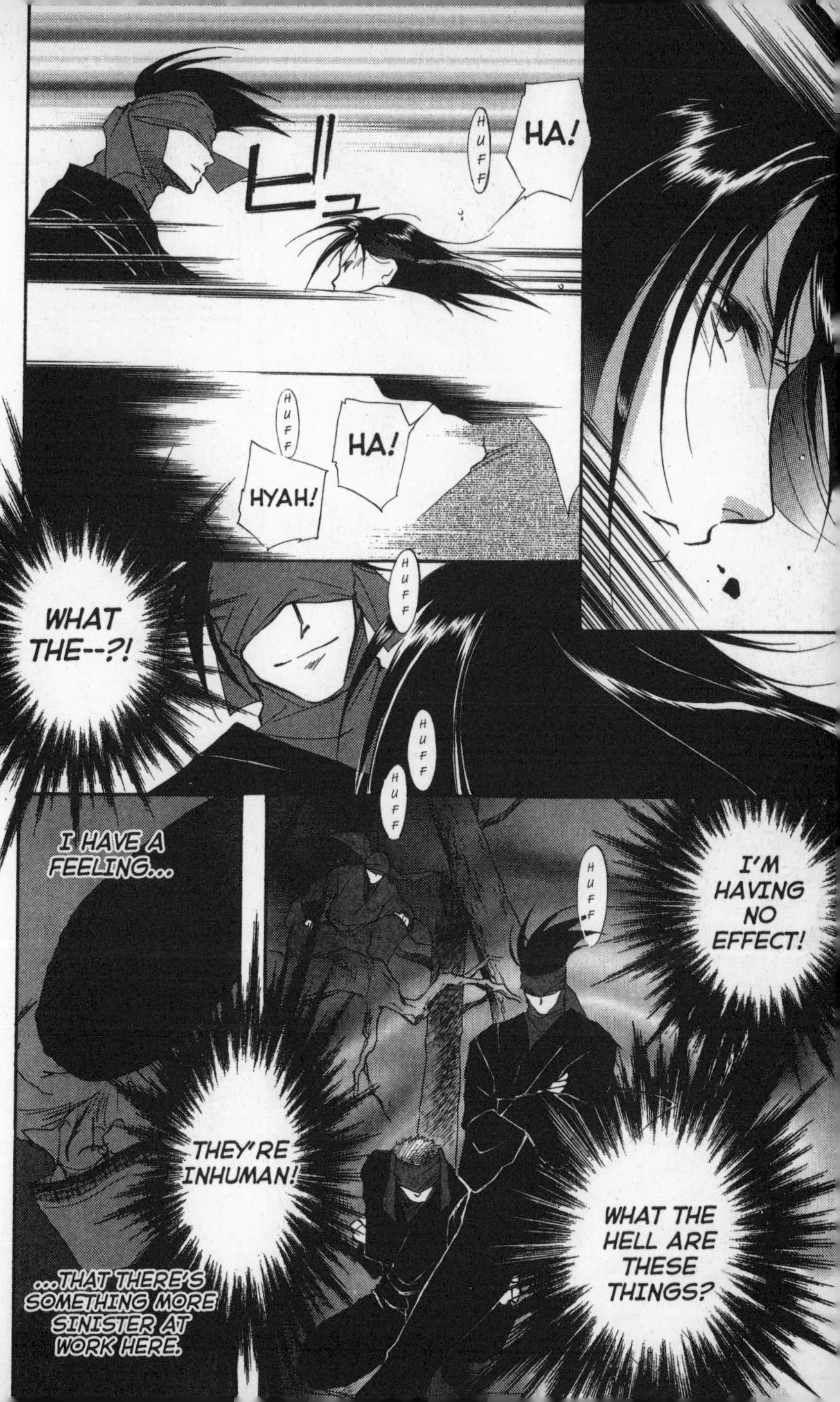
HA!
HUFF
ビュ
HA!
HUFF
HYAH!
HUFF
WHAT THE--?!
HUFF
HUFF
I'M HAVING NO EFFECT!
HUFF
WHAT THE HELL ARE THESE THINGS?
THEY'RE INHUMAN!
I HAVE A FEELING...
...THAT THERE'S SOMETHING MORE SINISTER AT WORK HERE.

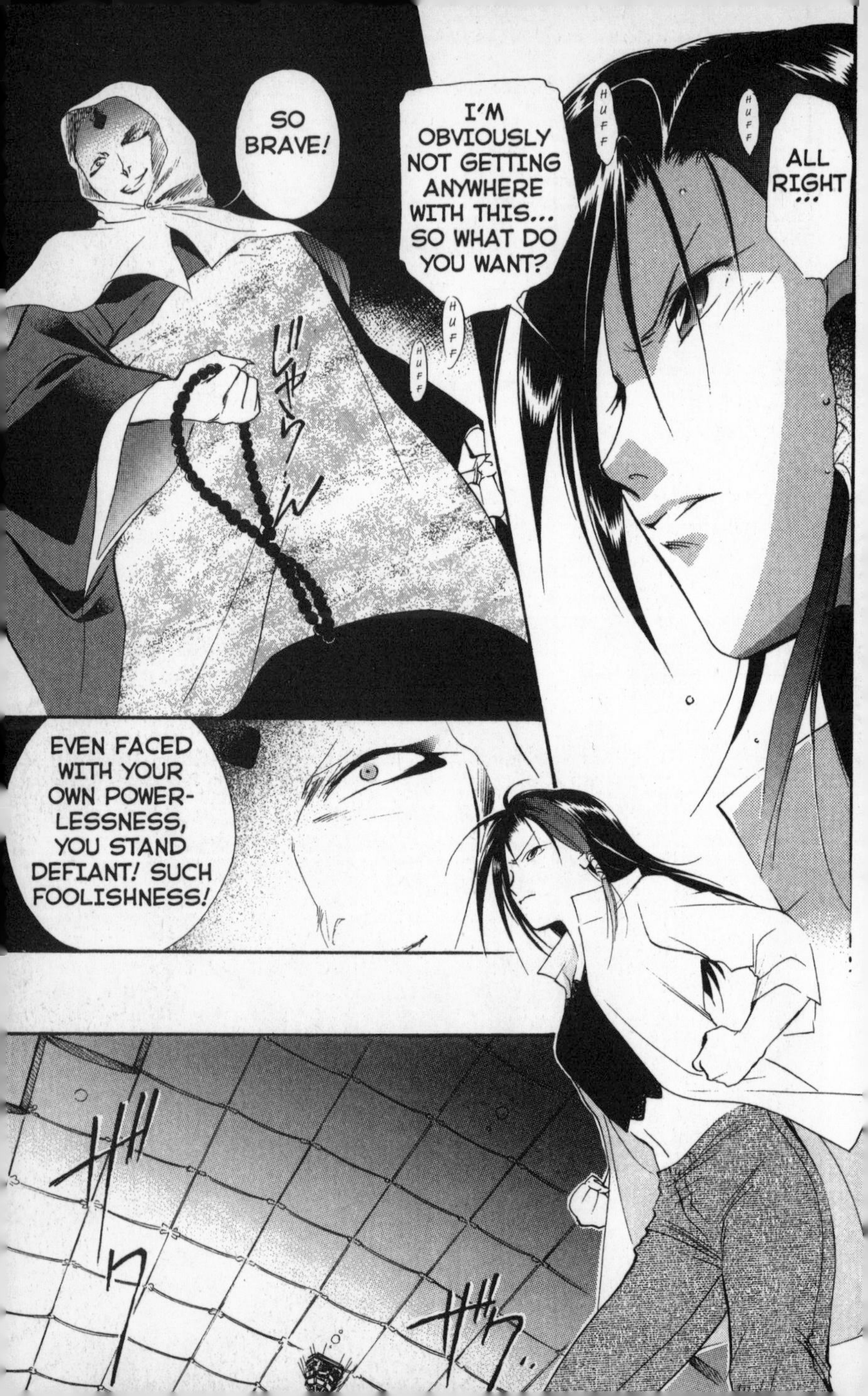
HUFF
HUFF
ALL RIGHT...
I'M OBVIOUSLY NOT GETTING ANYWHERE WITH THIS... SO WHAT DO YOU WANT?
HUFF
HUFF
SO BRAVE!
EVEN FACED WITH YOUR OWN POWER-LESSNESS, YOU STAND DEFIANT! SUCH FOOLISHNESS!

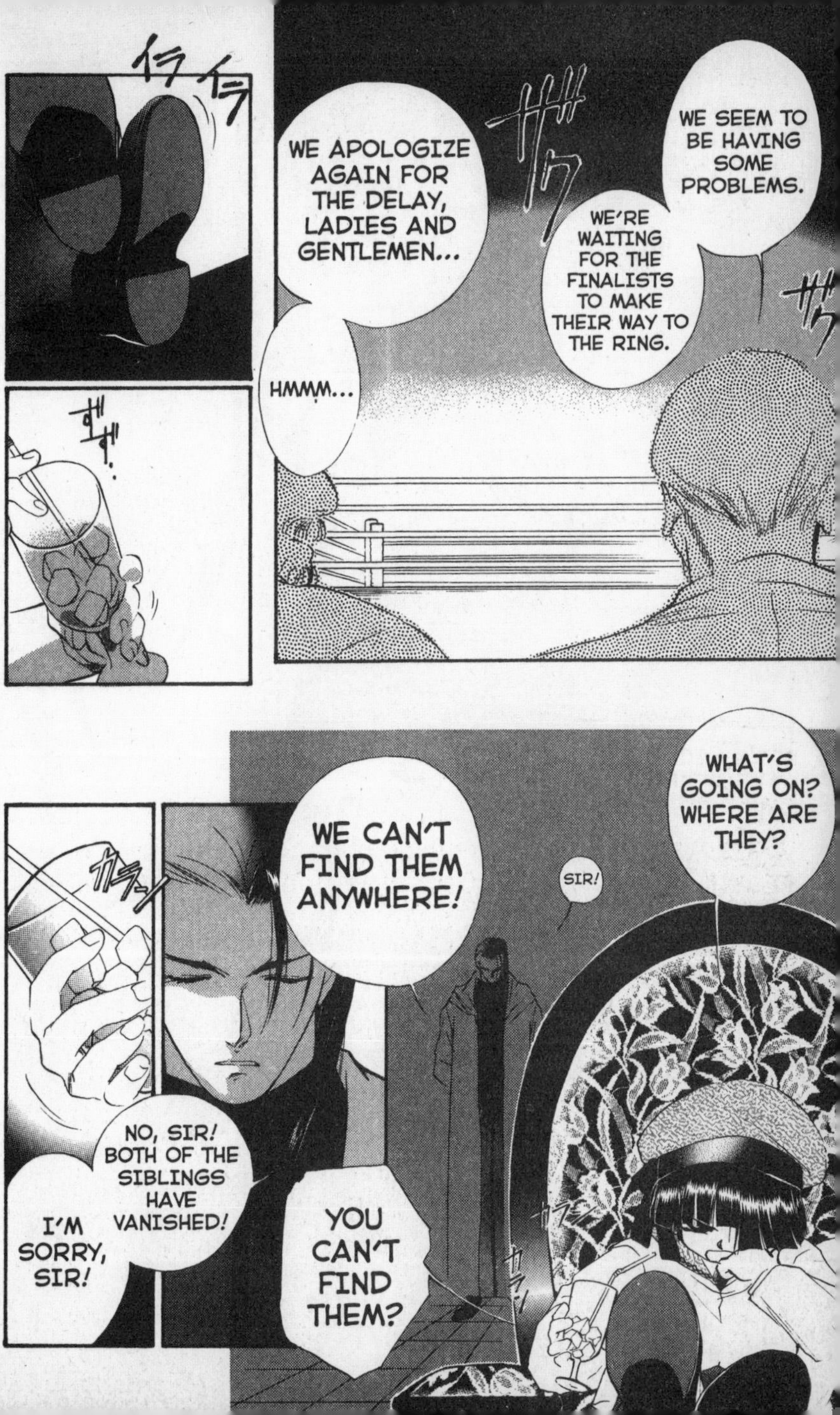

WE SEEM TO BE HAVING SOME PROBLEMS.
WE'RE WAITING FOR THE FINALISTS TO MAKE THEIR WAY TO THE RING.
WE APOLOGIZE AGAIN FOR THE DELAY, LADIES AND GENTLEMEN...
HMMM...
イラ イラ
WHAT'S GOING ON? WHERE ARE THEY?
SIR!
WE CAN'T FIND THEM ANYWHERE!
YOU CAN'T FIND THEM?
NO, SIR! BOTH OF THE SIBLINGS HAVE VANISHED!
I'M SORRY, SIR!

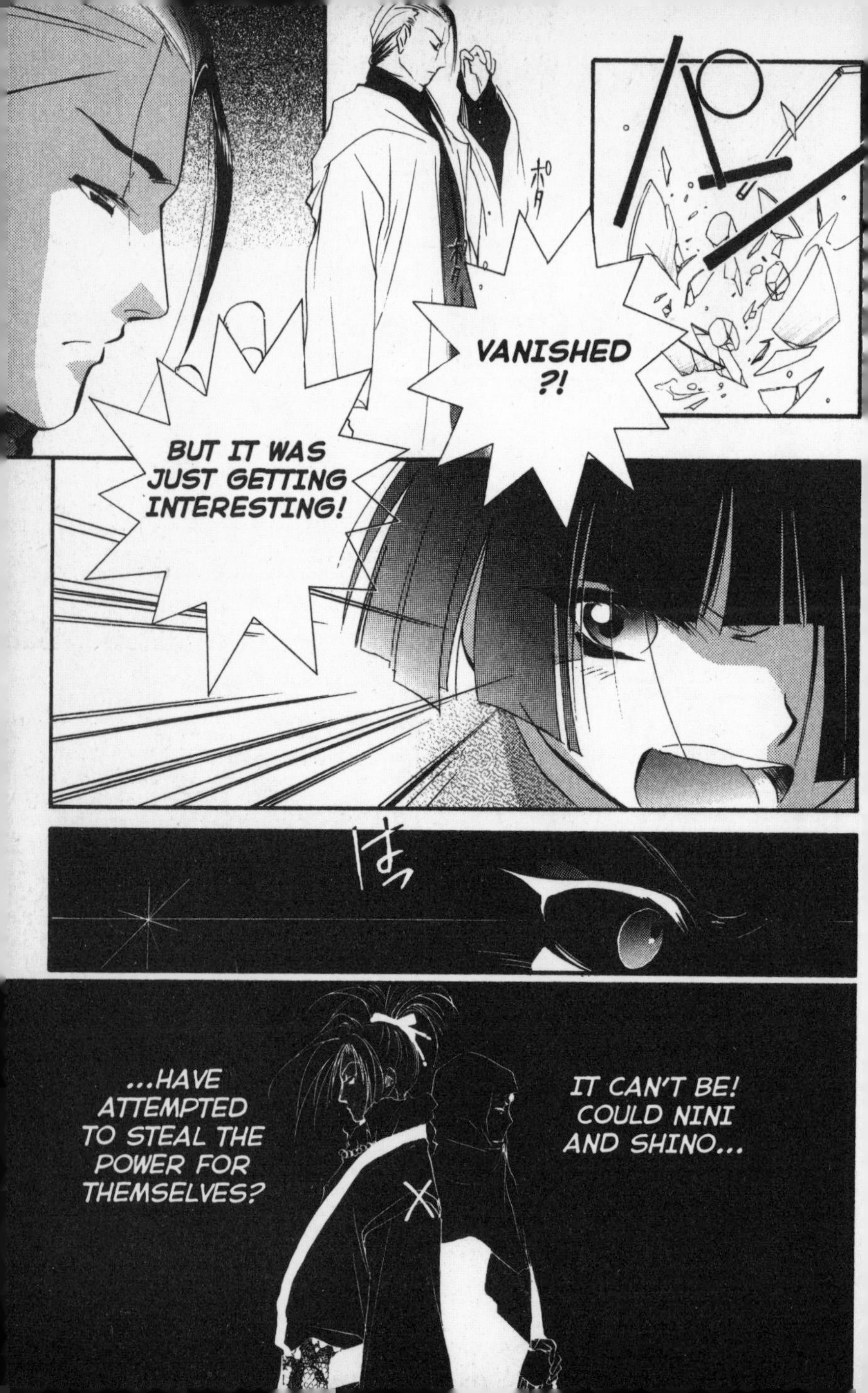
VANISHED ?!
ポタ
BUT IT WAS JUST GETTING INTERESTING!
はっ
IT CAN'T BE! COULD NINI AND SHINO...
...HAVE ATTEMPTED TO STEAL THE POWER FOR THEMSELVES?

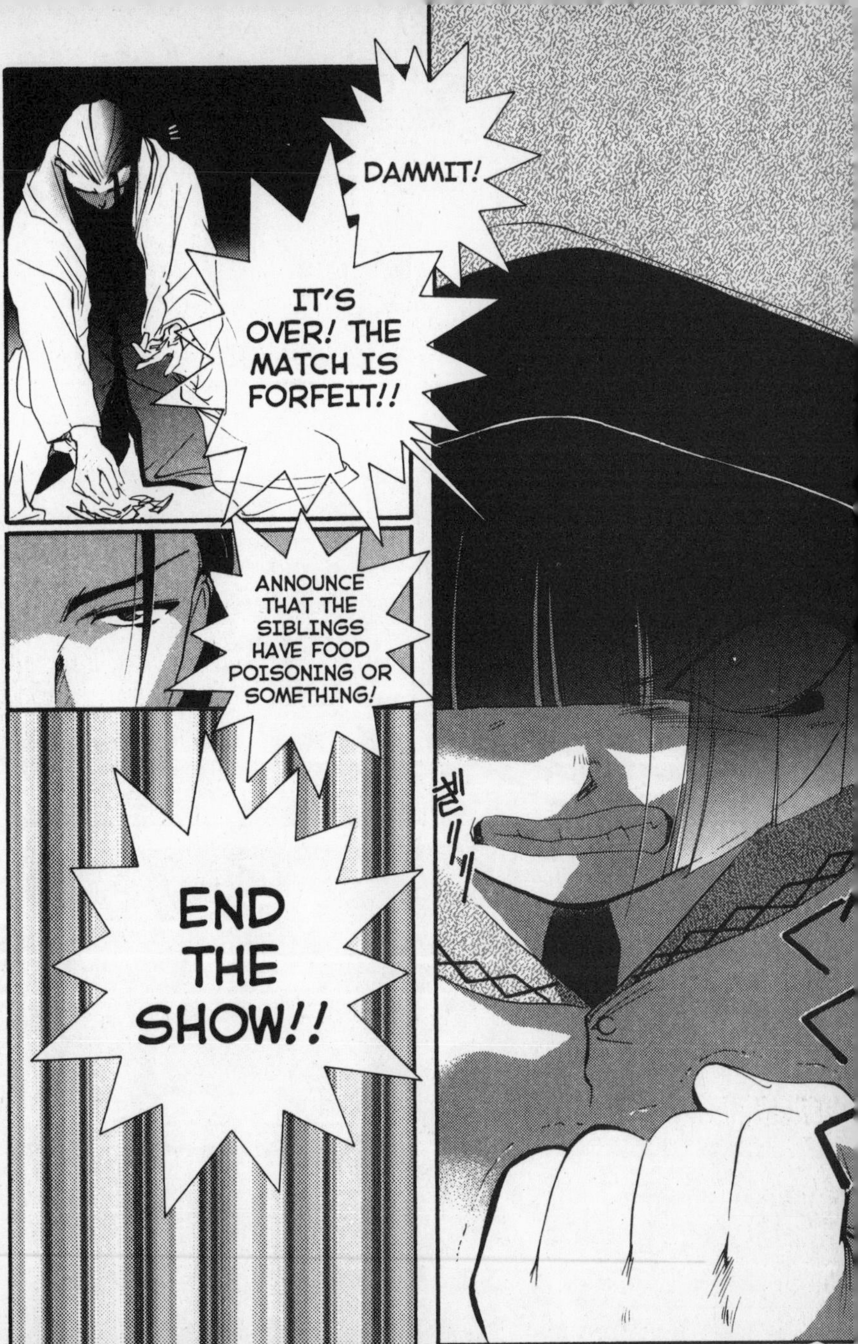
DAMMIT!
IT'S OVER! THE MATCH IS FORFEIT!!
ANNOUNCE THAT THE SIBLINGS HAVE FOOD POISONING OR SOMETHING!
END THE SHOW!!

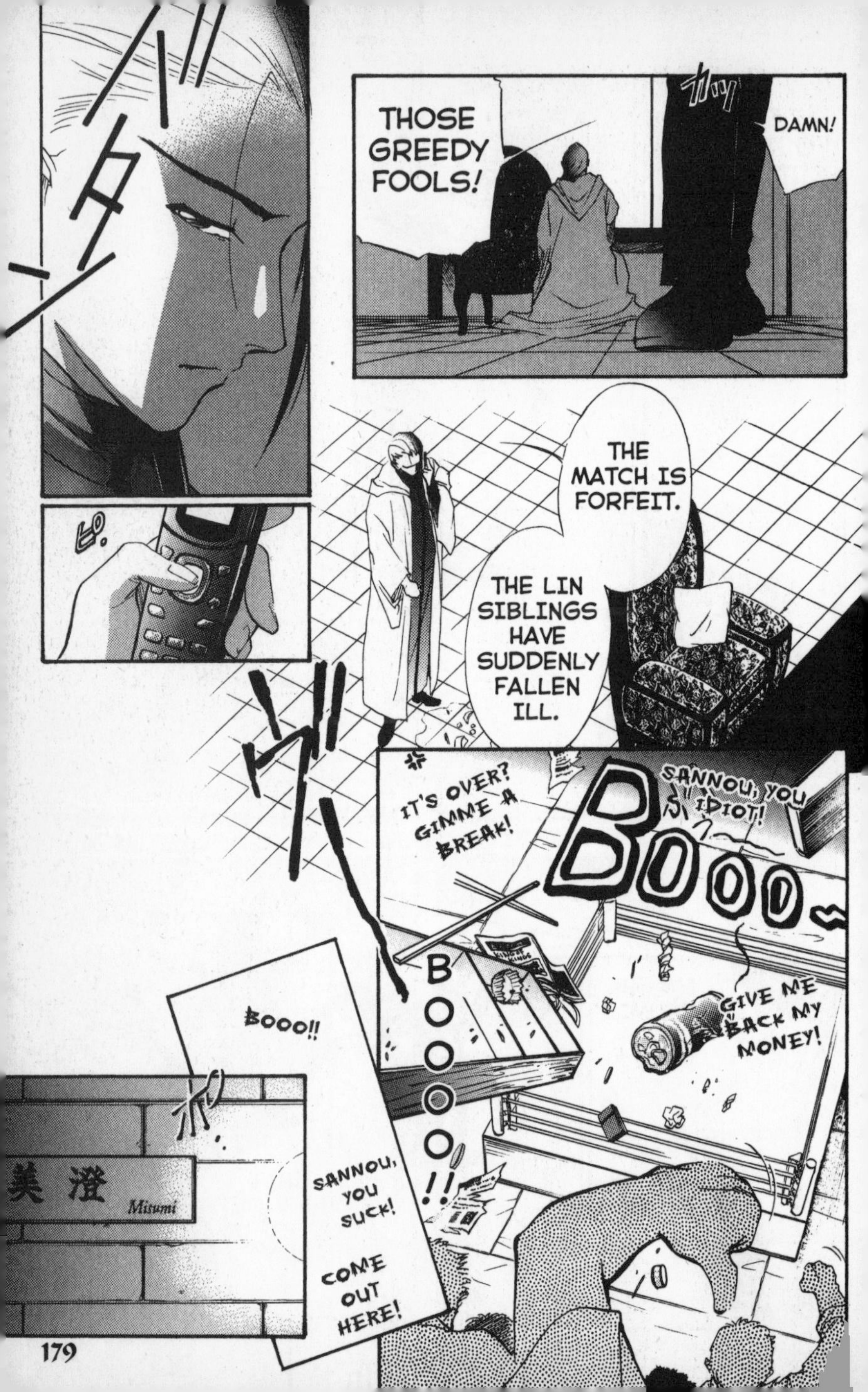
DAMN!
THOSE GREEDY FOOLS!
THE MATCH IS FORFEIT.
THE LIN SIBLINGS HAVE SUDDENLY FALLEN ILL.
SANNOU, YOU IDIOT!
BOOO~
IT'S OVER? GIMME A BREAK!
GIVE ME BACK MY MONEY!
BOOOOO!!
BOOO!!
SANNOU, YOU SUCK!
COME OUT HERE!
美澄
Misumi

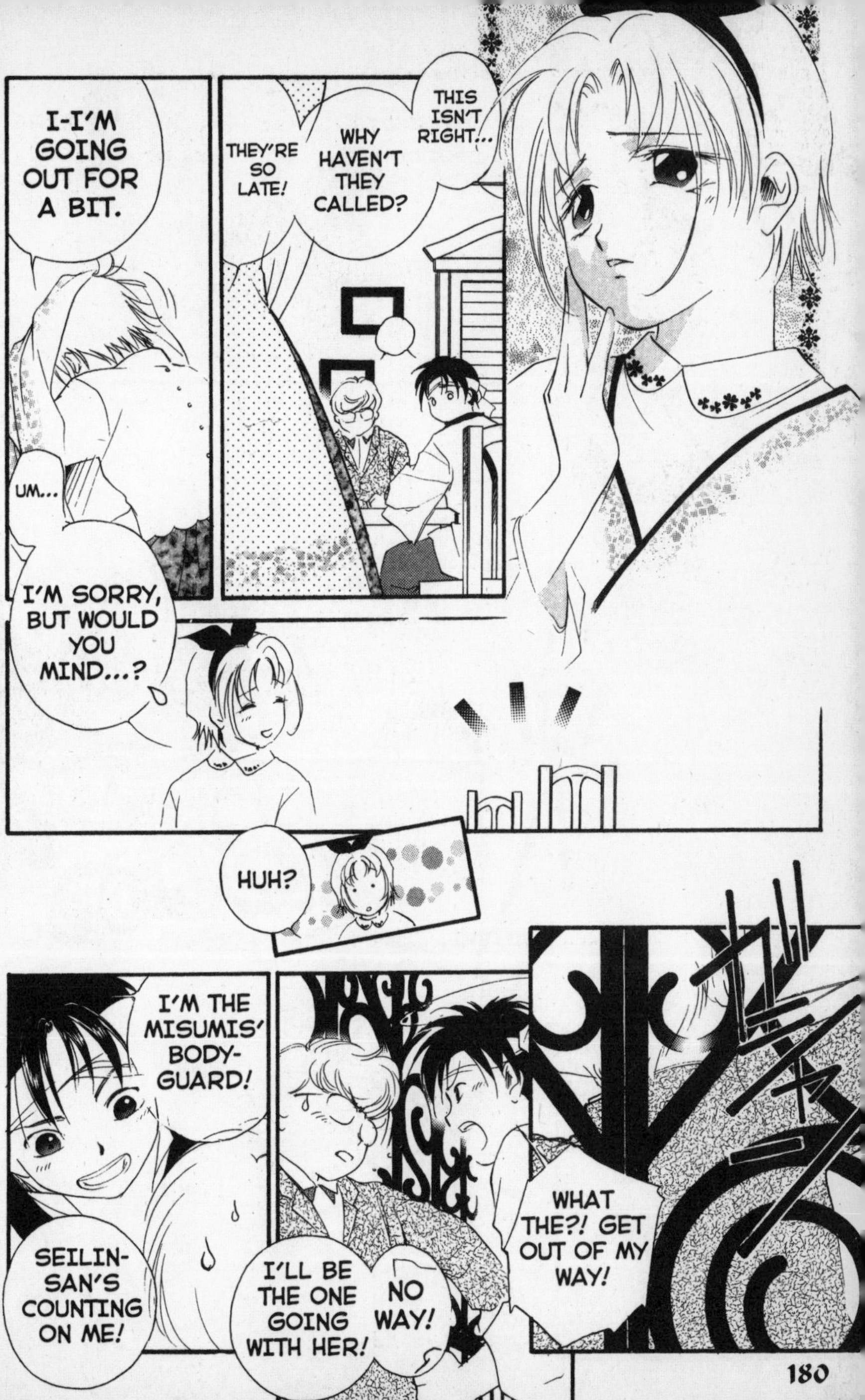
THIS ISN'T RIGHT...
WHY HAVEN'T THEY CALLED?
THEY'RE SO LATE!
I-I'M GOING OUT FOR A BIT.
UM...
I'M SORRY, BUT WOULD YOU MIND...?
HUH?
WHAT THE?! GET OUT OF MY WAY!
NO WAY!
I'LL BE THE ONE GOING WITH HER!
I'M THE MISUMIS' BODY-GUARD!
SEILIN-SAN'S COUNTING ON ME!

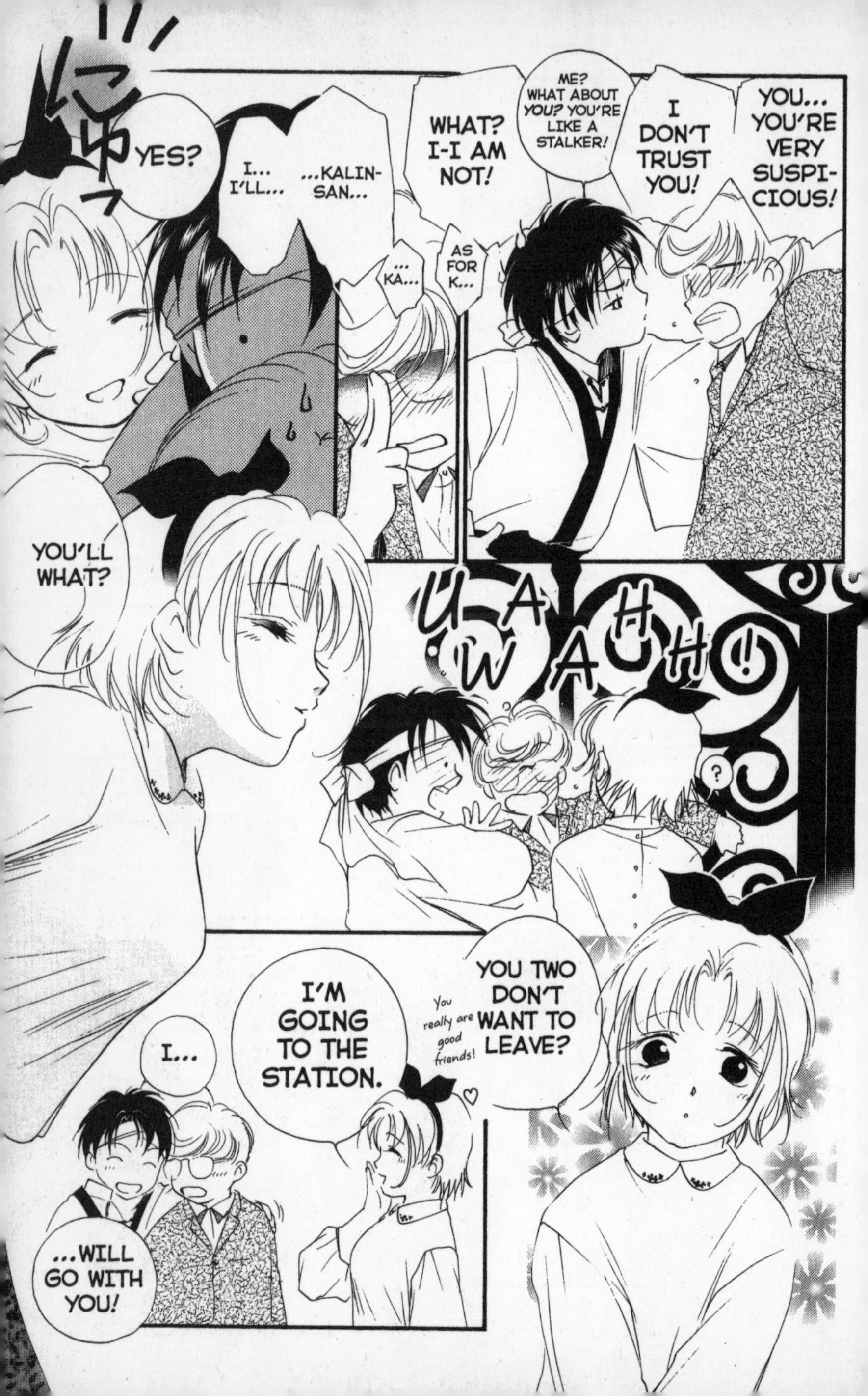
YOU... YOU'RE VERY SUSPICIOUS!
I DON'T TRUST YOU!
ME? WHAT ABOUT *YOU?* YOU'RE LIKE A STALKER!
WHAT? I-I AM NOT!
AS FOR K...
...KA...
...KALIN-SAN...
I... I'LL...
YES?
YOU'LL WHAT?
UWAAHHH!
?
YOU TWO DON'T WANT TO LEAVE?
You really are good friends!
I'M GOING TO THE STATION.
I...
...WILL GO WITH YOU!

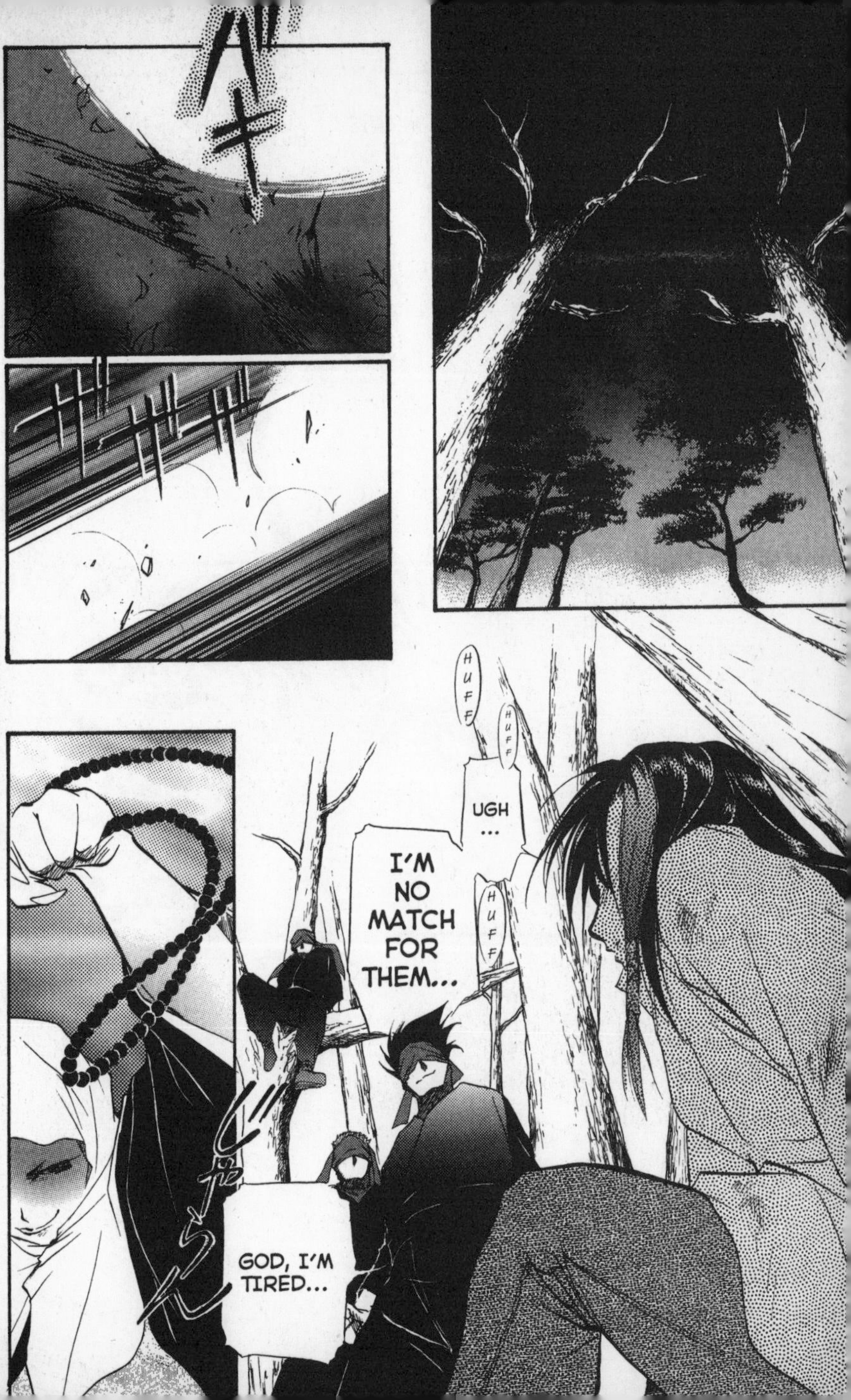
HUFF
HUFF
UGH...
I'M NO MATCH FOR THEM...
HUFF
GOD, I'M TIRED...

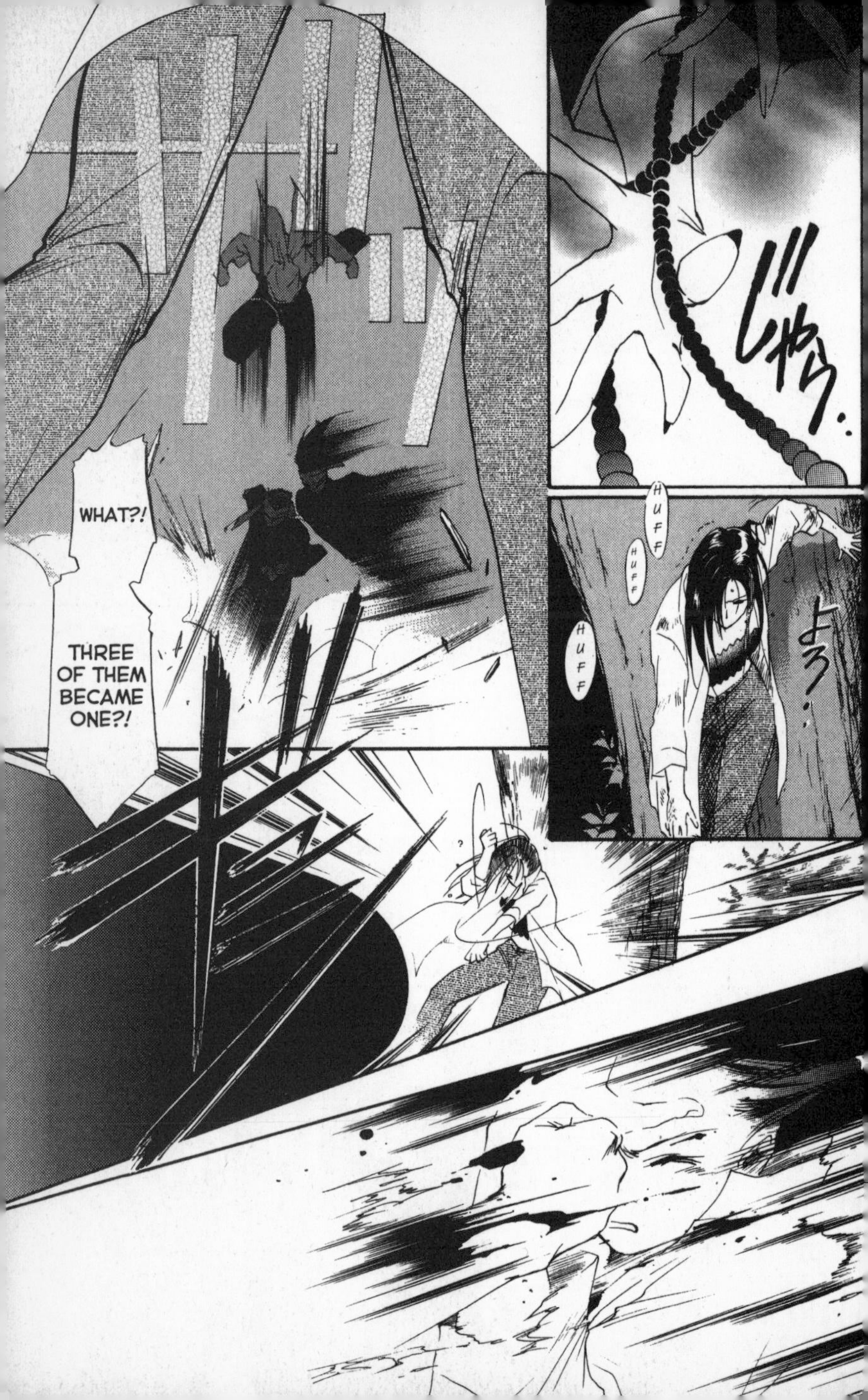

HUFF
HUFF
HUFF
よろ…
WHAT?!
THREE OF THEM BECAME ONE?!

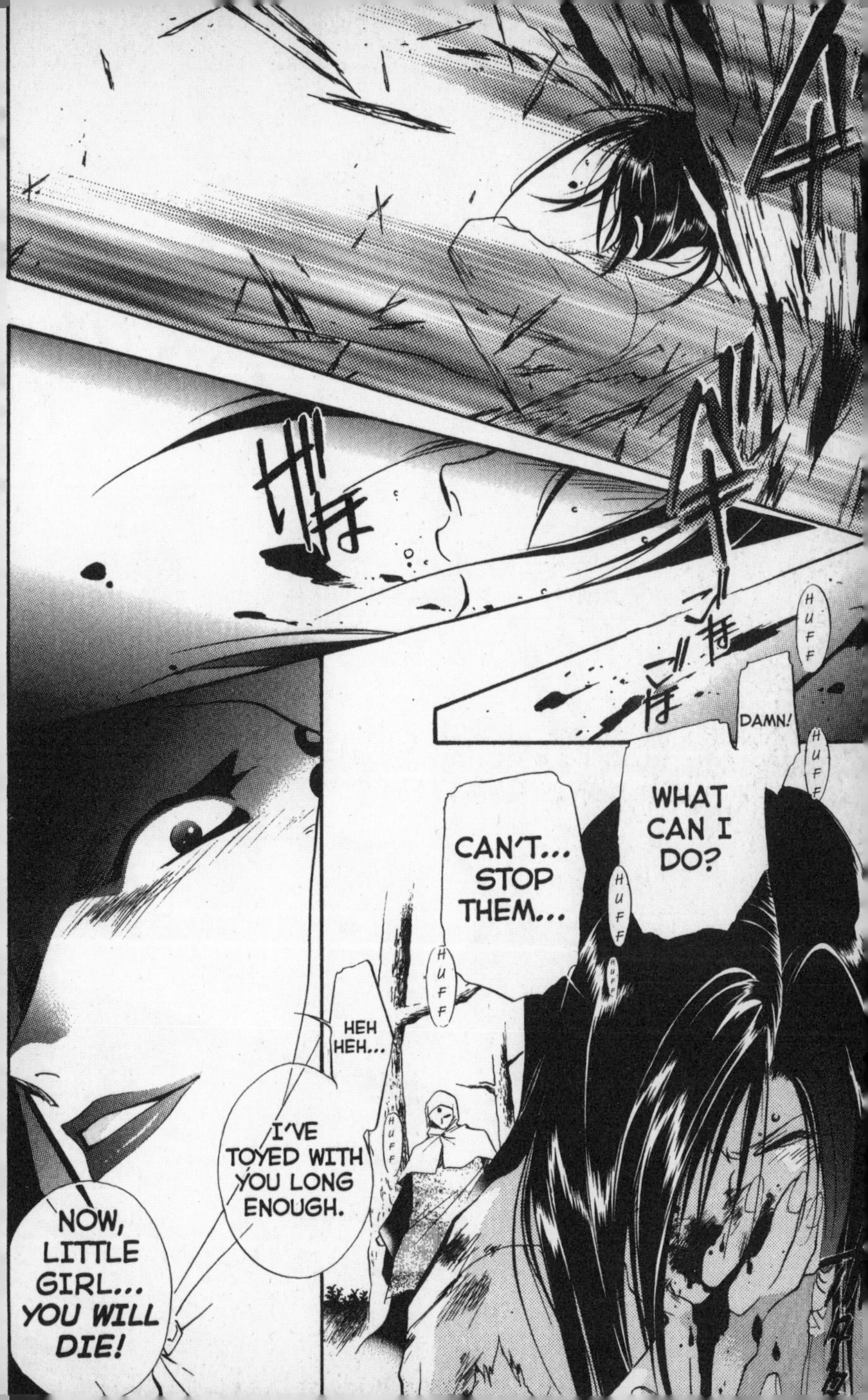
HUFF
DAMN!
HUFF
WHAT CAN I DO?
CAN'T... STOP THEM...
HUFF
HUFF
HUFF
HEH HEH...
I'VE TOYED WITH YOU LONG ENOUGH.
HUFF
NOW, LITTLE GIRL... YOU WILL DIE!

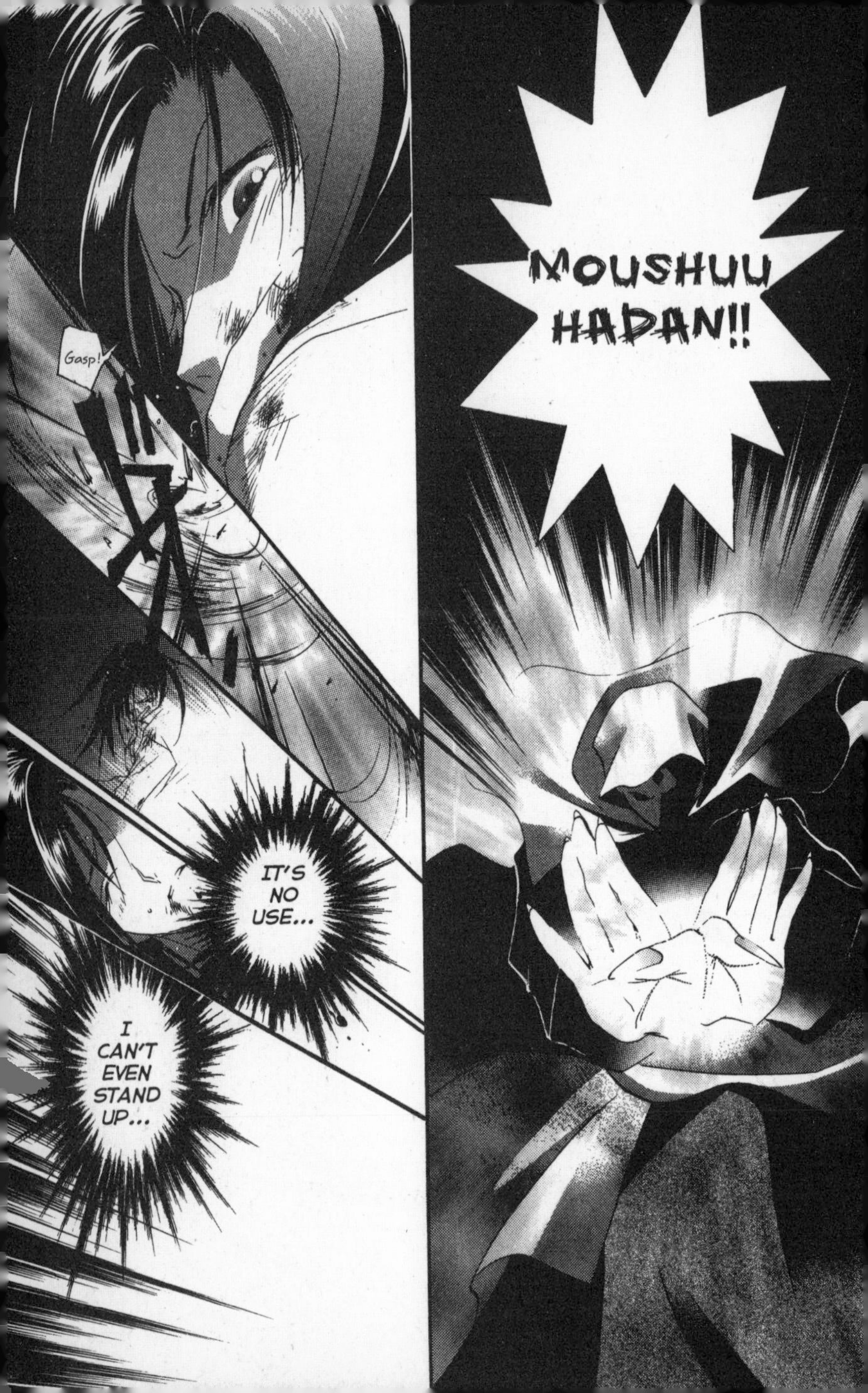
MOUSHUU HADAN!!
Gasp!
IT'S NO USE...
I CAN'T EVEN STAND UP...

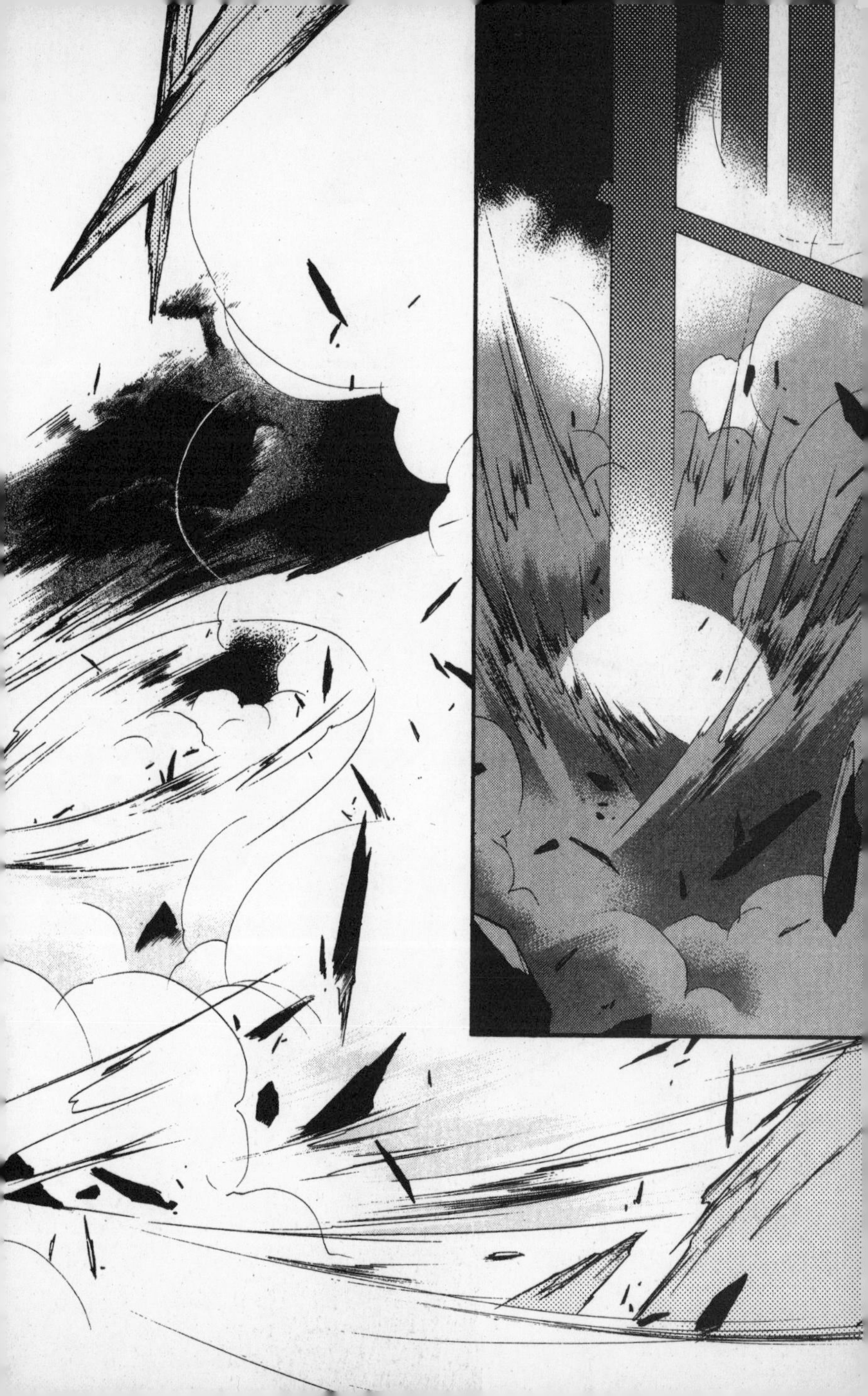

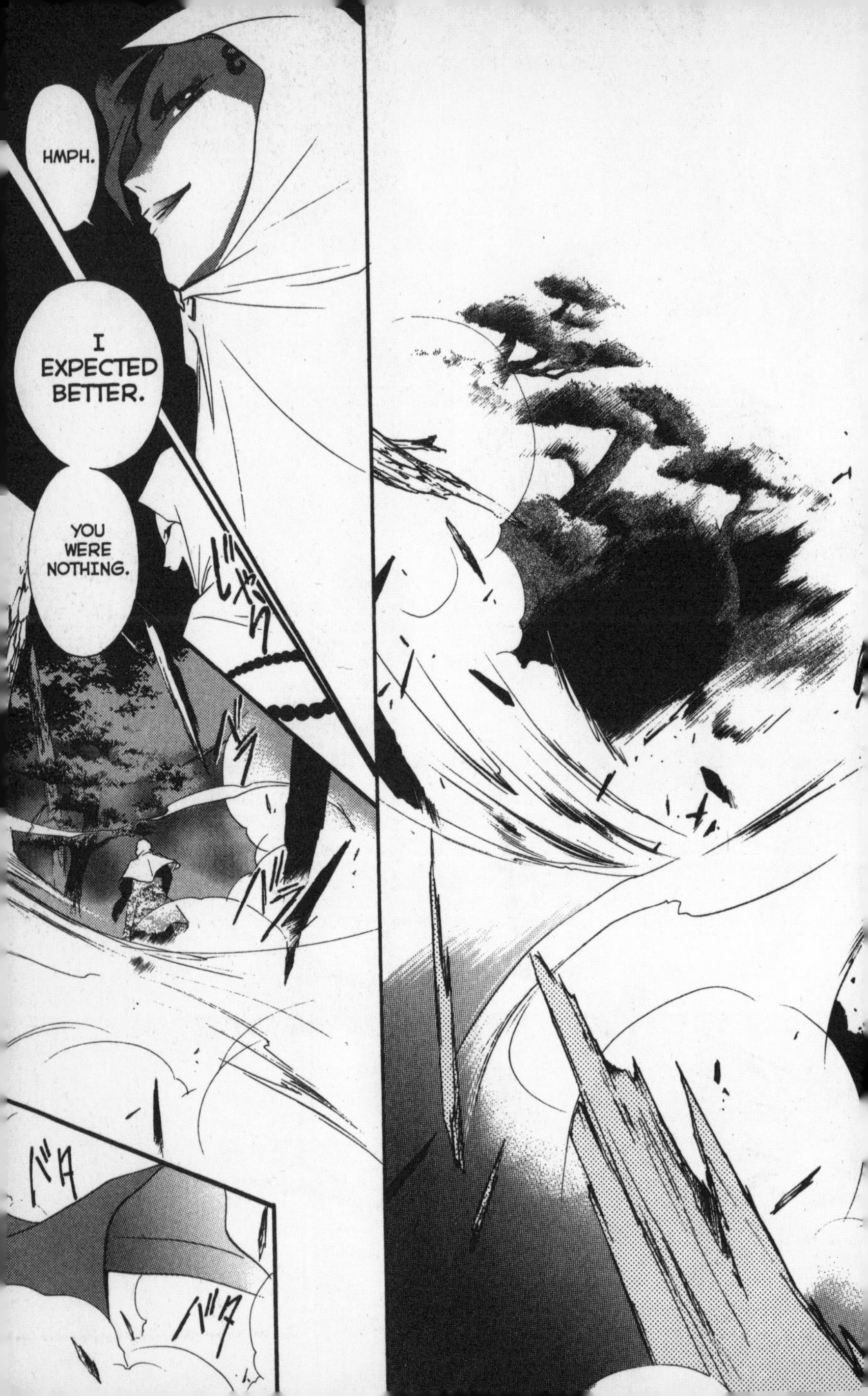
HMPH.
I EXPECTED BETTER.
YOU WERE NOTHING.

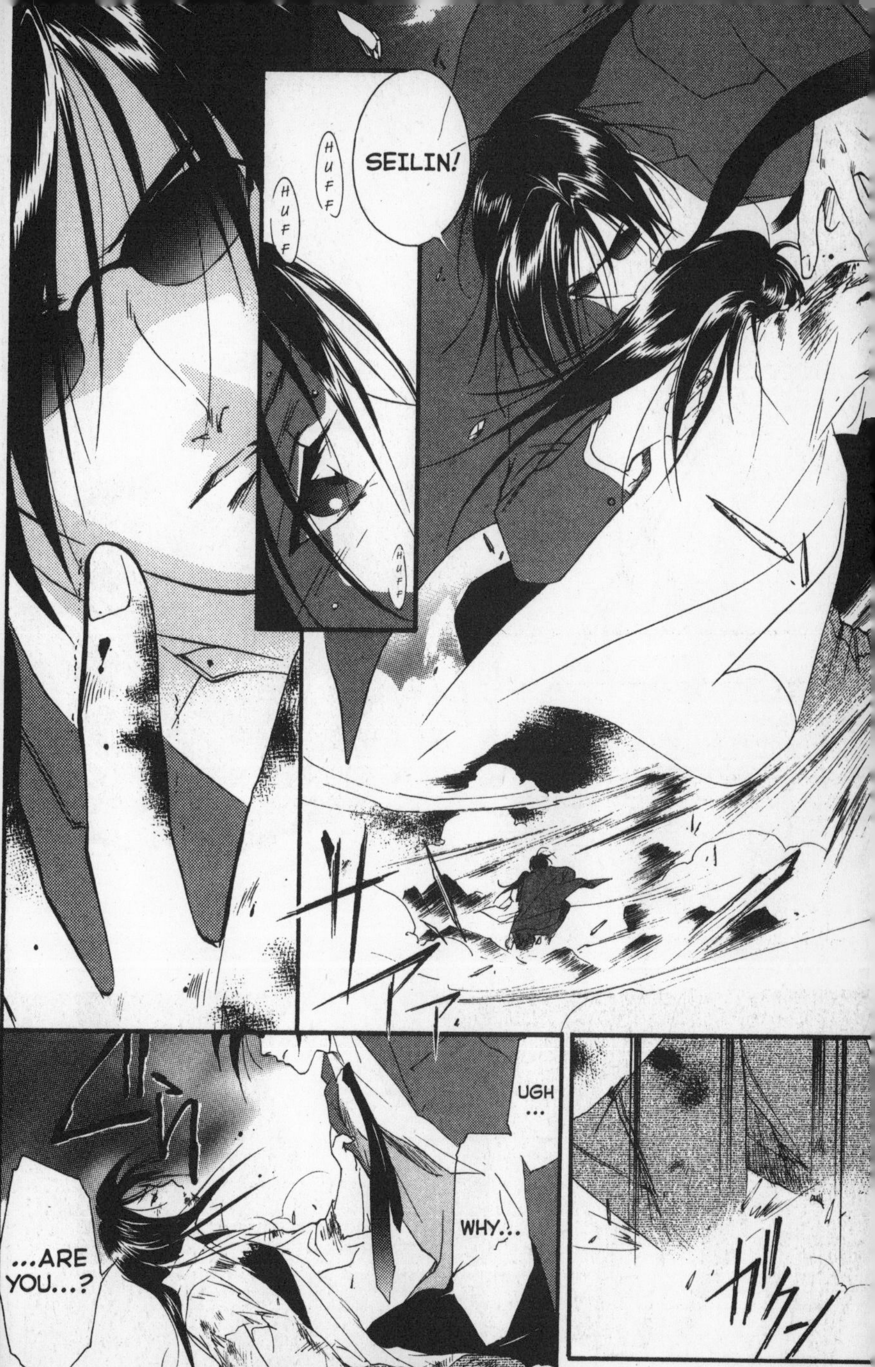

SEILIN!
HUFF
HUFF
HUFF
ガクン
UGH...
WHY...
...ARE YOU...?

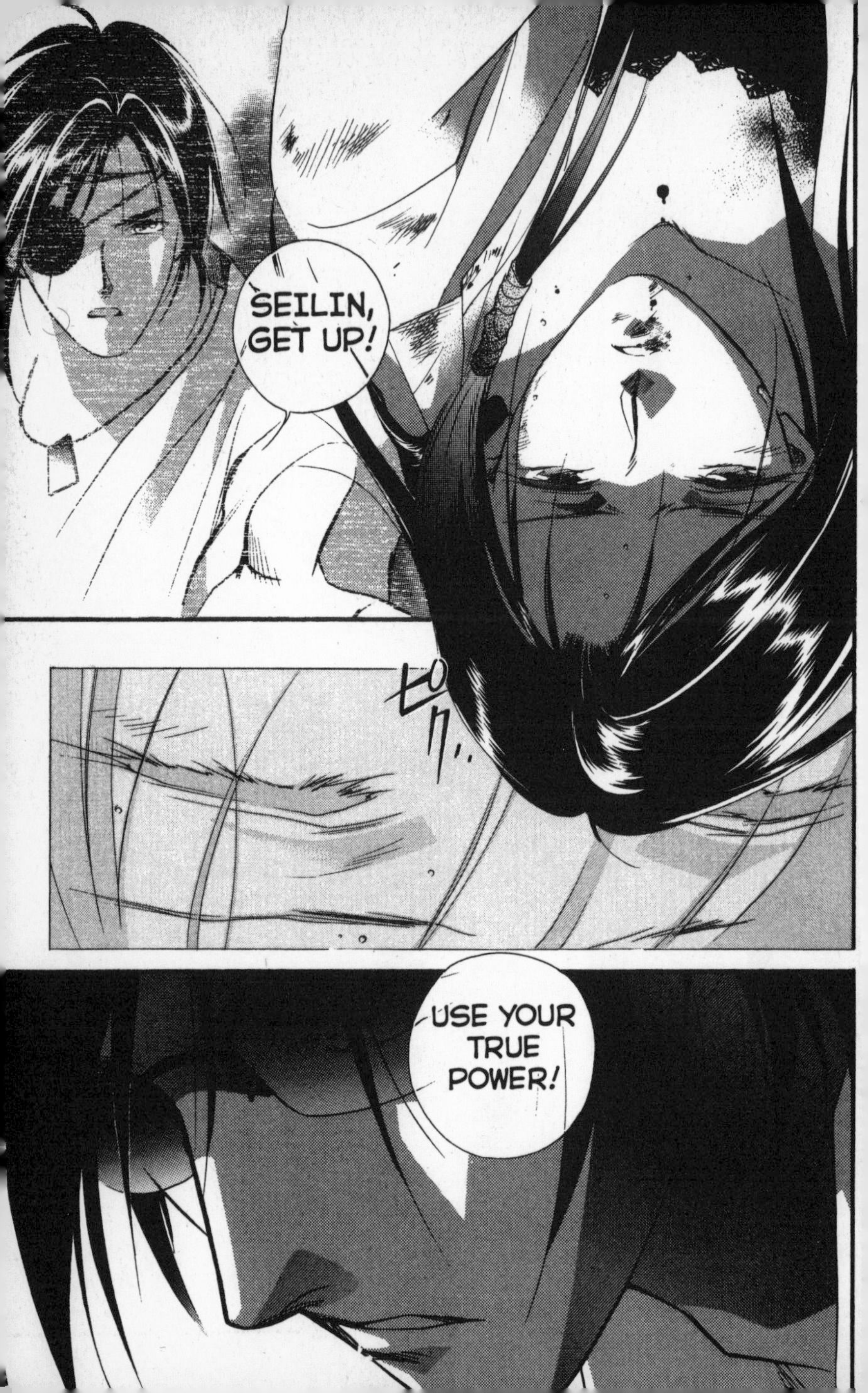
SEILIN, GET UP!
USE YOUR TRUE POWER!

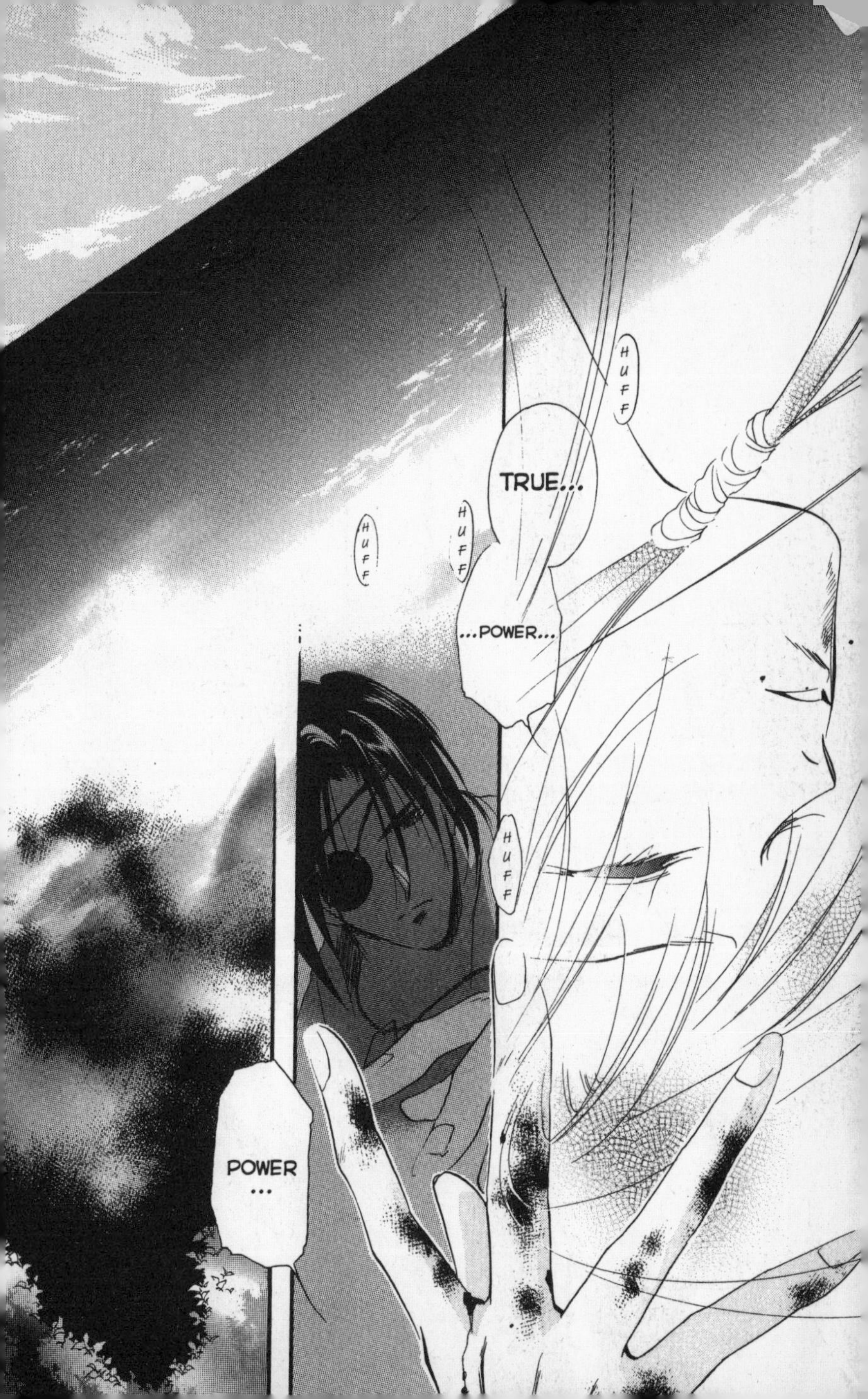
HUFF
TRUE...
HUFF
HUFF
...POWER...
HUFF
POWER
...

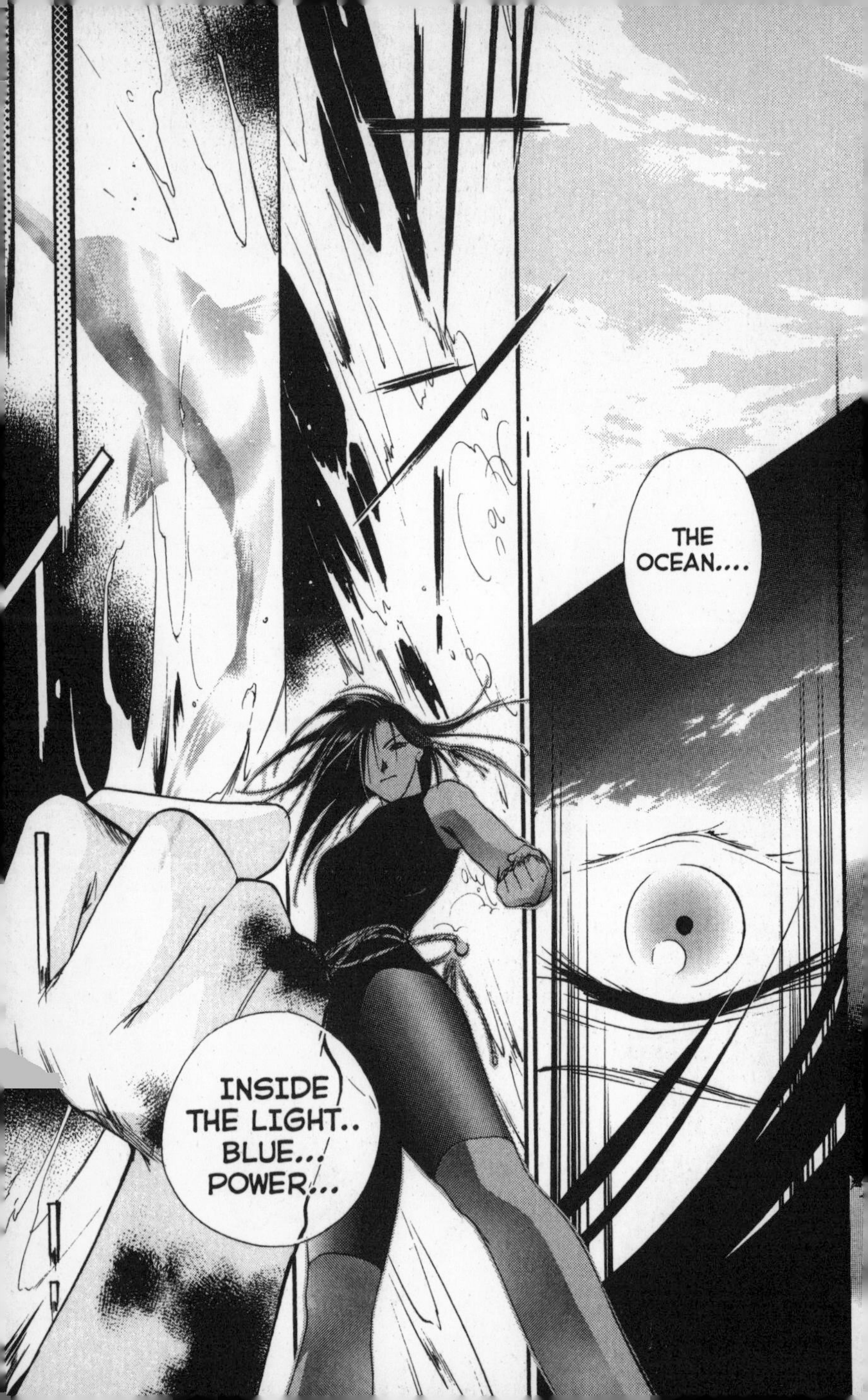
THE OCEAN....
INSIDE THE LIGHT.. BLUE... POWER...

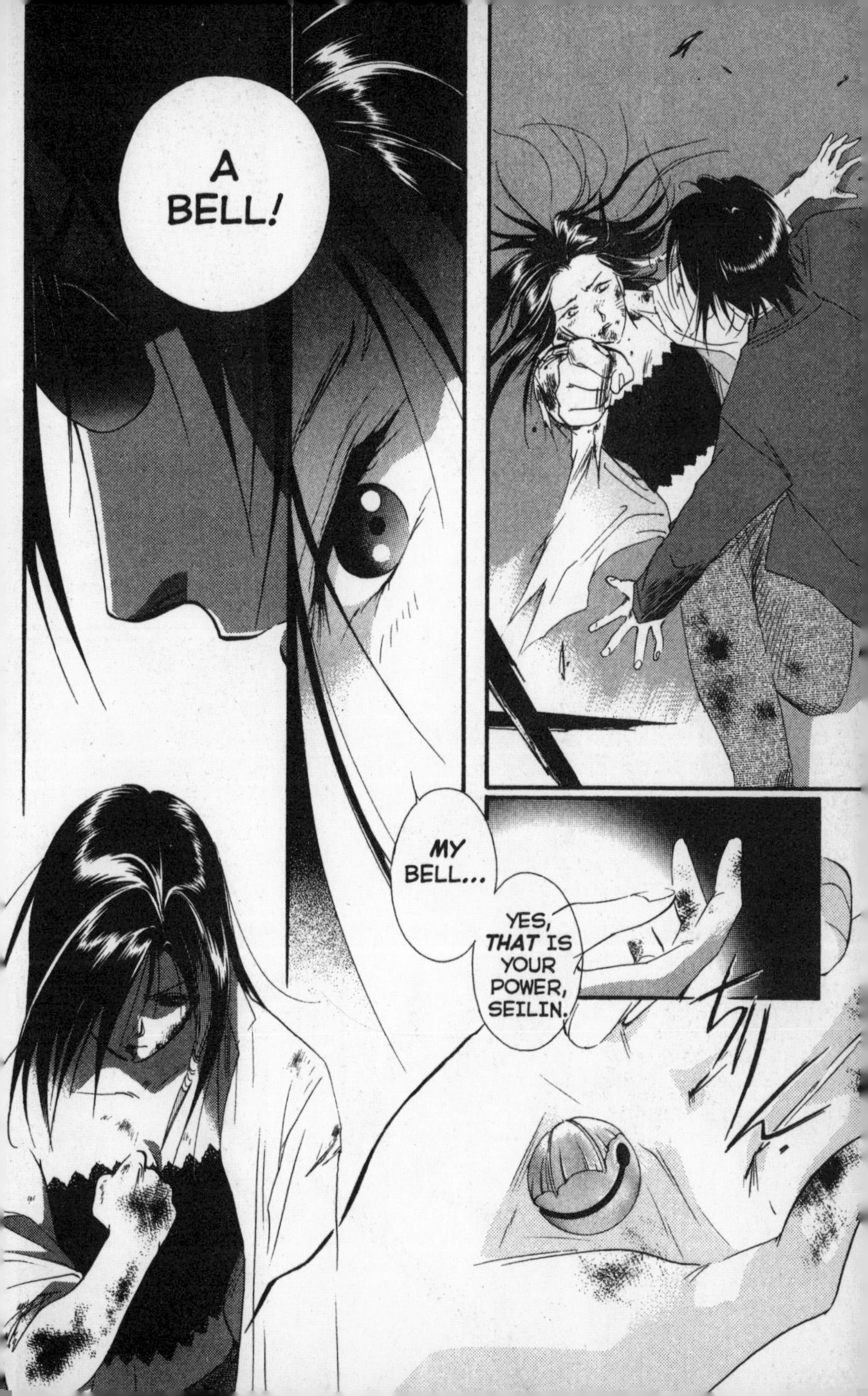
A BELL!
MY BELL...
YES, THAT IS YOUR POWER, SEILIN.

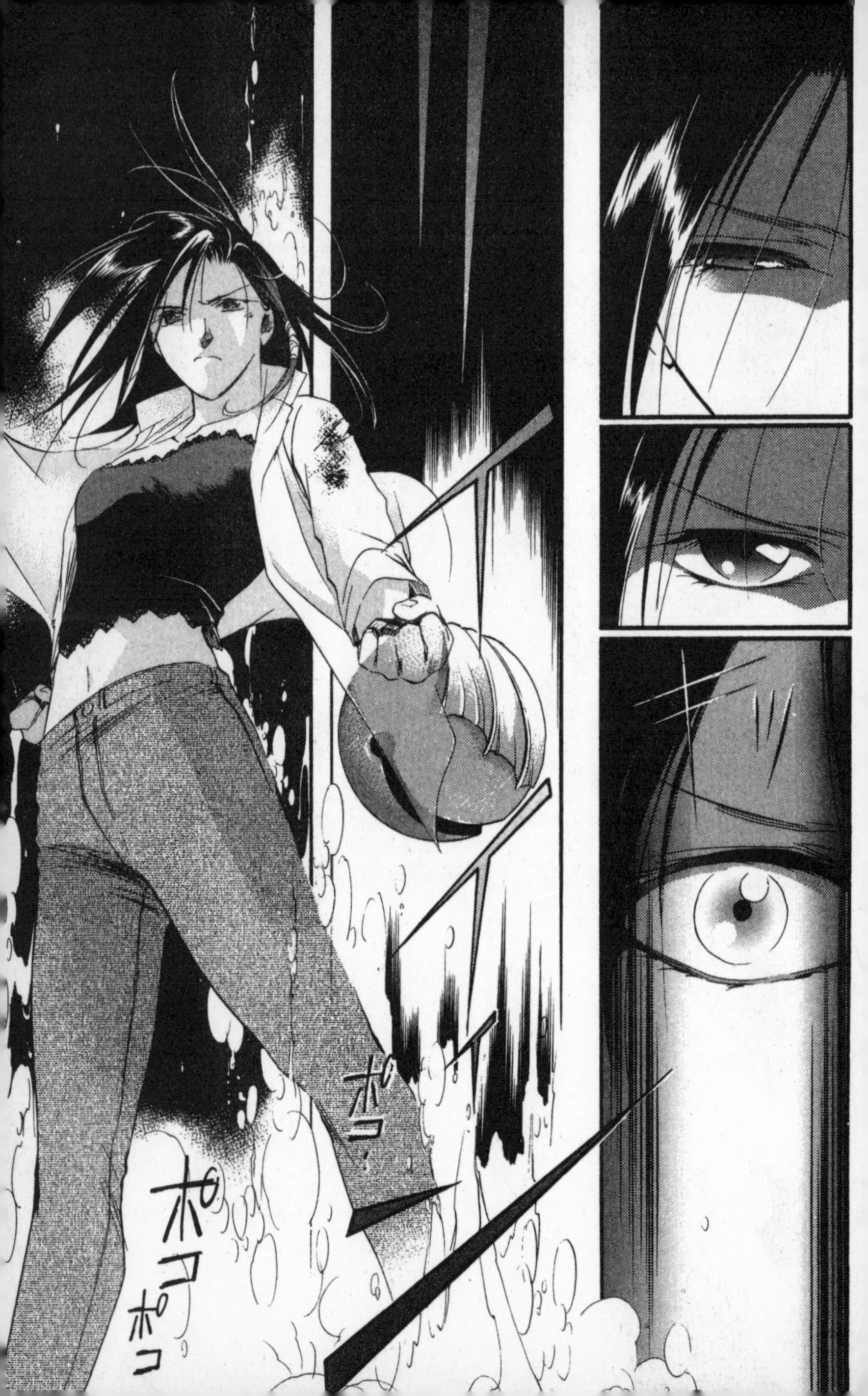
ポコ
ポコポコ

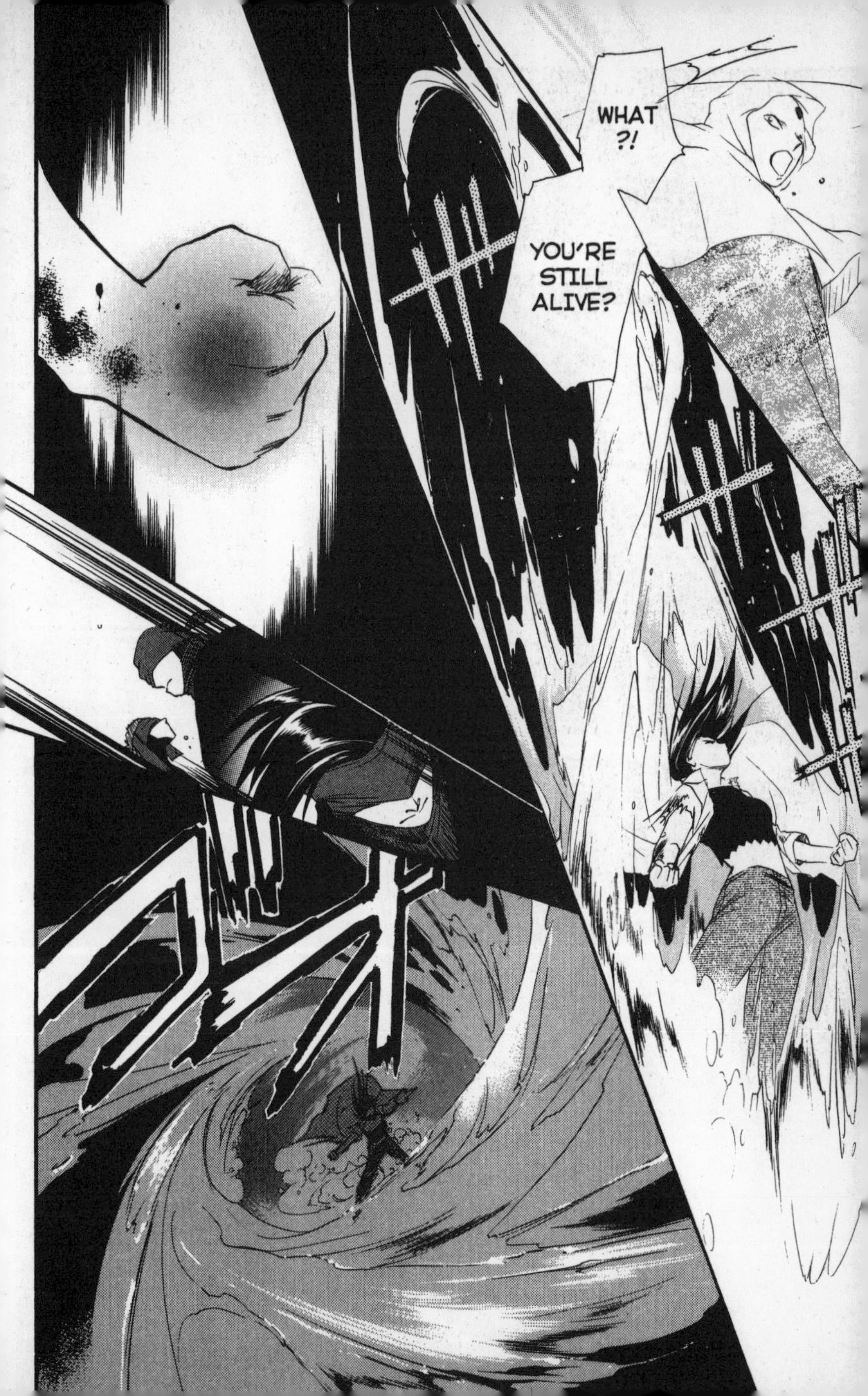
WHAT ?!
YOU'RE STILL ALIVE?

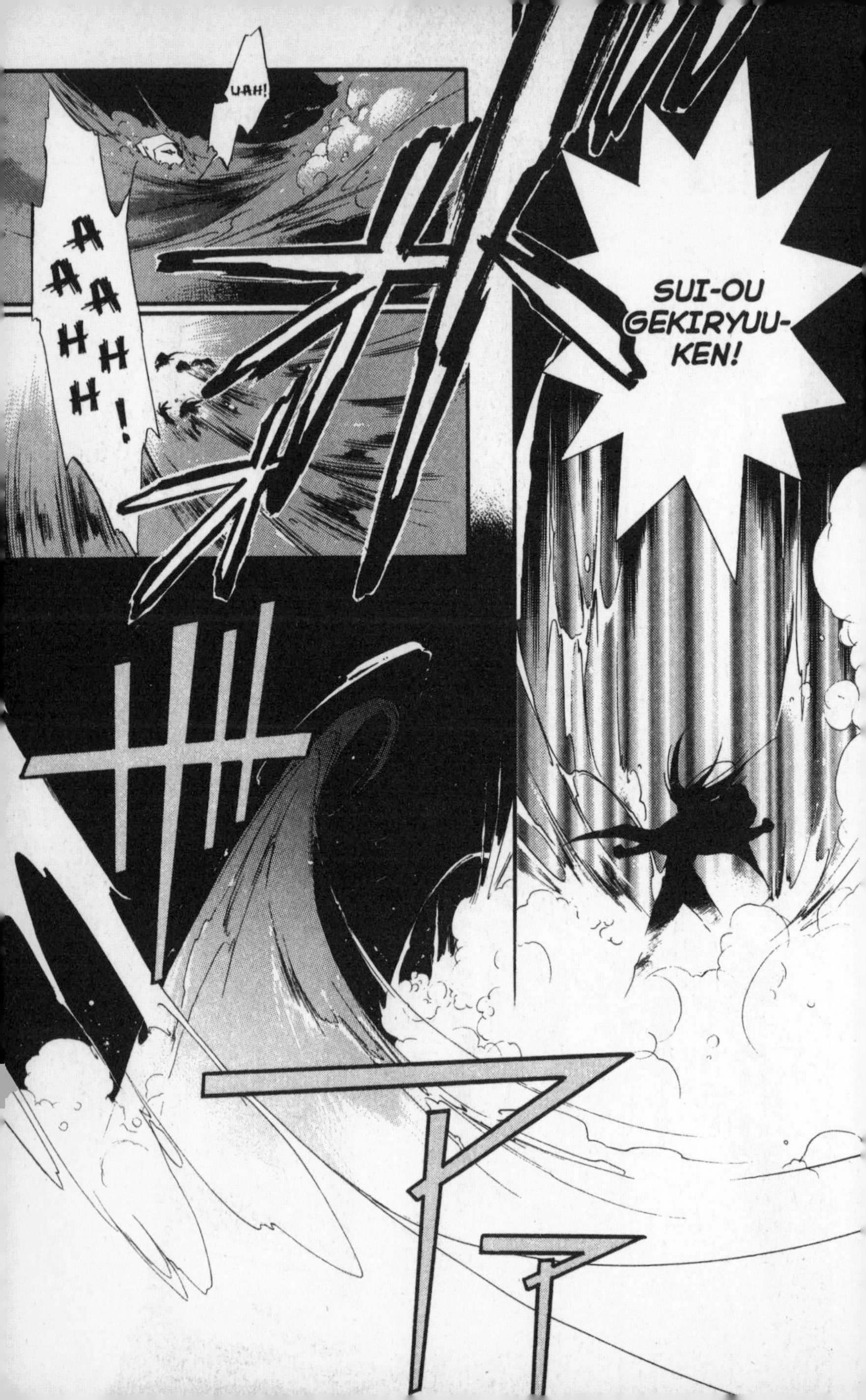
SUI-OU GEKIRYUU-KEN!
UAH!
AAAHHH!

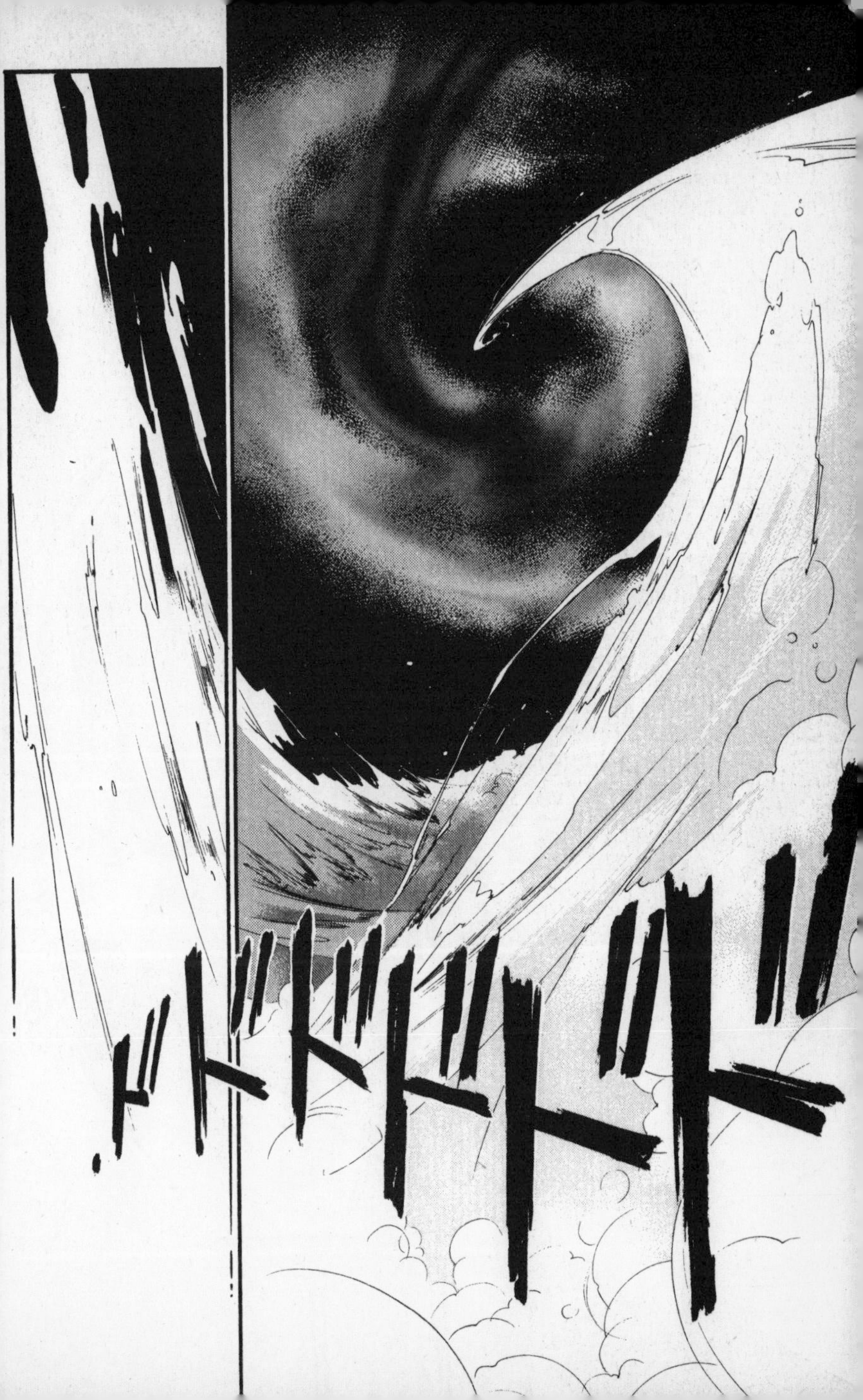
ドドドドドド

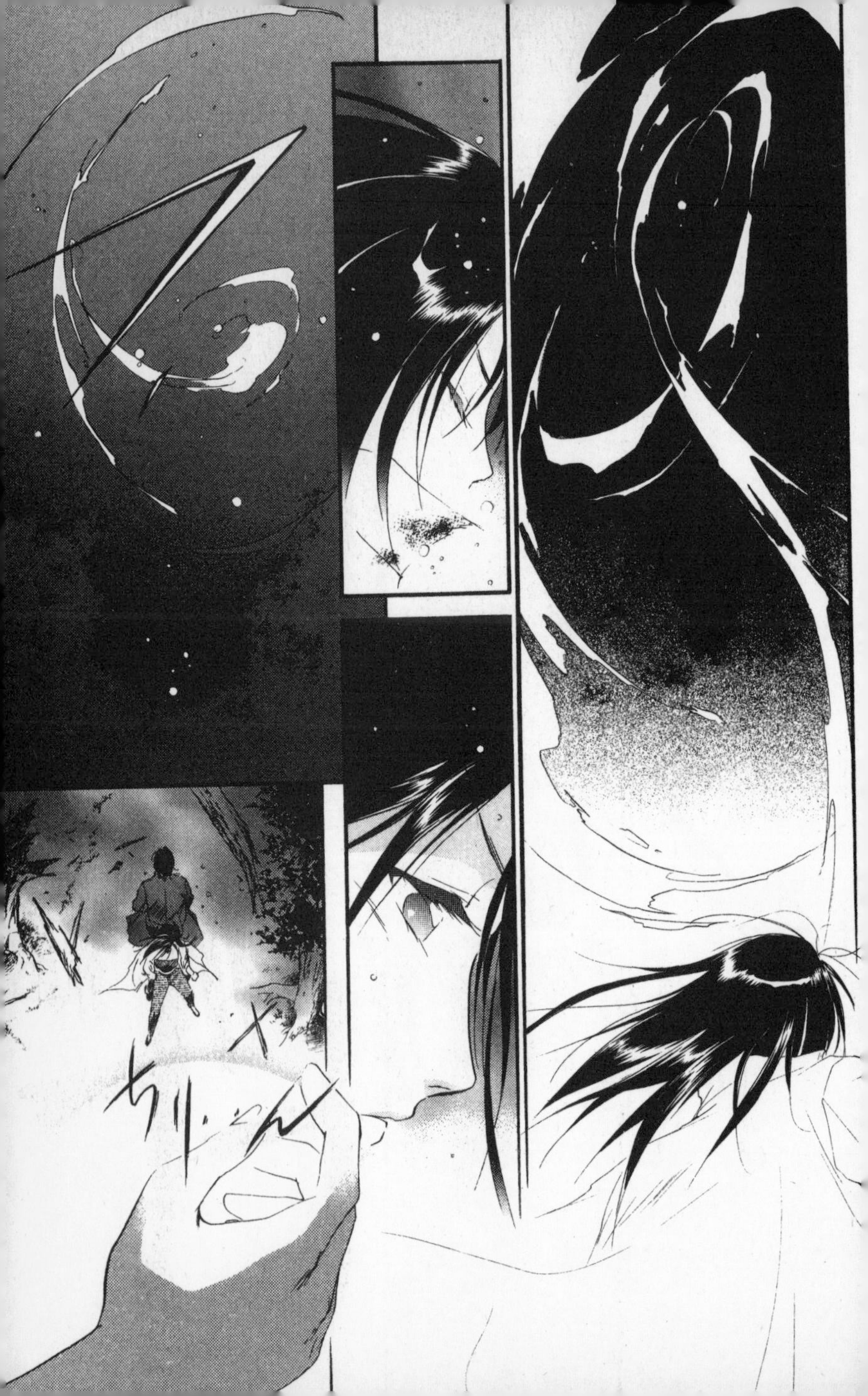
ちり・・ん

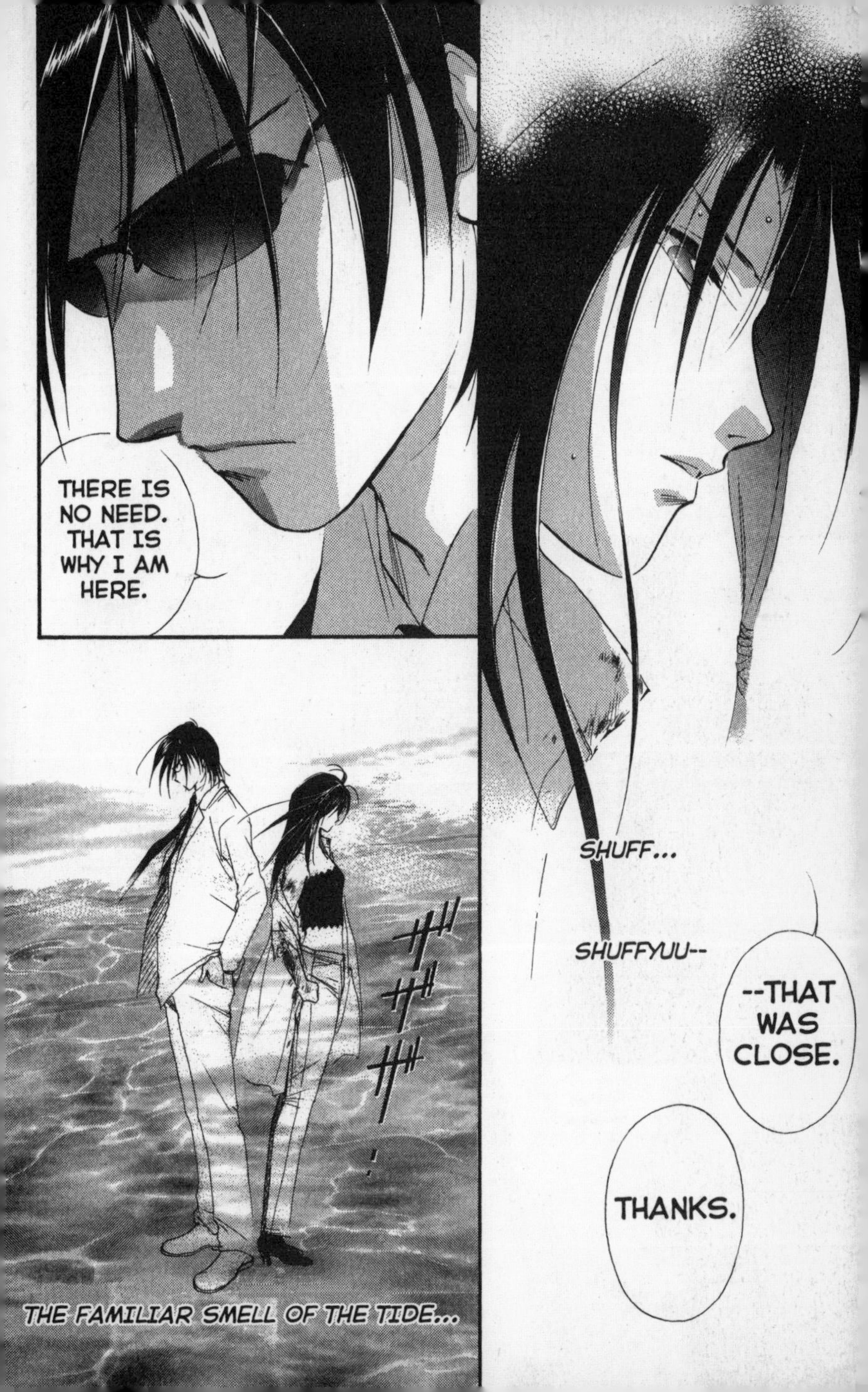
SHUFF...
SHUFFYUU--
--THAT WAS CLOSE.
THANKS.
THERE IS NO NEED. THAT IS WHY I AM HERE.
THE FAMILIAR SMELL OF THE TIDE...

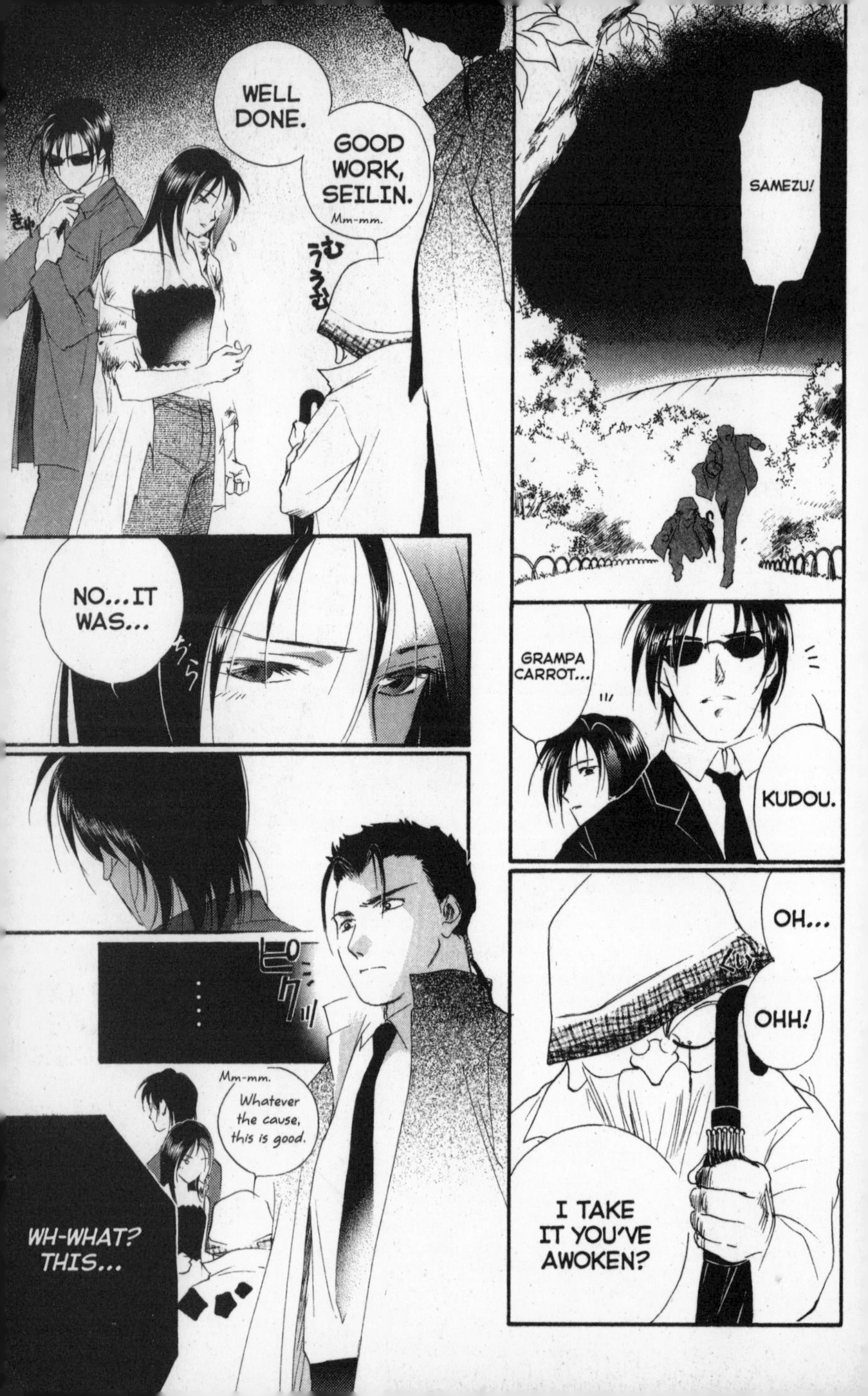
SAMEZU!
GRAMPA CARROT...
KUDOU.
OH...
OHH!
I TAKE IT YOU'VE AWOKEN?
WELL DONE.
GOOD WORK, SEILIN.
Mm-mm.
うむうむ
きゅ
NO...IT WAS...
ちら
ピクッ
....
Mm-mm.
Whatever the cause, this is good.
WH-WHAT? THIS...

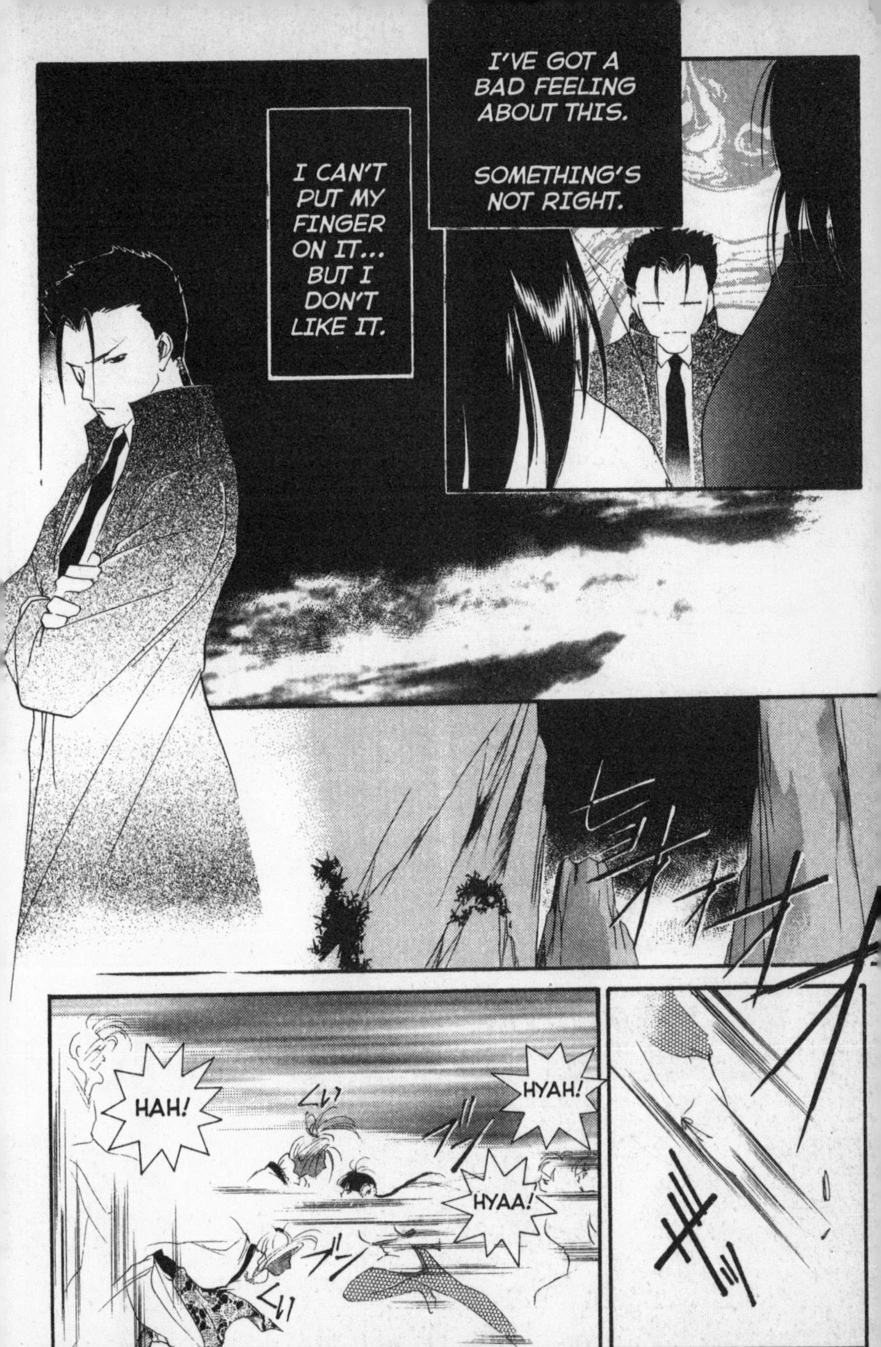
I'VE GOT A BAD FEELING ABOUT THIS.
SOMETHING'S NOT RIGHT.
I CAN'T PUT MY FINGER ON IT... BUT I DON'T LIKE IT.
HYAH!
HAH!
HYAA!

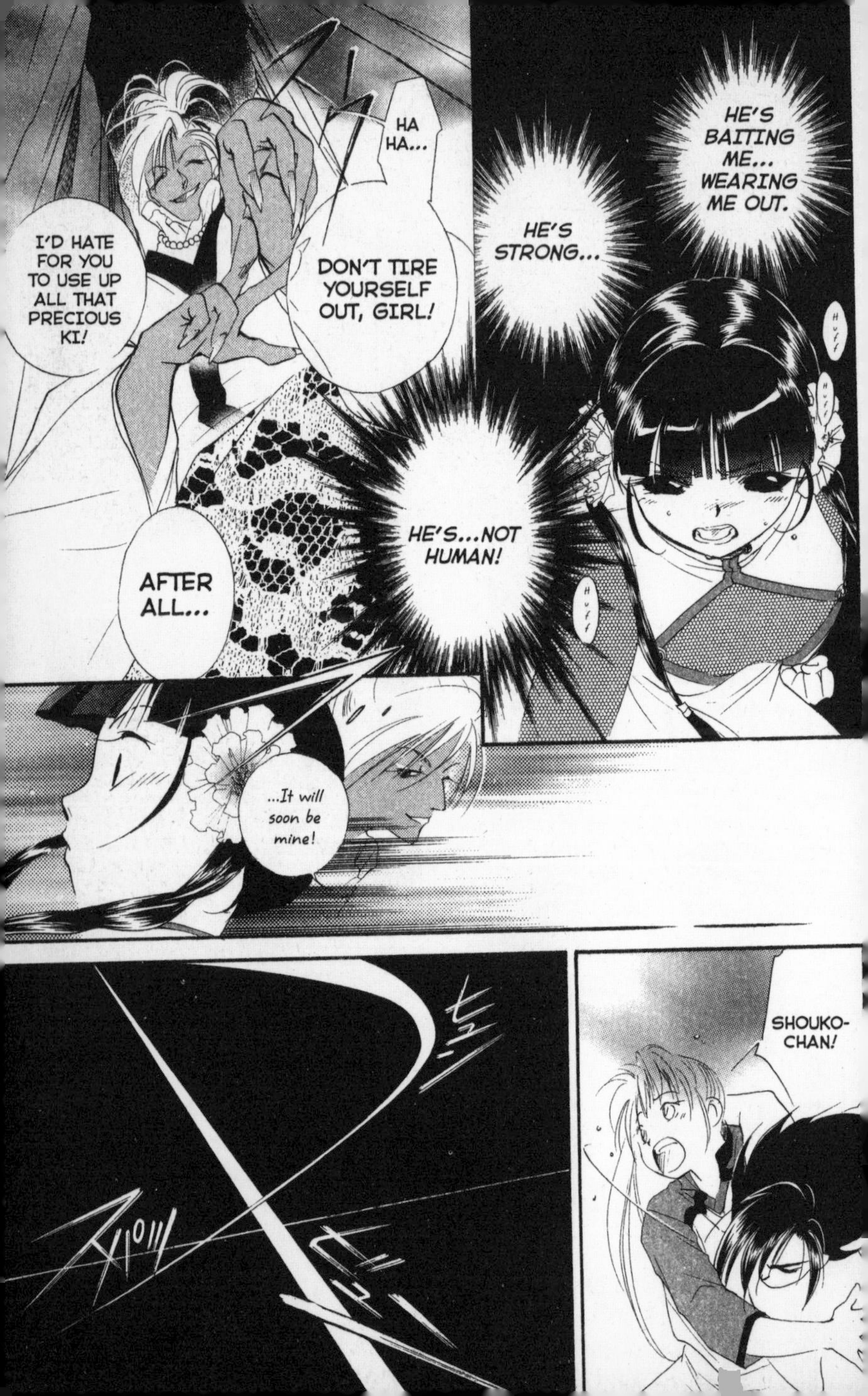
HE'S BAITING ME... WEARING ME OUT.
HE'S STRONG...
Huff
Huff
HE'S...NOT HUMAN!
Huff
HA HA...
DON'T TIRE YOURSELF OUT, GIRL!
I'D HATE FOR YOU TO USE UP ALL THAT PRECIOUS KI!
AFTER ALL...
...It will soon be mine!
SHOUKO-CHAN!

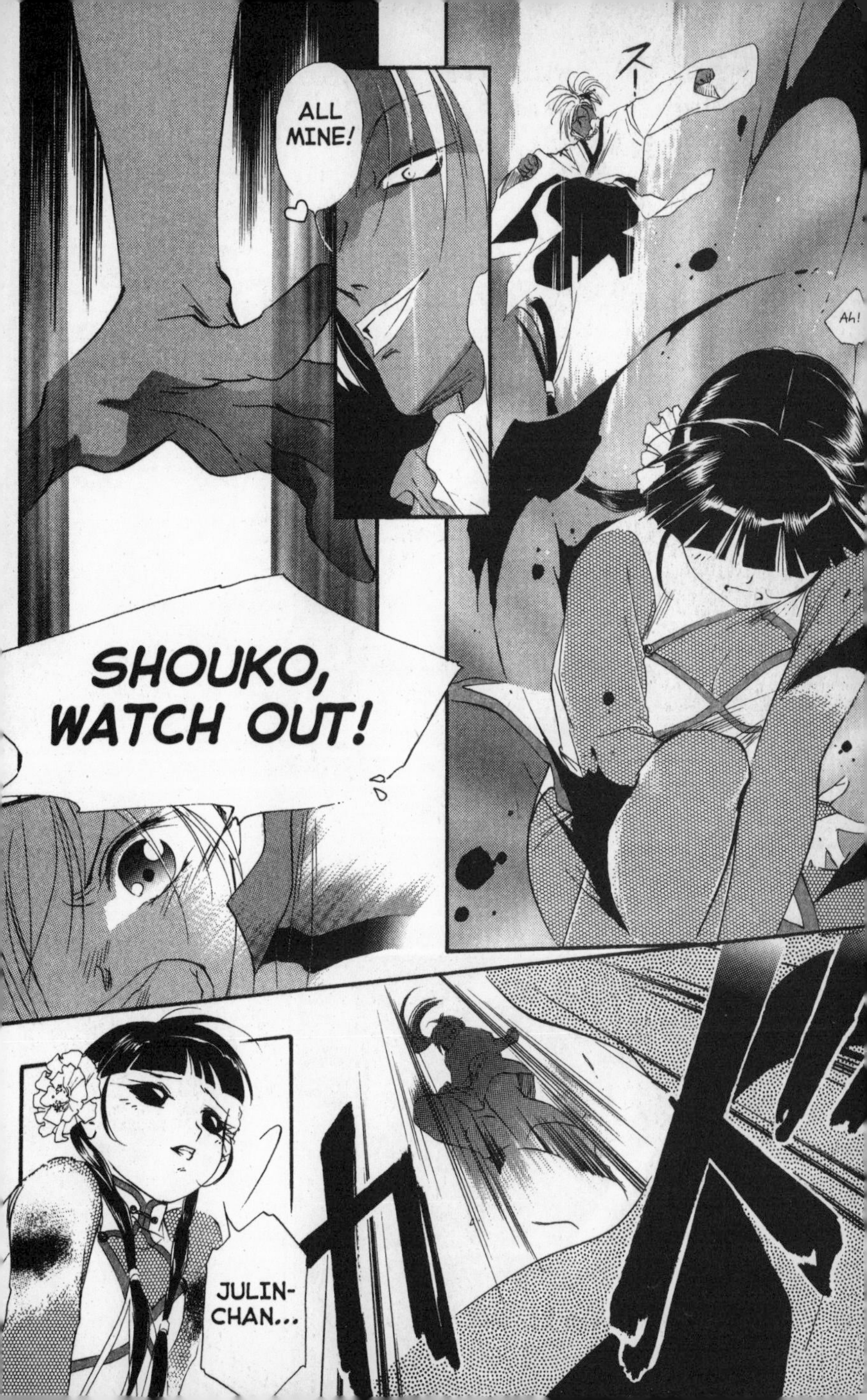
スー
Ah!
ALL MINE!
SHOUKO, WATCH OUT!
JULIN-CHAN...

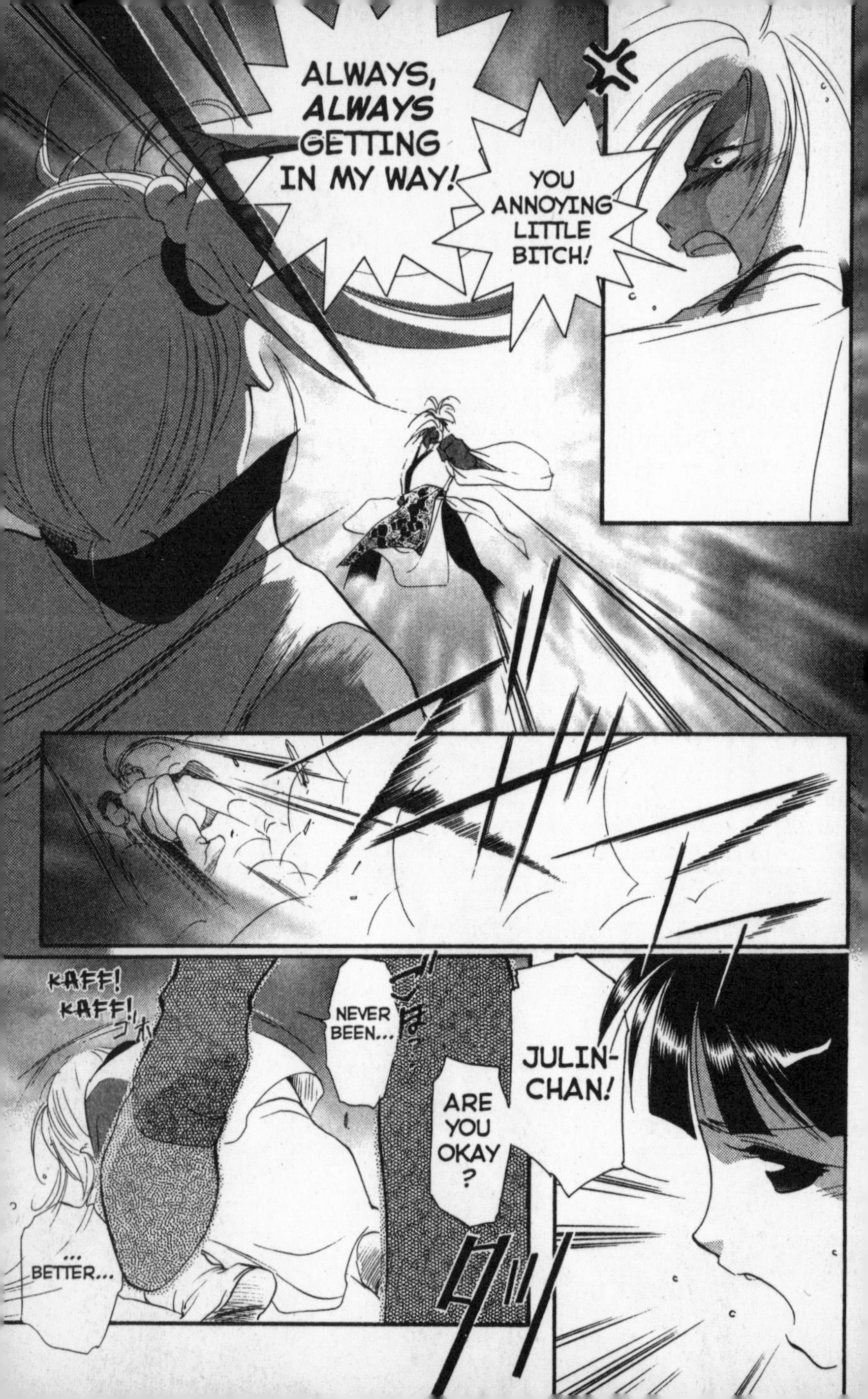
YOU ANNOYING LITTLE BITCH!
ALWAYS, ALWAYS GETTING IN MY WAY!
JULIN-CHAN!
ARE YOU OKAY?
NEVER BEEN...
KAFF! KAFF!
...BETTER...

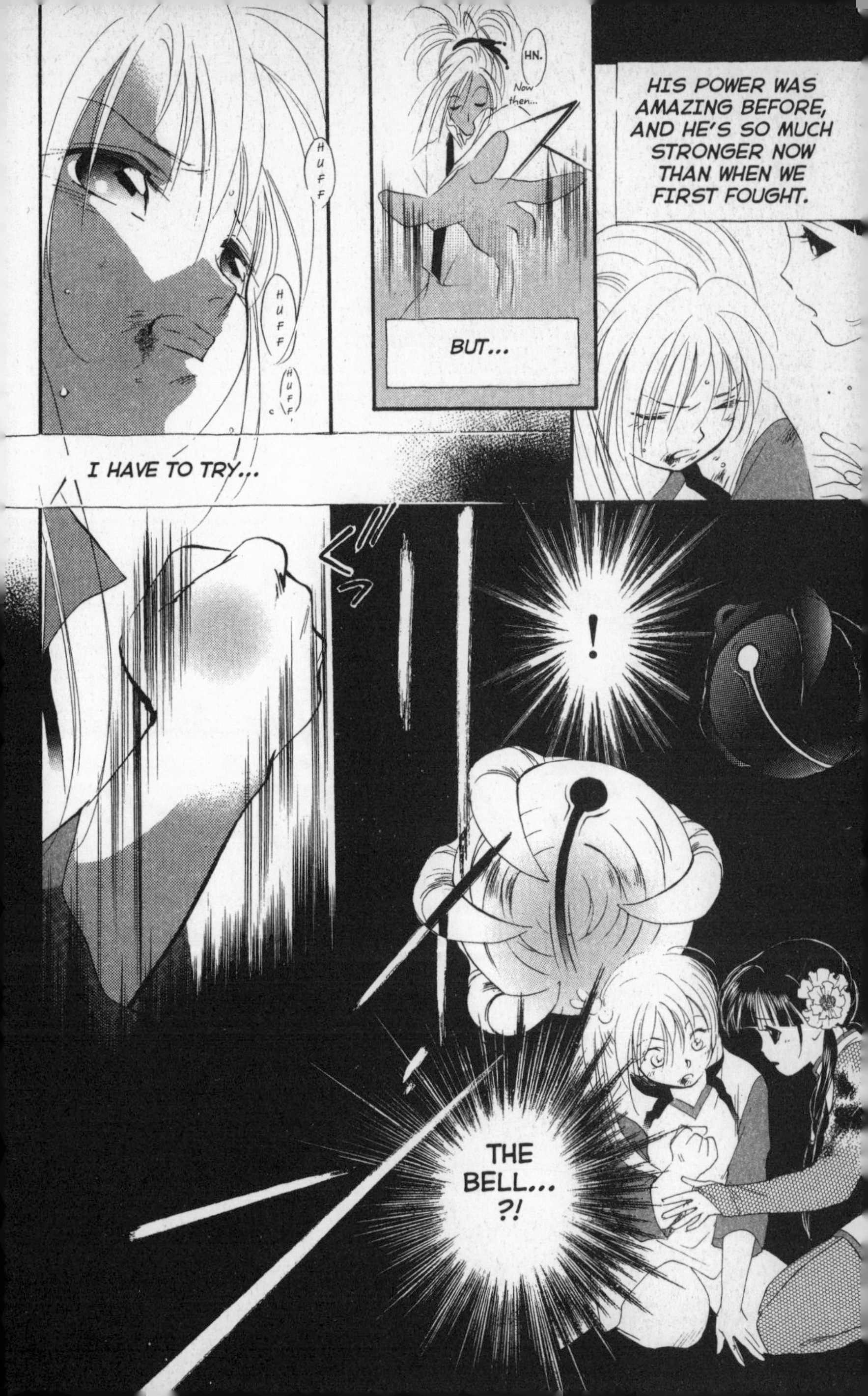
HIS POWER WAS AMAZING BEFORE, AND HE'S SO MUCH STRONGER NOW THAN WHEN WE FIRST FOUGHT.
HN.
Now then...
BUT...
HUFF
HUFF
HUFF
I HAVE TO TRY...
!
THE BELL... ?!

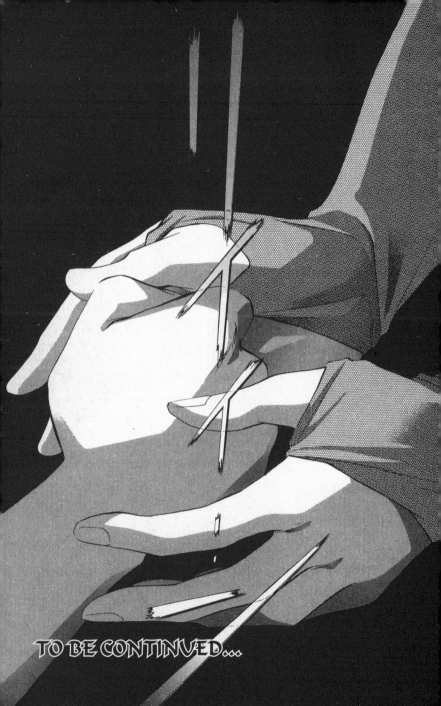

TO BE CONTINUED...

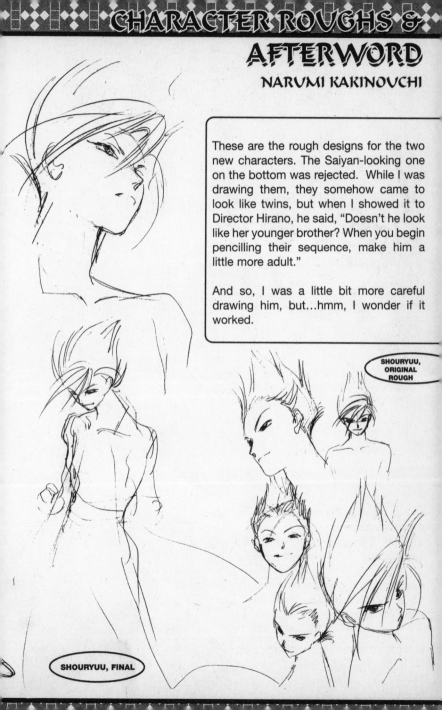

CHARACTER ROUGHS & AFTERWORD

NARUMI KAKINOUCHI

These are the rough designs for the two new characters. The Saiyan-looking one on the bottom was rejected. While I was drawing them, they somehow came to look like twins, but when I showed it to Director Hirano, he said, "Doesn't he look like her younger brother? When you begin pencilling their sequence, make him a little more adult."

And so, I was a little bit more careful drawing him, but…hmm, I wonder if it worked.

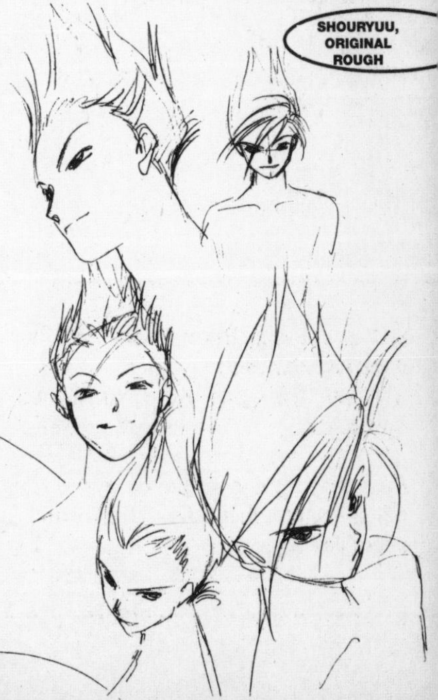

SHOURYUU, ORIGINAL ROUGH

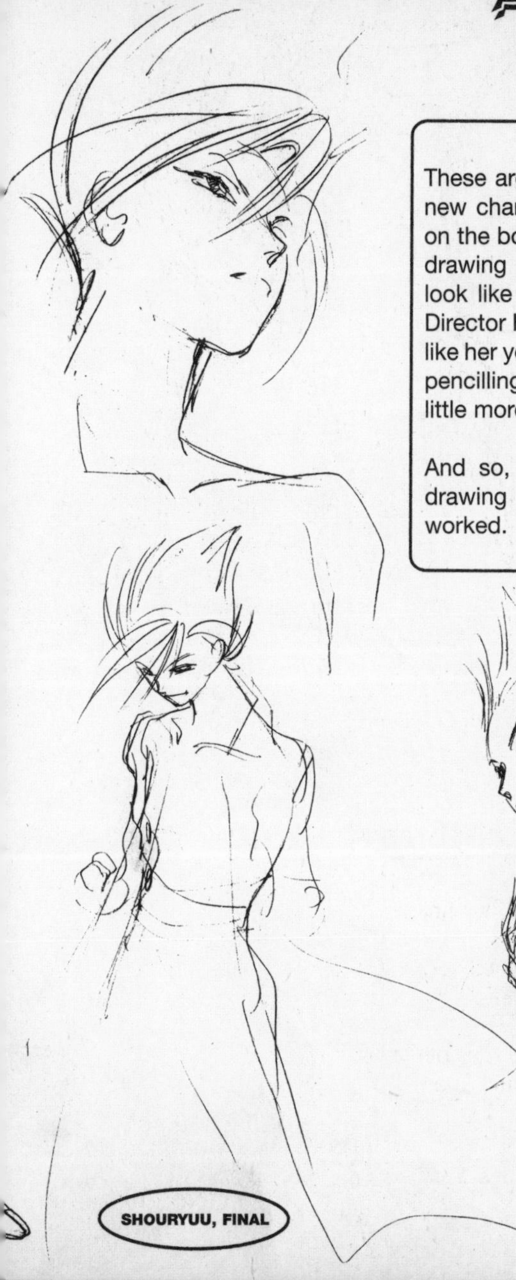

SHOURYUU, FINAL

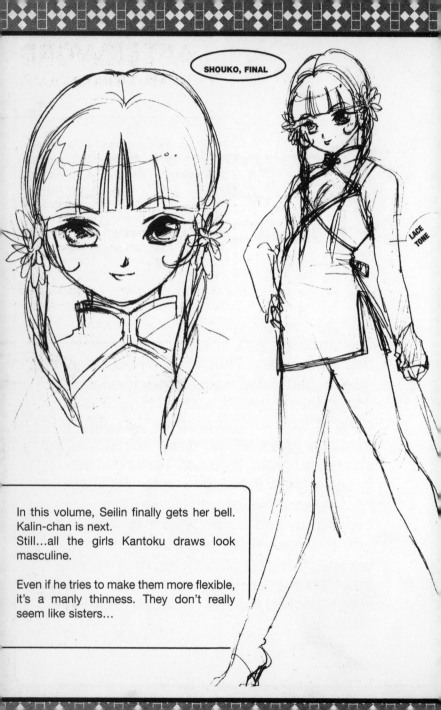

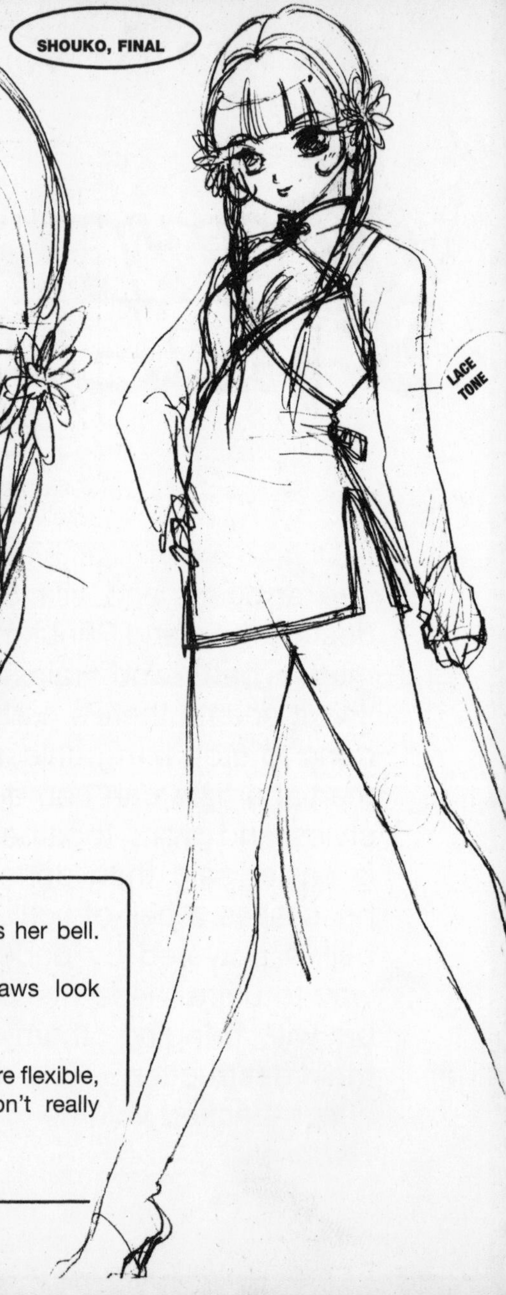
SHOUKO, FINAL
LACE TONE

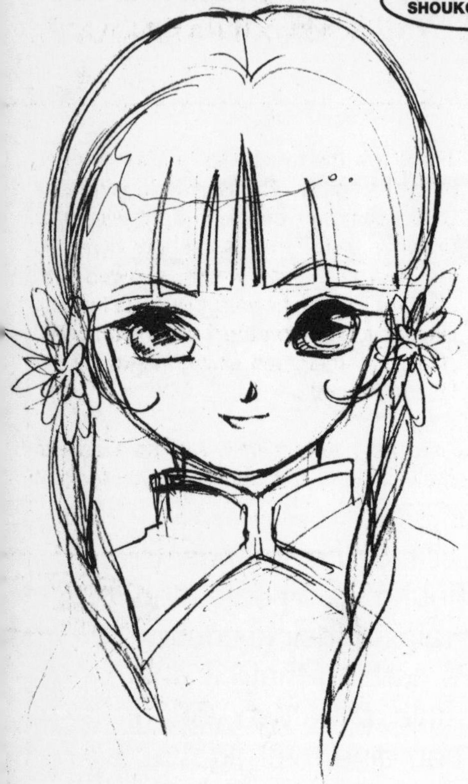

In this volume, Seilin finally gets her bell. Kalin-chan is next.
Still...all the girls Kantoku draws look masculine.

Even if he tries to make them more flexible, it's a manly thinness. They don't really seem like sisters...

In the Next Volume of...

Shaolin Sisters Reborn

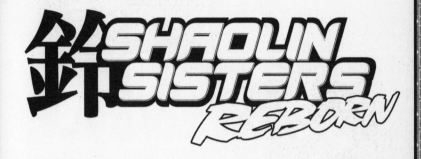

The arrogant and vile Shino intends to destroy Julin and Shouko Lin by defeating them in battle and draining their ki energy, and it seems there's nothing that can be done to stop him…unless the two young martial artists can combine their fighting styles and work together. However, this is easier said than done. After all, Julin possesses a bell of light, while Shouko's bell is powered by darkness. Is there a way to unite these two opposing forces, or will bringing them together spell their destruction? Find out in our next action-packed volume of *Shaolin Sisters: Reborn!*

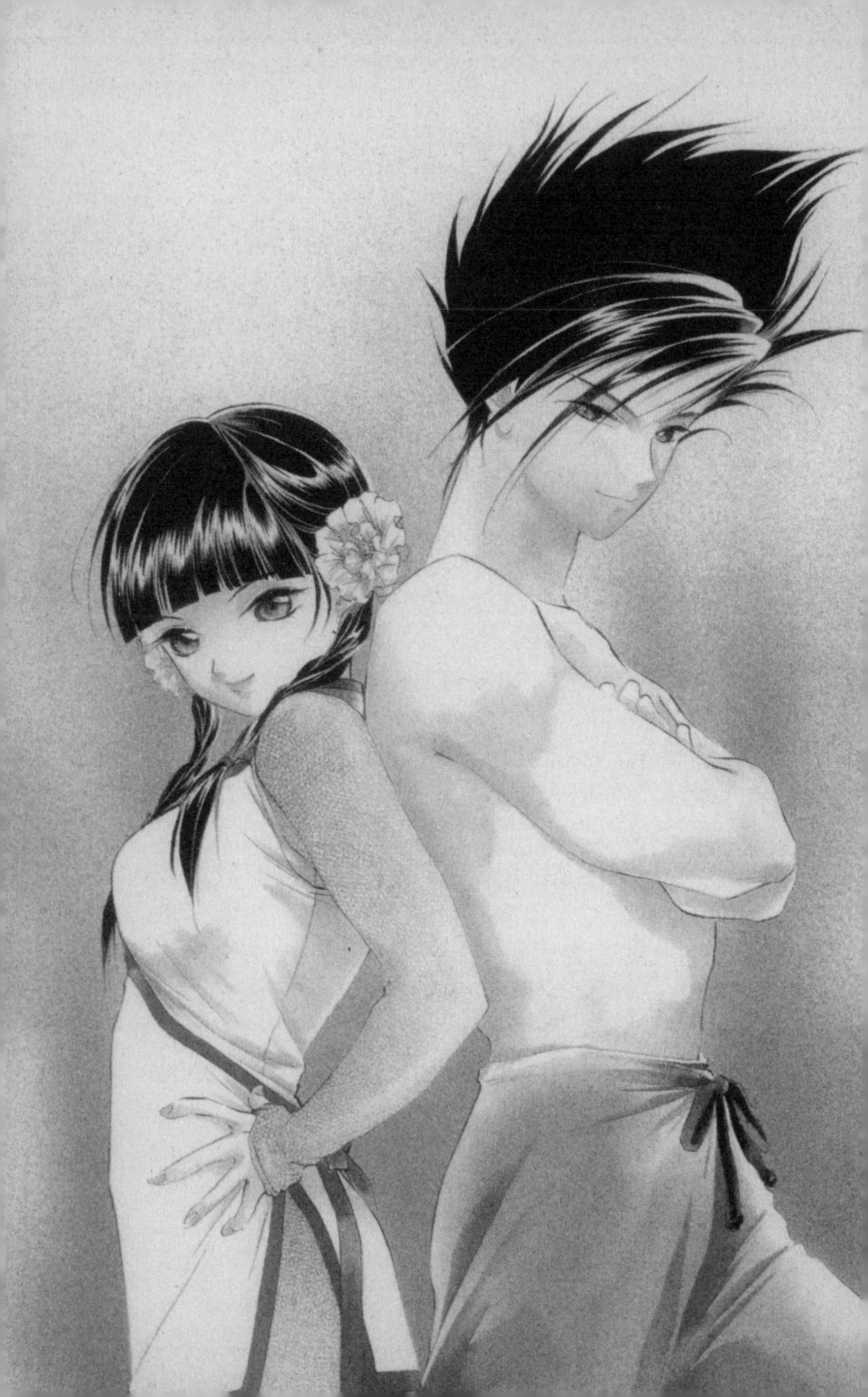

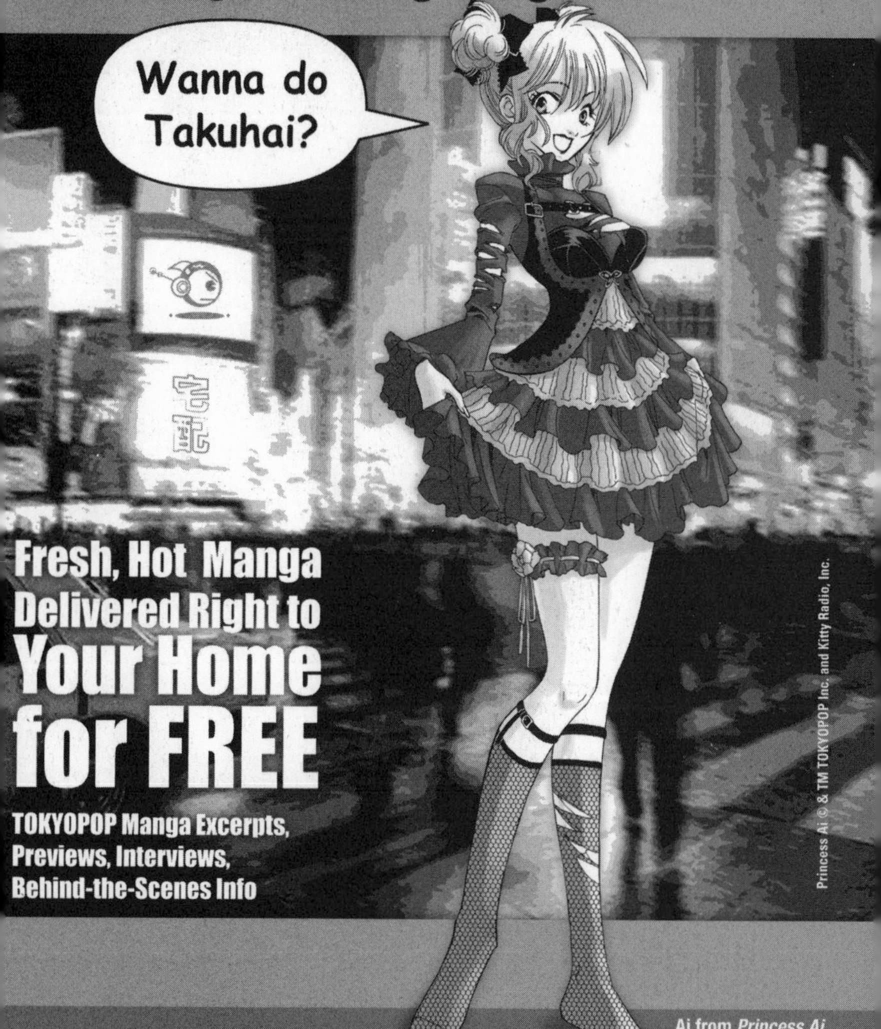
Wanna do Takuhai?
宅配
Fresh, Hot Manga Delivered Right to Your Home for FREE
TOKYOPOP Manga Excerpts, Previews, Interviews, Behind-the-Scenes Info
Princess Ai © & TM TOKYOPOP Inc. and Kitty Radio, Inc.
Ai from *Princess Ai*

TOKYOPOP SHOP

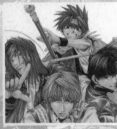
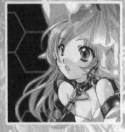

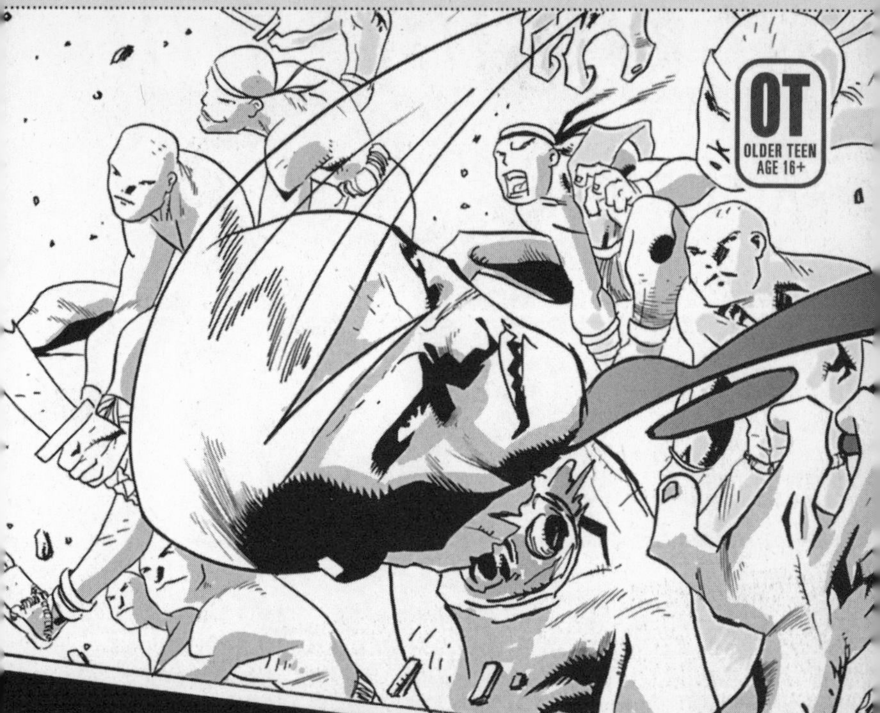
OT
OLDER TEEN
AGE 16+

In the deep South, an ancient voodoo curse unleashes the War on Flesh—a hellish plague of voracious Ew Chott hornets that raises an army of the walking dead. This undead army spreads the plague by ripping the hearts out of living creatures to make room for a Black Heart hive, all in preparation for the most awesome incarnation of evil ever imagined… An unlikely group of five mis-matched individuals have to put their differences aside to try to destroy the onslaught of evil before it's too late.

VOODOO MAKES A MAN NASTY!

Preview the manga at:
www.TOKYOPOP.com/waronflesh

WAR ON FLESH

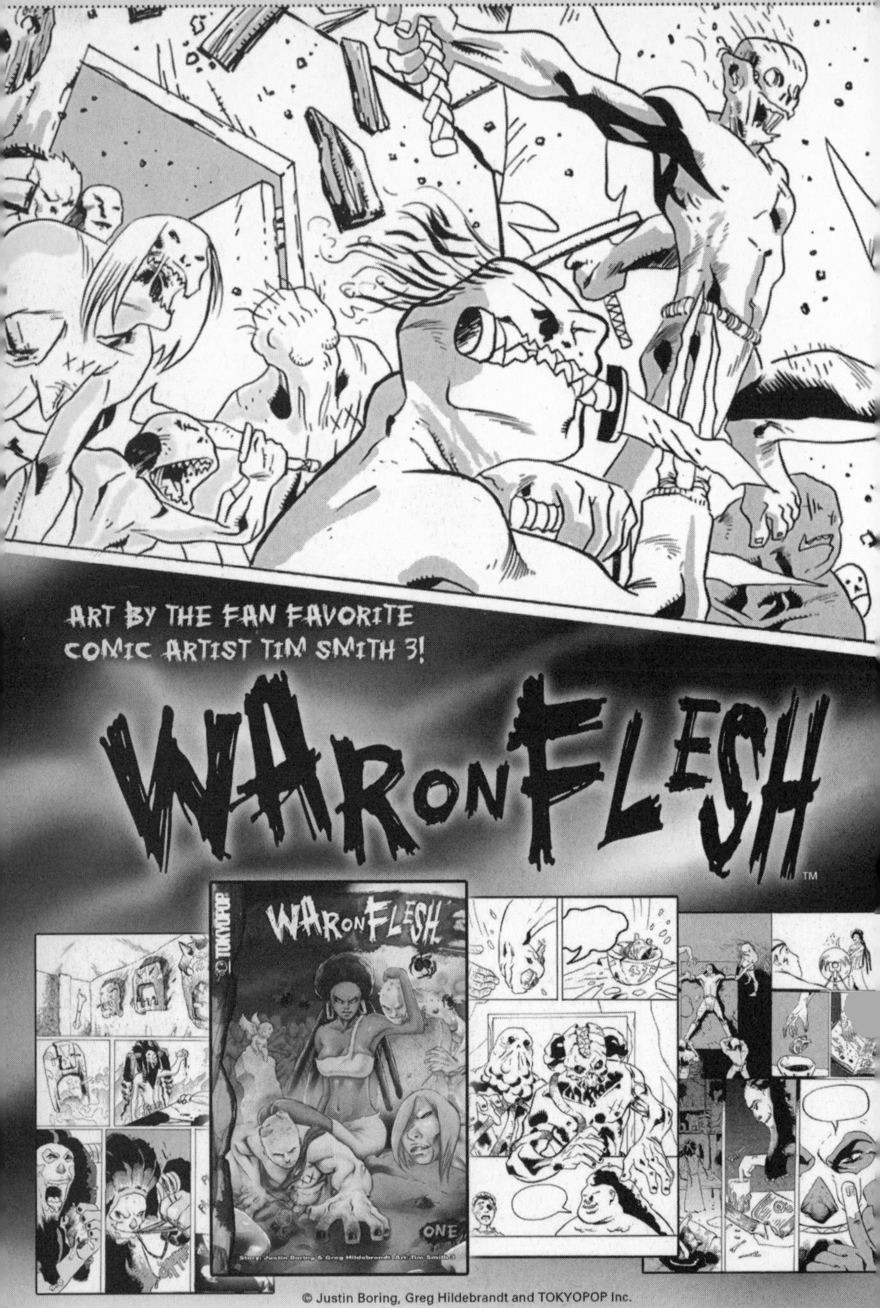
ART BY THE FAN FAVORITE
COMIC ARTIST TIM SMITH 3!
WAR ON FLESH™
WAR ON FLESH
TOKYOPOP
ONE
Story: Justin Boring & Greg Hildebrandt Art: Tim Smith 3

SPOTLIGHT TOKYOPOP MANGA SUPPLEMENT

GIRLS BRAVO

BY MARIO KANEDA

T
TEEN
AGE 13+

BOY MEETS GIRL. BOY BREAKS OUT IN HIVES.
BOY STUMBLES ONTO ALIEN PLANET FULL OF GIRLS...

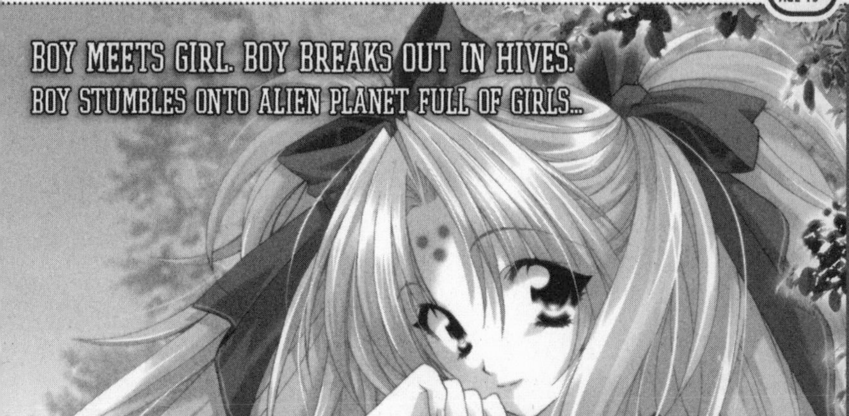

Meet Yukinari Sasaki, an average high school boy who has extreme girl phobia—and an allergic reaction when girls touch him. One day, he befriends an alien named Miharu, who comes from a planet that is inhabited by only women. Remarkably, Yukinari is able to touch Miharu, without breaking out. He returns to his own world accompanied by Miharu, but shortly thereafter, other girls follow them to his world...and his life turns into one big mess!

THE LAUGH-OUT-LOUD MANGA THAT INSPIRED THE POPULAR ANIME ADAPTATION!

FOR MORE INFORMATION VISIT: WWW.TOKYOPOP.COM

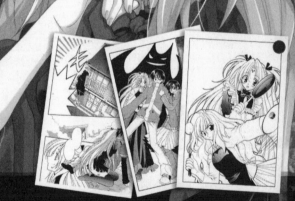

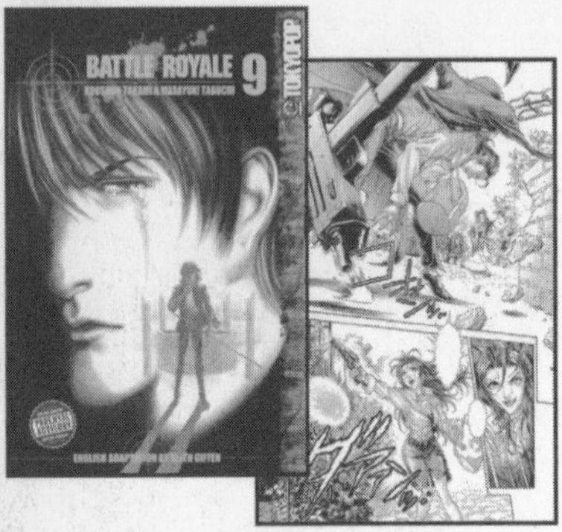
BATTLE ROYALE 9
TOKYOPOP

BY KOUSHUN TAKAMI & MASAYUKI TAGUCHI

BATTLE ROYALE

As far as cautionary tales go, you couldn't get any timelier than *Battle Royale*. Telling the bleak story of a class of middle school students who are forced to fight one another to the death on national television, Koushun Takami and Masayuki Taguchi have created a dark satire that's sickening, yet undeniably exciting as well. And if we have that reaction reading it, it becomes alarmingly clear how the students could be so easily swayed into *doing* it.

~Tim Beedle, Editor

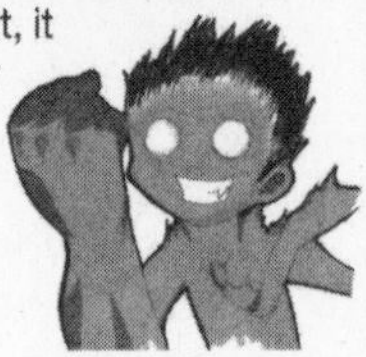

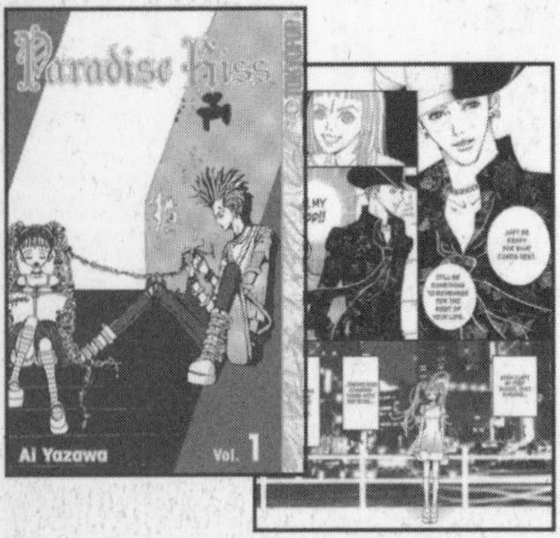
Paradise Kiss
Ai Yazawa
Vol. 1

BY AI YAZAWA

PARADISE KISS

The clothes! The romance! The clothes! The intrigue! And did I mention the clothes?! *Paradise Kiss* is the best fashion manga ever written, from one of the hottest shojo artists in Japan. Ai Yazawa is the coolest. Not only did she create the character designs for *Princess Ai*, which were amazing, but she also produced five fab volumes of *Paradise Kiss*, a manga series bursting with fashion and passion. Read it and be inspired.

~Julie Taylor, Sr. Editor

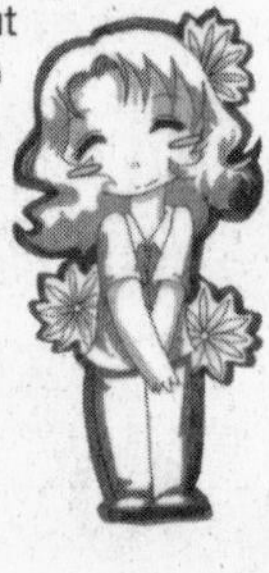

OAKLEY

P9-BJW-976

STOP!

This is the back of the book.
You wouldn't want to spoil a great ending!

This book is printed "manga-style," in the authentic Japanese right-to-left format. Since none of the artwork has been flipped or altered, readers get to experience the story just as the creator intended. You've been asking for it, so TOKYOPOP® delivered: authentic, hot-off-the-press, and far more fun!

DIRECTIONS

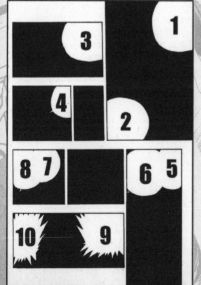

If this is your first time reading manga-style, here's a quick guide to help you understand how it works.

It's easy... just start in the top right panel and follow the numbers. Have fun, and look for more 100% authentic manga from TOKYOPOP®!

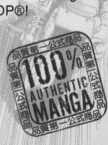